In Defence of Global Capitalism

To Steve,
The Liberty!

Johan

D0817138

In Defence of Global Capitalism

Johan Norberg

Timbro

© The author and AB Timbro 2001
Swedish title: Till världskapitalismens försvar
English translation: Roger Tanner
Cover design and cover photo: Åsa Ölander, Pennywise Productions
Typesetting: Ateljé Typsnittet L&R AB
Printing: Kristianstads Boktryckeri AB, 2001
ISBN: 91-7566-503-4
info@timbro.se
www.timbro.com
tel. +46-(0)8-587 898 00
fax +46-(0)8-587 898 50

Contents

Preface

Our anarchist party won the school election!

It was the autumn term 1988 at my school – we were about 16 at the time – in a western suburb of Stockholm. As usual when it was election year, we were to stage a "school election" of our own. But Markus, my best pal, and I didn't believe in the system. Majority polls, to our way of looking at things, were like two wolves and a lamb voting on what to have for dinner. The school wanted us to elect someone to rule us, but we wanted to rule our own lives.

Partly, I suppose, we did it because we felt different from the others. I was dead keen on listening to synthesizer music and goth, preferably dressed in black and with backcombed hair. We wanted to play music and read books, while the others seemed mostly preoccupied with gizmos and fitting in. The right wing, it seemed to us, was upper class establishment, dead against anything different. But we didn't feel any more at home with the left, which to us meant drab governmental bureaucracy and regimentation. Even if we preferred Sisters of Mercy and the Swedish punk singer Thåström, it was John Lennon's "imagine there's no countries" we believed in. National states must be abolished and people allowed to move freely and co-operate of their own free will everywhere in the world. We wanted a world without compulsion, without rulers. Clearly, then, we were neither right wing nor left wing, neither Conservatives nor Social Democrats. We were anarchists!

So we started "Anarchist Front" and put ourselves down as candidates in the school election on a radical, humorous ticket. We put up hand-written posters on the walls in school, proclaiming things like:

"Who's going to run your life – you or 349 MPs?" We demanded the abolition of the government and of the ban on bikes in the school yard. Most of the teachers took a dim view of this, feeling that we were making a farce of the election, whereas we thought that we were making our voices heard in true democratic spirit. Being called to the headmaster's study for a telling-off merely strengthened our rebellious spirit.

We did well in a tough campaign, polling 25 per cent of the votes. The Social Democrats came second with 19 per cent. We were over the moon, convinced that this would be the start of something big ...

That was thirteen years ago. In the meantime I have changed my mind on a number of things. I have come to realise that questions concerning individuals, society and freedom are more complicated than I then believed. There are too many aspects and problems involved for everything to be settled in one drastically Utopian stroke. I have come to realise that we need a government which protects liberty and prevents the powerful from oppressing individuals, and I have come to understand that representative democracy is preferable to all other systems, for this very purpose of protecting the rights of the individual. But my fundamental urge to liberty is the same today as in that wonderful election campaign of 1988. I want people to be allowed freedom, with no one oppressing anyone else, and with governments not being permitted to fence people in or exclude them with tariffs and frontiers.

This is why I love what is rather barrenly termed *globalisation*, the process whereby people, communications, trade, investments, democracy and the market economy are tending more and more to cross national boundaries. This internationalisation has made us less constricted by the map-makers' boundaries.

Political power has always been local, based on physical control of a certain territory. Globalisation is enabling us more and more to override these territories, by travelling in person and by trading or investing across national boundaries. Opportunities for choosing other solutions and foreign alternatives have multiplied as transport costs have fallen, we have acquired new and more efficient means of communication, and trade and capital movements have been liberalised.

We do not have to shop with the big local company, we can turn to a foreign competitor; we do not have to work for the village's one and only employer, we can be offered alternative opportunities; we do not have to make do with local cultural amenities, the world's culture is at our disposal; we do not have to spend our whole life in one place, we can travel and relocate. Above all, this leads to a liberation of our thinking. We no longer make do with local routine, we want to choose actively and freely. Companies, politicians and associations are having to exert themselves to elicit interest or support from people who are acquainted with a host of alternatives from the world's diversity. Our possibilities of controlling our own lives are growing, and prosperity is growing with them.

This is why I find it pathetic when people who call themselves anarchists engage in the globalisation struggle, but against it, not for! I visited Gothenburg, Sweden, in June 2001 during the big EU-summit. I went there in order to explain why the problem with the European Union is that in many ways it is fighting globalisation and liberalisation, and to present my view that borders should be opened and controls dismantled.

I never got the chance to hold my speech. The place where I was to speak was suddenly in the middle of a battle zone, when so called anti-globalisation anarchists were smashing shops and throwing stones at policemen who were trying to defend a democratic meeting. They are anarchists who demand prohibitions and controls and throw stones at people with different values. Anarchists who demand that the government resume control of those people and enterprises who no longer find their initiative restricted by national boundaries. They make a mockery of the idea of freedom. To our cheerful Anarchistic Front, people like that had nothing to do with anarchism. In our simplified teenage vocabulary they were, if anything, fascists.

But this is only the violent appendage of a broader movement which is critical of general globalisation. In the past few years more and more people have been complaining that the new liberty and internationalism have gone too far, amounting to a "hypercapitalism". The protest movement against this capitalism may call itself radical and profess to stand for exciting new ideas, but its actual standpoints belong to the same old opposition to free markets and free trade which has always been shown by national rulers. Many – authoritarian Third World régimes and Eurocrats, agrarian movements and monopoly corporations, conservative intellectuals and new left movements – are afraid of globalised humanity acquiring more power at the expense of politics. All of them are united in viewing globalism as a monster completely out of control. A monster that has to be rounded up and restrained.

Much of their criticism of globalisation is based on portraying it as something big and menacing. Often they do so, not by reasoned argument but through flat statements of fact, e.g. that 51 of the world's biggest economies are business enterprises or that something like 1.5 trillion dollars are moved around in financial markets every day. As if size itself were intrinsically dangerous and terrifying. This is mathematics, not argument. It remains to be proved that big enterprises or high turnover are a problem in themselves. Often the detractors forget to prove any such thing. In this book I propose pleading for the opposite. So long as we are at liberty to pick and choose, there is nothing wrong with certain forms of voluntary co-operation growing large through success.

Figures like this, and the abstract term "globalisation" – itself apparently little over ten years old – conjure forth the image of an anonymous, enigmatic, elusive force. Simply because it is governed by people's individual actions in different continents, and not from a control centre, it seems uncontrolled, chaotic. "There is no head office, no board of directors, no control panel," one critic complains.[1] Many feel powerless at the prospect of globalisation, and this feeling certainly comes easily when faced with the decentralised decisions of millions of people. If others are at liberty to run their own lives, we have no power over them, but in return we acquire a new power over our own lives. This kind of powerlessness is a good thing. There is no one in the driving seat, because all of us are steering.

The Internet would wither and die if we did not send e-mails, order books and download music every day through this global computer network, no company would collect goods from abroad if we didn't order them, and no one would invest money over the border if there were no entrepreneurs there willing to invest in response to customer demand. Globalisation consists of our everyday actions. We eat bananas from Ecuador, drink tea from Sri Lanka, watch American movies, order books from Britain, work for export companies selling to Germany and Russia, holiday in Thailand and save money for retirement in funds investing in South America and Asia. Resources may be channelled by finance corporations and goods carried across frontiers by business enterprises, but they only do these things because we want them to. Globalisation takes place from beneath, even though politicians come running after it with all manner of abbreviations and acronyms (EU, IMF, WB, UN, UNCTAD, OECD) in a bid to structure the process.

Of course, keeping up with times doesn't always come easily, especially to intellectuals in the habit of having everything under control. In a book about the 19th century Swedish poet and historian Erik Gustaf Geijer, the Swedish intellectual Anders Ehnmark writes, almost enviously, that Geijer was able to keep abreast of all principal

---

1. Elmbrant 2000, p. 98.

happenings in the world at large, just sitting in Uppsala reading the *Edinburgh Review* and the *Quarterly Review*.[2] That is how simple and intelligible the world can be when it is only a tiny élite in the capitals of Europe that makes any difference whatsoever to the course of world events. But how complex and confusing everything is becoming now that the other continents are awakening and developments are also beginning to be affected by ordinary people's everyday decision-making. No wonder then, that influential people, decision makers and politicians claim that "we" (i.e. they) lose power because of globalisation. They have lost some of it to us, ordinary citizens.

Not all of us are going to be global jet-setters, but we don't have to in order to be a part of the globalisation process. In particular, the poor and powerless can find their well-being vastly improved when inexpensive goods are no longer excluded by tariff barriers and when foreign investments offer employment and streamline production. Those still living in the place where they were born stand to benefit enormously from information being allowed to flow across frontiers, and from being free to choose their political representatives. But this requires more in the way of democratic reforms and economic liberalisation.

Demanding more liberty to pick and choose may sound trivial, but it isn't. I understand the objection, though. To us in the affluent world, the availability of non-local options may seem a luxury. Say what you will about herring and Swedish talk shows, but they aren't insupportable – not the herring, at any rate. But the existence from which globalisation delivers people in the Third World really is insupportable. To the poor it is often an existence in abject poverty, in filth, ignorance and impotence, always wondering where the next meal is coming from and whether the water you have walked so many miles to collect is lethal or fit to drink.

---

2. Ehnmark 1999, p. 60.

When globalisation knocks at the door of Bhagant, an elderly agricultural worker and untouchable in the Indian village of Saijani, this leads to houses being built of brick instead of mud, and to people getting shoes on their feet and clean clothes – not rags – on their backs. Outdoors, the streets now have drains, and the fragrance of tilled earth has replaced the stench of refuse. Thirty years ago Bhagant didn't know he was living in India. Today he watches world news on television.[3]

The new freedom of choice means that people are no longer consigned to working for the village's only employers, the powerful big farmers. When the women get work away from home, they also become more powerful within the family. New capital markets mean that Bhagant's children are not compelled to borrow money from usurers who collect payment in future labour. The yoke of usury, by which the whole village was once held in thrall, vanishes when people are able to go to different banks and borrow money from them instead.

Everyone in Bhagant's generation was illiterate. In his children's generation, just a few were able to attend school, and in his grandchildren's generation *everyone* goes to school. Things have improved, Bhagant finds. Liberty and prosperity have grown. Today the children's behaviour is the big problem. When he was young, children were obedient and helped in the home. Now they have grown so terribly independent, making money of their own. This can cause tensions, of course, but it isn't quite the same thing as the risk of having to watch your children die, or having to sell them to a loan shark.

The stand taken by you and me and other people in the privileged world on the burning issue of globalisation can decide whether more people are to share in the development which has taken place in Bhagant's village or whether that development is to be reversed.

---

3. Berg & Karlsson, 2000 chap. 1.

***

Critics of globalisation often portray economic internationalisation as a menace by hinting that it is governed by an underlying intention, invoked by ideological fundamentalists indifferent to the accuracy or otherwise of their map-making. The critics try to paint a picture of neo-liberal market marauders having secretly plotted for capitalism to assume world mastery. In a book targeting what is termed "hypercapitalism", the Swedish radio journalist Björn Elmbrant claims that in the past two decades we have witnessed "a species of ultra-liberal revolution".[4]

Deregulation, privatisation and trade liberalisation, however, were not invented by ultra-liberal ideologists. True, there were political leaders – Reagan and Thatcher, for instance – who have been inspired by economic liberalism. But the biggest reformists, entitling us to speak in terms of a globalisation of capitalism, were communists in China and the Soviet Union, protectionists in Latin America and nationalists in Asia. In many other countries – Sweden, for example – the progress has been spurred by Social Democrats. In short, the notion of conspiratorial ultra-liberals making a revolution of shock therapy is completely wide of the mark. Instead, it is pragmatic, often anti-liberal politicians, being of the opinion that their governments have gone too far in the direction of control-freakery, have for this very reason begun liberalising their economies. The allegation of liberal-capitalist world dominion has to be further tempered by the observation that we today probably have the biggest public sectors and the heaviest pressures of taxation the world has ever known. The liberalisation measures introduced have been concerned with abolishing a number of centralist excesses occurring previously, not with introducing a system of *laissez-faire*. And because the rulers have

---

4. Elmbrant 2000, p. 195.

retreated on their own terms and at their own speed, there is also reason to ask whether things really have gone too far or whether they have not even gone far enough.

In defending capitalism, what I have in mind is the capitalist freedom to proceed by trial and error, without having to ask rulers and frontier officials first. This is fundamentally the liberty which I once thought anarchy would bring, but under the control of laws ensuring that one person's freedom will not encroach on other people's. I want everyone to have that liberty in plenty. If the critics of capitalism feel that we already have a superabundance of that liberty today, I would like to have more still – a super-duper-abundance if possible. Especially for the poor of the world's population, who as things now stand have little say regarding their work and consumption. That is why I do not hesitate to call this book *a defence of global capitalism*, even though that world capitalism is more a possible future than a genuinely existing system.

By capitalism I do not specifically mean an economic system of capital ownership and investment opportunities. Those things can also exist in a command economy. What I mean is the liberal market economy, with its free competition based on the right of using one's property, the freedom to negotiate, to conclude agreements and to start up business activities. What I am defending, then, is individual liberty in the economy. Capitalists are dangerous when, instead of capitalist ownership, they join forces with the government. If the state is a dictatorship the enterprises can actually be a party to human rights violations, as for example in the case of a number of western oil companies in African states. By the same token, capitalists frequenting the corridors of political power in search of benefits and privileges are not capitalists either. On the contrary, they are a threat to the free market and as such must be criticised and counteracted. It often happens that businessmen want to play politics and politicians want to play at being businessmen. This is not a market economy, it is a mixed economy in which entrepreneurs and politicians have confused their roles. Free capitalism exists when politicians pursue liberal policies and entrepreneurs do business.

There is a further point I would like to make in penning this defence of capitalism. Basically, what I believe in is neither capitalism nor globalisation. It is not systems or regulatory codes that achieve all we see around us in the way of prosperity, inventions, communities and culture. These things are created by people. I believe in man's capacity for achieving great things and in the combined force which results from encounters and exchanges. I plead for greater liberty and a more open world, not because I believe one system happens to be more efficient than another, but because I can see it provides a setting which liberates individuals and their creativity as no other system can. That it spurs the dynamism which has led to human, economic, scientific and technical advances, and which will go on doing so. Believing in capitalism does not mean believing in growth, the economy or efficiency. Desirable as they may be, these are only the results. Belief in capitalism is, fundamentally, belief in mankind.

This also means that, in common, presumably, with most other liberals, I can endorse the opinion of French socialist prime minister Lionel Jospin that we must have a "market economy, not a market society". My aim is not for economic transactions to supplant all other human relations. My aim is freedom and voluntary relations in all fields. The market economy is a result of this in the economic field, in the cultural field it means freedom of expression and press freedom, in politics it means democracy and the rule of law, in social life it means the right to live according to one's own values and to choose one's own company.

It is not the intention that we should put price tags on everything. The important things in life – love, the family, friendship, one's own way of life – cannot be valued in money. Those who believe that to the liberal mind everyone does everything with the aim of maximising their income know nothing about liberals, and any liberal of such persuasions knows nothing of human nature. It is not a desire for better payment that moves me to write a book about the value of globalisation instead of, say, coarse fishing. I am writing because this is something I believe in, because to me it matters. And I wish to live in a liberal society because it gives people the right to choose what matters to them.

Last of all, my heartfelt thanks to the friends who helped me to marshal my thoughts on these matters, for the simple reason that this subject also matters to them, especially in the case of Fredrik Erixon, Sofia Nerbrand and Mauricio Rojas. A great thanks also to Barbro Bengtson, Kristina von Unge and Charlotte Häggblad for their efficiency in making my manuscript possible to publish.

Stockholm, September 2001
Johan Norberg

I

Every day in every way...

The half-truth

At least ever since 1014, when Archbishop Wulfstan, preaching in York, declared that "The world is in a rush and is getting close to its end", people have believed that everything is growing worse, that things were better in the old days. Much of the discussion surrounding globalisation presupposes that the world is rapidly going to the dogs. Last year, Archbishop K. G. Hammar of Sweden echoed his colleague of a thousand years ago by summing up world development in the following terms:

People can see that we are going off the rails and there isn't the slightest little communication cord for anyone to pull. [5]

In particular, the world is said to have become increasingly unfair. The chorus of the debate on the market economy runs: "The rich are getting richer and the poor are getting poorer." If anything this is regarded as a dictate of natural law, not a thesis to be argued. If we look beyond the catchy slogans and study what has actually happened in the world, we find this thesis to be a half-truth. The first half is true: the rich have indeed grown richer. Not all of them everywhere, but generally speaking. Those of us who are privileged to live in affluent countries have grown appreciably richer in the past few decades. So too have the Third World rich. But the second half is, quite simply, wrong. The poor have not, generally speaking, come to be worse off in recent decades. On the contrary, extreme poverty has

---

5. Wulfstan, cit. Giddens 1999, p. 1, Hammar was interviewed in *Arena* 6/2000.

diminished, and where it was quantitatively greatest – in Asia – many hundreds of millions of people who, barely twenty years ago, were struggling to make ends meet have begun to achieve a secure existence and even a modest degree of affluence. Global misery has diminished and the great injustices have started to tremble. This opening chapter will contain a long succession of figures and trend descriptions, but it has to in order to refute the very widespread fallacy that exists concerning the world's condition.[6]

One of the most important books published in recent years is *I Asiens tid*, a reportage book in which Swedish author Lasse Berg and documentary film-maker Stig Karlsson describe new visits to Asian countries where they travelled during the 1960s. On that occasion they saw poverty, abject misery and imminent disaster. Like many other travellers to the same countries, they could not bring themselves to believe in a hopeful future, and they thought socialist revolution, possibly, was the only way out. Returning to India and China in the 1990s, they cannot help seeing how wrong they were. More and more people have extricated themselves from poverty, the problem of hun-

---

6. Unless otherwise indicated, the facts and figures quoted in this chapter come from the UN Development Programme (UNDP) and the World Bank, especially the respective annual publications of these two institutions, *Human Development Report and World Development Report*, and the compilation entitled *World Development Indicators*, 2000. Figures, it should be noted, sometimes vary from one source to another, due to differences in the methods of measurement, and so care must be taken to employ one and the same method when studying a certain change over time.

In this book, when contrasting developing countries with industrialised countries, I refer to the commonly accepted definition of developing (or underdeveloped) countries as those suffering, for example, from a low standard of living, poor public health and education, low productivity, shortage of capital, heavy economic dependence on agriculture and raw materials, and instability and dependence on the international arena. Cf. Todaro 1997, p. 38. By this definition, about 135 of the poorest states are counted as developing countries. It is important to remember that the differences between these countries are so great that it is hard to speak of them as one group. The concept lumps together dictatorships and democracies, war zones and growth markets, abysmally poor, famine-wracked countries, and countries heading for the ranks of the industrialised nations.

ger is steadily diminishing, the streets are cleaner. Mud huts have given way to brick buildings which are wired up for electricity and have television aerials on their roofs.

When the two Swedes first visited Calcutta, a tenth of its inhabitants were homeless, and every morning lorries from public authorities or missionary societies went round collecting the bodies of dossers who had died in the night. Thirty years later, setting out to photograph people living on the streets, they have difficulty in finding any. And the stereotypes come tumbling down. The rickshaw, that remarkable conveyance known to many of us from the Tintin albums, consisting of a passenger cart with a barefoot man between the shafts, is disappearing from the urban scene, and people are travelling by car, motorbike and subway instead.

When Lasse Berg and Stig Karlsson show young Indians photographs of what things looked like on their last visit, the youngsters refuse to believe that it is even the same place. Could things really have been so dreadful? Developments are highlighted for the reader by two photographs on page 42 in their book. In the old one, taken in 1976, Satto, a twelve-year-old Indian girl, holds up her hands. They are already furrowed and worn, prematurely aged by many years' hard work. Beneath it is a recent picture of Satto's thirteen-year-old daughter Seema, also holding up her hands. They are young and soft, the hands of a child whose childhood has not been taken away from her.

The biggest change of all is in people's thoughts and dreams. Television and newspapers bring ideas and impressions from the other side of the globe, widening people's notions of what is possible. Why should one have to spend all one's life in one place? Why must a woman be forced to have children early and sacrifice her career? Why must marriages be arranged and the untouchables excluded from them when family relations in other countries are so much freer? Why make do with this policy when there are alternative political systems available?

Lasse Berg writes, self-critically:

Reading what we observers, foreigners as well as Indians, wrote in the 60s and 70s, nowhere in these analyses do I see anything of present-day India. Often nightmare scenarios – overpopulation, tumult, upheaval or stagnation – but not this calm and steady forward-jogging, and least of all this modernisation of thoughts and dreams. Who foresaw that consumerism would penetrate so deeply in and among the villages? Who foresaw that both economy and prosperity would do so well? Looking back, what the descriptions have in common is an overstatement of the extraordinary, frightening, uncertain (most writers had their personal hobby-horses and favourites) and an understatement of the force of normality.[7]

This development has resulted, not from socialist revolution but, on the contrary, from a move in the past few decades towards greater individual liberty. The freedom to choose and the international exchange have grown, investments and development assistance have transmitted ideas and resources. In this way benefit has been derived from the knowledge, wealth and inventions of other countries. Imports of medicines and new health care systems have improved living conditions. Modern technology and new methods of production have moved production forward and improved the food supply. Individual citizens have become more and more free to choose their own occupations and to sell their products. We can tell from the statistics how this enhances national prosperity and reduces poverty among the population. But the most important thing of all is liberty itself, the independence and dignity which autonomy confers on people who have been living under oppression.

Slavery, which a couple of hundred years ago was a worldwide phe-

---

7. Berg & Karlsson, p. 96.

nomenon, has been beaten down in one continent after another, concomitantly with the spread of humanist ideas. It lives on today, illegally, but since the liberation of the Arab Peninsula in 1970 has been forbidden practically everywhere on earth. The forced labour of precapitalist economies is being rapidly superseded by freedom of contract and freedom of movement where the market breaks through.

Poverty reduction

Between 1965 and 1998, the average world citizen's income practically doubled, from 2,497 to 4,839 dollars, corrected for purchasing power and in fixed money terms. This has *not* come about through the industrialised nations multiplying their incomes. During this period the richest one-fifth of the world's population increased their average income from 8,315 to 14,623 dollars, i.e. by roughly 75 per cent. For the poorest one-fifth of the world's population, the increase has been faster still, with average income rising during the same period from 551 to 1,137 dollars, i.e. more than doubling.[8] World consumption today is more than twice what it was in 1960.

Material developments in the past half-century have resulted in the world having over three billion more people liberated from poverty. This is historically unique. UNDP, the UN Development Programme, has observed that, all in all, world poverty has fallen more during the past 50 years than during the preceding 500. In its 1997 *Human development report*, the UNDP notes that humanity is in the midst of "the second great ascent". The first began in the 19th century, with the industrialisation of the USA and Europe and the rapid spread of prosperity. The second began during the post-war era and is now in full swing, with first Asia and then the other developing countries noting ever-greater advances in the war against poverty, hunger, disease and illiteracy.

---

8. Melchoir, Telle & Wiig 2000, kap 2.

The great success in reducing poverty in the 20th century shows that eradicating severe poverty in the first decades of the 21st century is feasible, the UNDP argues.[9]

Poverty is still rapidly diminishing. If a person's income is less than one dollar a day, we usually term this extreme poverty. Between 1990 and 1998 the number of the extremely poor fell from just below 1.3 billion to about 1.2 billion. These are uncertain figures, of course, due to the impossibility of compiling income data for all the world's population, and so the reduction may be either greater or smaller than given, but either way it signals what has happened. The interesting thing is that during the same period the world's population grew rapidly, so that the proportion of the extremely poor fell heavily, from 29 to 23.4 per cent. World Bank forecasts point to a continuation of this development and to the present-day percentage of poor being halved by 2015. This hinges on continuing, preferably faster, economic growth. It is in places where prosperity has grown fastest that poverty has been most effectively combated. In East Asia (China excluded), extreme poverty has fallen from 15 to just over 9 per cent, in China from 32 to 17 per cent. Six Asians in ten were extremely poor in 1975. Today's figure is fewer than two out of ten.

"But," the sceptic asks, "what do people in the developing countries want consumption and growth for, why must we force our way of life upon them?" The answer is that we must not force a particular way of life on anyone, but whatever their values generally, the great majority of people the world over desire better material conditions, for the simple reason that they will then have more options, regardless of what priorities they then opt for. As Amartya Sen, Indian economist and Nobel laureate, has emphasised, and others with him, poverty is not just a material problem. Poverty is something wider, it

9. UNDP 1997, Overview.

is about powerlessness, about being deprived of basic opportunities and freedom of choice. Small incomes are often symptomatic of the absence of these things, of people being subjected to coercion and marginalization. Human development means leading a reasonably healthy and secure life, with a good standard of living and freedom to shape one's own life. The investigation of material development is important both because it suggests how these conditions have developed and also because it contributes to development as such. It is material resources, individual and societal, which enable people to feed themselves, be educated, obtain health care and be spared watching their children die. These are relatively universal human instincts, one finds, when people are allowed to choose for themselves.

Average life expectancy is increasing.

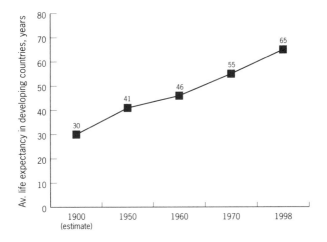

Source: UNDP.

The worldwide improvement is reflected, for example, by a very rapid growth of average life expectancy throughout the world. At the beginning of the 20th century, average life expectancy in the developing countries was about 30, in 1960 it had risen to 46, and in 1998 it was 65. Longevity in the developing countries today is higher than it was a hundred years ago in what was then the world's leading economy, Britain. Development has been slowest in Africa south of Sahara, but even there life expectancy has risen, from 41 to 51 years since the 1960s. Average life expectancy remains highest, however, in the most affluent countries, and in the OECD countries it is 78. But the fastest improvement has been in the poor countries. In 1960 their average life expectancy was 60 per cent of that of the affluent countries, today it is more than 80 per cent. Nine out of every ten people in the world today can expect to live beyond 60, which is more than twice the average only a hundred years ago.

In *I Asiens tid* Lasse Berg describes returning to Malaysia thirty years after his first visit and suddenly realising that in the meantime the average life expectancy of its population has risen by 15 years. This means that the people he meets there have been able to celebrate *every* birthday since his last visit by only coming half a year closer to death.[10]

The improvement in health has been partly due to better eating habits and living conditions, but also to improved care. Twenty years ago there was one doctor for every thousand inhabitants, today there are 1.5. In the very poorest countries there was 0.6 of a doctor per thousand inhabitants in 1980, and this has almost doubled to 1.0. Perhaps the most dependable indicator of the living conditions of the poor is infant mortality, which in the developing countries has fallen drastically. Whereas 18 per cent of new-borns – almost one in five! – died in 1950, by 1976 this had fallen to 11 per cent and in 1995 was

---

10. Berg & Karlsson, p. 300.

only 6 per cent. In the past thirty years alone, mortality has been almost halved, from 107 deaths for thousand births in 1970 to 59 per thousand in 1998. More and more people, then, have been able to survive despite poverty. The statistics nevertheless show a progressively smaller proportion of the world's population to be poor, which in turn suggests that the reduction of poverty has been still greater than is apparent from a superficial study of the statistics.

Infant mortality is declining.

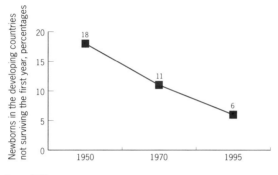

Source: UNDP.

Hunger

The fact of people living longer and in better health is partly connected with the reduction of one of the cruellest manifestations of underdevelopment: hunger. Calorie intake in the Third World has risen by 30 per cent per capita since the 60s. According to FAO, the UN Food and Agriculture Organisation, 960 million people in the developing countries were undernourished in 1970. In 1991 the figure was 830 million, falling by 1996 to 790 million. In proportion to population this is an immensely rapid improvement. Thirty years ago nearly 37 per cent of the population of the developing countries were afflicted with hunger. Today's figure is 18 per cent. Many? Yes. Too many? Of course. But the number is rapidly declining. It took the first two decades of the 20th century for Sweden to be declared free from chronic malnutrition. In only 30 years the proportion of hungry in the world has been reduced by half, and it is expected to decline further, to 12 per cent, by 2010. There have never been so many of us on earth, and we have never had such a good supply of food. Things have moved fastest in East and Southeast Asia, where the proportion of hungry fell during this period from 43 to 13 per cent. In Latin America it has fallen from 19 to 11 per cent, in North Africa and the Middle East from 25 to 9 per cent, in South Asia from 38 to 23 per cent. The worst development has occurred in Africa south of the Sahara, where the proportion of hungry has actually increased, from 89 to 180 million people. But even there the hungry percentage of population has declined, albeit marginally, from 34 to 33 per cent.

World hunger is declining.

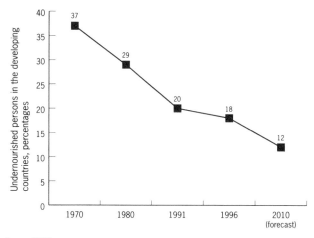

Source: UNDP.

Global food production has doubled during the past half-century, and in the developing countries it has tripled. Compared with the beginning of the 1960s, per capita food production is up by 22 per cent worldwide, and the developing countries are producing no less than 49 per cent more grain per capita. Very little of this development is due to new land having been broken. Instead it is the old land that is being farmed more efficiently. The yield per hectare of arable land has virtually doubled. Wheat, maize and rice prices have fallen by over 60 per cent. Since the beginning of the 1980s alone, food prices have halved and production from a certain area of land has risen by 25 per cent – a process which has been swifter in poor countries than in affluent ones.

This is the triumph of "the green revolution". Higher-yield, more resistant crops have been developed, at the same time as sowing, irrigation, manuring and harvesting methods have improved dramatically. New, efficient strains of wheat account for over 75 per cent of production in the developing countries, and farmers there are estimated to have earned nearly 5 billion dollars by the change. In southern India the green revolution is estimated to have boosted farmers' real earnings by 90 per cent and those of landless peasants by 125 per cent in 20 years. Its impact has been least in Africa, but even there it has raised maize production per hectare by between 10 and 40 per cent. Without this revolution, it is estimated that world prices of wheat and rice would be nearly 40 per cent higher than today and that roughly 2 per cent of the world's children who are now getting enough to eat would have suffered from chronic undernourishment. Today's food problem has nothing to do with overpopulation, it is due to not everyone being able to afford to buy food or being free to produce it in secure conditions and having access to the knowledge and technology available. If modern farming techniques were applied in all the world's agriculture, we would already be able here and now to feed another billion or so people, many researchers claim.[11]

The incidence of major famine disasters has also declined dramatically, very much due to many states having become democracies. Starvation has occurred in states of practically every kind – communist régimes, colonial empires, technocratic dictatorships and ancient tribal societies. In all cases they have been centralised, authoritarian states suppressing free debate and the workings of the market. As Amartya Sen remarks, there has never been a famine disaster in a democracy. Even poor democracies, like India and Botswana, have avoided starvation despite having a poorer food supply than many countries where disaster of this kind has struck. By contrast, communist states like China, the Soviet Union, Cambodia, Ethiopia and North Korea, and colonies like India under the British Raj, have evo-

---

11. *Forbes* 16th Nov. 1998, p. 36, World Bank 2000a, p. 184.

ked starvation. Which goes to show that famine is caused by dictatorship, not by food shortage. Famine is induced by leaders destroying production and trade, making war and ignoring the plight of the starving population.

Amartya Sen maintains that democracies are spared starvation for the simple reason that it is easily prevented, if the rulers of society wish to prevent it. Rulers can refrain from impeding the distribution of food and they can create jobs for people who would not be able to afford food purchases in times of crisis. But dictators are under no pressure, because they can always eat their fill. Democratic leaders are under pressure, because otherwise they will be unseated. Added to which, a free press makes the general public aware of the problems, so that they can be tackled in time. In a dictatorship, even the leaders can be deceived by censorship. There is much to suggest that China's leaders were reassured by their own propaganda and their subordinates' cosmeticised statistics while 30 million people died of starvation during "the Great Leap Forward" between 1958 and 1961.[12]

At the same time as more people are getting the food they need, the supply of potable drinking water has doubled, which is hugely important for the reduction of disease and infection in the developing countries. Worldwide, eight people in ten now have access to pure water. A generation ago, 90 per cent of the world's rural population were without pure water, today this applies to only 25 per cent. At the beginning of the 1980s, little more than half of India's population had access to pure water, while ten years later the figure was over 80 per cent. In Indonesia the same percentage rose from 39 to 62. Countries like Kuwait and Saudi Arabia today derive large parts of their water supply from desalination of seawater, which is available in practically unlimited quantities. Desalination is a costly process, but it shows that growing prosperity can solve even problems of resources.

------

12. Sen 1999, chap. 7.

Education

Education is one of the most reliable methods of increasing people's development and earning prospects. At the same time, many people are debarred from it. This is very much a gender issue. Roughly 65 per cent of those who are not allowed to attend school, and thus remain illiterate, are girls. It is also a poverty problem. In many countries the poorest people have no education at all. Poor families cannot afford to send their children to school, because their earnings are indispensable, school is too expensive or the return on education is insufficient. In India, children from the 15 per cent of wealthiest families receive 10 years more schooling than those from the poorest 15 per cent. And so it is no surprise that education is quickly extended when the economy gathers speed. This in turn acts as a spur to economic growth.

Participation in junior school education has come close to 100 per cent the world over. The big exception, once again, is Africa south of the Sahara, and even there it has risen to three-quarters. Participation in further education rose from 27 per cent in 1960 to 67 per cent in 1995. During that time the proportion of children allowed to attend school rose by 80 per cent. Today there are nearly 900 million illiterate adults. That sounds a lot, and indeed it is, but it represents a heavy decrease, from 70 per cent of the population of the developing countries in the 1950s to between 25 and 30 per cent today. The very rapid spread of literacy in the world today is readily apparent from an examination of literacy rates for different generations. Where the youngest people are concerned, illiteracy is rapidly disappearing.

Illiteracy is diminishing

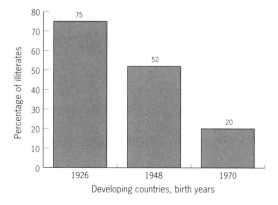

Source: UNESCO

Democratisation

The accelerating spread of information and ideas throughout the world, coupled with rising education standards and growing prosperity, is also accentuating demands for genuine political rights. Critics of globalisation maintain that a dynamic market and international capital are a threat to democracy, but what they really see threatened is the use they would like to make of democracy, namely as a means of augmenting governmental power. Never before in human history have democracy, universal suffrage and the free formation of opinion been as widespread as they are today.

A hundred years ago, no country on earth had universal and equal suffrage. The world was ruled by empires and monarchies. Even in the western countries women were excluded from the democratic process. During the 20th century, large parts of the world were subjugated by communism, fascism or nazism, ideologies which have led to major wars and the political assassination of more than a hundred million people. With just a few exceptions, those systems have fallen. The totalitarian states have collapsed, the dictatorships have been democratised and the absolute monarchies have been deposed. A hundred years ago, one-third of the world's population was governed by remote colonial powers. Today the colonial empires have been dismantled. In the past few decades alone, dictatorships have fallen like ninepins, especially following the tearing down of the communist Iron Curtain. The end of the Cold War also put an end to the unpleasant American strategy of supporting Third World dictatorships as long as they opposed the Soviet bloc.

According to the American think tank Freedom House there are today 120 democracies with multi-party systems and with universal, equal suffrage. Living in those democracies are 3.5 billion people, i.e. roughly 60 per cent of the world's population. 86 countries with a total of 2.5 billion inhabitants are regarded as "free", i.e. democratic countries with civic rights. That is more than 40 per cent of the world's inhabitants, the biggest proportion ever. That many, in other words, are living in states which guarantee the rule of law and permit free debate and an active opposition.

The world is being democratised.

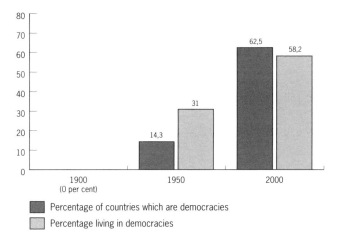

Percentage of countries which are democracies
Percentage living in democracies

Source: Freedom House, 2000

At present there are 47 states which are violating basic human rights. Worst among them are Afghanistan, Burma, Equatorial Guinea, Iraq, Cuba, Libya, North Korea, Saudi Arabia, Sudan, Syria and Turkmenistan – that is, countries least affected by globalisation and least oriented in favour of the market economy and liberalism. While deploring and combating their oppression, suppression of opinion, government-controlled media and wire-tapping, we should still remember that this was the normal state of affairs for most of the world's population only a few decades ago. In 1973 only 20 countries with populations of more than a million were democratically governed.[13]

During the 1990s the number of "free" states in the world increased by 21, at the same time as the number of unfree ones declined by 3. This has proceeded parallel to the formation of many new states, following the disintegration of old ones like the Soviet Union. The democratic trend continues. And there is no reason to expect it to end now. Now and then it is alleged that democracy is hard to reconcile with Islam, and so it may seem in the world today. But we should remember that many researchers were saying the same about Catholicism as recently as the 70s, when Catholic countries included, for example, the military régimes of Latin America, the communist states of eastern Europe and dictatorships like the Philippines under Marcos.

The number of wars has diminished by half during the past decade, and today less than one per cent of the world's population are directly affected by military conflicts, one reason being that democracies simply do not make war on each other, and another being that international exchange makes conflict less interesting. With freedom of movement and free trade, an inhabitant is not all that interested in the size of his or her country. Prosperity is created, not by annexing land from another country but by being able to carry on trade with that land and its resources. If, on the other hand, the world consists of self-contained national states, the land of other countries has no value until one is able to seize it.

---

13. Freedom House, 2001.

"The ox made peace" is a 16th century saying from the border country between Denmark and Sweden. What happened was that the farmers of Småland (Sweden) and Blekinge (Denmark) made peace with each other, against the wishes of their rulers, because they wanted to trade meat and butter for herring and spices. Or, as the 19th century French liberal Frédéric Bastiat put it: "If goods do not cross borders, soldiers will." Mutual dependence means fewer potential causes of conflict between states. Cross-ownership, foreign corporations and investments and privately owned natural resources make it hard to tell where one country really begins and the other one ends. Several centuries ago, when the Swedes ravaged the continent, it was other people's resources they stole. If we were to do the same thing today, Swedish companies, Swedish capital and Swedish export markets would bulk large among our victims.

It has been asserted that the globalist challenge to national states leads to separatism and to local and ethnic conflicts. There is indeed a risk of separatist activity when national power is called into question, and the tragedy of the former Yugoslavia is evidence of the bloody conflicts which can follow. But the number of major internecine conflicts – costing over a thousand lives – fell from 20 to 13 between 1991 and 1998. Nine of those conflicts occurred in Africa, the world's least democratised, least globalised and least capitalist continent. The conflicts following upon the collapse of totalitarian states are above all power struggles in temporary vacuums. In several countries, centralisation has prevented the evolution of stable, democratic institutions and civil societies, and when centralisation disappears, chaos ensues pending the establishment of new institutions. There is no reason for believing this to be a new trend in a more internationalised and democratic world.

Oppression of women

One of the world's cruellest injustices concerns the oppression of women. There are parts of the world where the woman is regarded as the man's property. A father is entitled to marry off his daughter, and it is the husband who decides what work his wife is to do. In many countries it is the husband who owns the woman's passport or ID card, with the result that she cannot even travel freely in her own country. Laws disqualify women from divorce, from ownership of property and from work outside the home, and deny their daughters the same rights of inheritance as their sons. Girls receive nothing like the same education as boys, and very often no education at all. Women are abused and subjected to genital mutilation and rape without any intervention by the authorities.

It is true, as many complain, that globalisation upsets old traditions and habits. How, for example, do you maintain patriarchal family traditions when the children are suddenly earning more than the head of the family? One of the traditions challenged by globalisation is the longstanding subjugation of women. Through cultural contacts and the interchange of ideas, new hopes and ideals are disseminated. Indian women who can see on television that western women are not necessarily housewives themselves begin to contemplate careers in law or medicine. Chinese women who were previously isolated are inspired to press demands and to make decisions of their own when they are able to read, at the gaogenxie.com website (the name means "high-heeled shoes", a symbol of freedom contrasting with the tradition of bound feet), about sexuality and the challenges of motherhood. When women begin making their own decisions and are enabled to decide their own consumer behaviour and choose their own employment, they become more insistent in demanding equal liberty and power in other fields.

> "My parents brought me up to be pretty and well-behaved. I was to be obedient and polite, submissive to them and my teachers ... When I eventually have children, I want to go in for equality within the family, between man and woman, between children and parents. It wasn't like that for us. To my parents' generation it went without saying that the married woman's life took place within the four walls of the home, where she did everything, even if she was working. I think that age will soon be gone forever."
>
> *Shang Ying, a 21-year-old Chinese girl employed as a bank clerk in Shanghai.*[14]

Growing prosperity gives women more opportunity of becoming independent and providing for themselves. Experience from Africa and elsewhere shows that women are often leading entrepreneurs for various kinds of small-scale production and dealing in the informal sector, which suggests that, barring discrimination and regulation by the government, the market is their oyster. And indeed, the worldwide spread of freer conditions of service and freer markets has made it increasingly difficult for women to be kept out of things. Women today constitute 42 per cent of the world's work force, as against 36 per cent twenty years ago. Capitalism doesn't care whether the best producer is a man or a woman. On the contrary, discrimination is expensive, implying as it does the rejection of certain people's goods and labour. All studies have shown that respect for women's rights and their ability to exert influence in the home are closely bound up with their prospects of employment outside the home and of independent earning.

---

14. Berg & Karlsson 2000, p. 202.

41

Technology can often be a force for renewal. Women in Saudi Arabia are prevented from showing themselves in public unless they cover their whole body except the hands, eyes and feet, and they are disqualified from car driving, among other things. The practical effect of this has been to exclude them from all economic activity. But now the Internet and the telephone have suddenly made it possible for women to carry on business from home, at the computer, and within a short space of time a welter of women's enterprises have come into being, dealing for example in fashion, travel bookings and conference and party arrangements. This is one reason why something like two-thirds of Internet users in Saudi Arabia are women. When several thousand women suddenly show that they are every bit as competitive as men, discrimination notwithstanding, the prohibitions applying to them are made to look increasingly absurd. Awareness and criticism of gender discrimination is growing.[15]

Democratisation gives women a voice in politics, and in more and more countries the laws have been reformed in favour of greater equality between the sexes. Divorce laws and rights of inheritance are becoming less and less biased. Equality before the law spreads with democracy and capitalism. The idea of human dignity knocks out discrimination. This too is accentuated by prosperity. In the poorest one-fifth of Indian households, the difference between the proportion of girls and boys respectively obtaining education is 11 per cent, while in the wealthiest one-fifth it is less than half that, namely 4.7. per cent. In the most unequal parts of the world – South Asia, Africa and the Middle East – the proportion of girls attending school has doubled in the past 25 years. The global difference between the proportion of women and men respectively enabled to attend school has diminished by more than half in two decades. On average in basic education, worldwide, 46 per cent of the pupils are girls.

---

15. "How Women Beat the Rules", *The Economist*, 2nd October 1999.

This is important, not only for the women but also for their children, because better education and extra earnings for a mother quickly result in the children becoming better-nourished and educated, whereas paternal status does not present the same connection. In South Asia, where an inhuman attitude concerning the value of women resulted – and still does – in high mortality among girls during the first years of life, girls now have a greater life expectancy at birth than boys. The average life expectancy of women in the developing countries has increased by 20 years during the past half-century. Development is also giving women more power over their own bodies. Increased power for women in poor countries, and improved availability of contraception, go hand in hand with reduced nativity.

Helen Rahman of Shoishab, an Oxfam-funded organisation working in Dhaka, Bangladesh, with disadvantaged and homeless children, and with working women, maintains that it is the emergence of the country's textile industry during the past 20 years that has given women better status: "The garment industry has stimulated a silent revolution of social change. It used not to be acceptable for a woman to work outside her neighbourhood. Before, anyone who left the countryside to go to the city was in disgrace; they were assumed to be involved in prostitution. Now it is acceptable for five girls to rent a house together." Helen has noticed changes in social behaviour too: "The income the women earn gives them social status and bargaining power. One very positive thing is that the average marriage age has increased." [16]

16. OXFAM: "The clothes trade in Bangladesh".

China

About half of the world's poor live in the most densely populated countries – India and China – hence the great importance of what happens in those countries. Both their economies have been extensively liberalised in the past twenty years. China's communist dictatorship realised at the end of the 1970s that collectivisation was impeding development. Controls and the compulsory delivery of their produce by farmers were detracting from renewal and crop yields. Deng Xiaoping, China's ruler, wanted to keep faith with the distributive ideas of socialism, but at the same time realised he would have to distribute either poverty or prosperity, and that the latter could only be achieved by giving people more freedom. And so in December 1978, two years after the death of Chairman Mao, he embarked on a programme of liberalisation. Rural families which had previously been forced into collective farming now became entitled to set aside part of their produce for sale at market prices, a system which became increasingly liberal as time went on. In this way the Chinese were impelled to invest in agriculture and improve its efficiency. The possibility of opting out of the collective and formally leasing land from the government was utilised to such a huge extent that in practice nearly all land passed into private hands in what may have been the biggest privatisation in history. It paid off, with crop yields rising between 1978 and 1984 by an incredible 7.7 per cent annually. The country which, twenty years earlier, had been hit by the worst famine in human history now had a food surplus.

Before long this successful kind of market incentive began to be introduced in the rest of the economy. Trade was permitted in the countryside, and also between town and country. The formerly self-sufficient villages were integrated with regional and even national markets. Increased productivity and purchasing power induced many farmers to invest their capital in starting up private and co-operative industrial production. Since then, more and more previously inconceivable phenomena – a freer labour market, foreign trade, direct foreign investments – have become accepted wisdom.

Information about these developments is partly contradictory, owing to the difficulty of obtaining hard facts in an immense dictatorship. But all observers agree that the economic growth and the rise in incomes have been unique. There has been talk of almost 10 per cent growth annually in the twenty years following the reforms, and GDP has more than quadrupled. Economically China remains a dwarf, with a GDP roughly equalling that of the Nordic countries combined. But the dwarf is growing fast! The available income of a city-dweller in China has skyrocketed from 40 to 657 dollars, and in the countryside available income has risen from 16 to 259 dollars. The 1978 liberalisation enabled 800 million Chinese farmers to double their incomes in only six years. The analyst Shuije Yao contends that extreme poverty was long concealed by China's official statistics, but in terms of actual development, half a billion Chinese have left extreme poverty behind them. The World Bank has spoken of "the biggest and fastest poverty reduction in history."[17]

Dramatic economic reverses may very well happen in China. Under the protection of capital regulations, colossal loans have been channelled into the inefficient national government sector and favoured enterprises, while SMEs are under-capitalised. The authorities have impeded insight into banks and corporations, which could precipitate a crisis of huge proportions. But the economy has undergone too much of a fundamental transformation for a reversion to the pre-

17. Yao 2000, World Bank 2000b.

1978 situation, as regards both reforms and prosperity, to be possible.

The Tiananmen Square massacre, the ban in many regions on having more than two children, oppression in Tibet and Sinkiang, the persecution of the Falun Gong movement, labour camps for political prisoners – these phenomena show that not everything has changed in China, unfortunately. Communist party oppression lives on, but fewer and fewer people expect it to survive economic liberalisation in the long term. Through economic liberalisation alone citizens have come to enjoy important liberties. Whereas formerly they had to work wherever they were ordered to, today the Chinese can choose their own employment. Travel and relocation used to be almost impossible, and moving from countryside to town or city was out of the question. Now the Chinese can travel almost freely, they can wear whatever clothing they like and they can spend their money almost as they please.

In the villages they have been more extensively enabled to choose their local representatives. Most often the elections are still controlled by the communist party, but where they are not, the people have shown that a change is what they want, and in nearly one-third of the villages the party system has collapsed. Combining increased local democracy with central dictatorship will be difficult in the long term. Although people can still be arrested for dissent, a wide diversity of opinion has become audible, due very much to international influence and the Internet. Independent organisations are emerging and information is no longer controllable. Even the newspapers are showing greater independence, and corrupt officials can be criticised.

India

Unlike China, India has been a democracy ever since Independence in 1947, but at the same time it has gone in for a strictly regulated economy. The government invested in large-scale industry which has been protected by fierce import and export barriers, with a view to self-sufficiency. This turned out to be a very expensive fiasco. All economic activity was ensnared by regulations and required permits which were practically unobtainable without pulling strings and paying bribes. Any wishing to engage in business had to devote a great deal of their time to buttering up officials, and if successful they were rewarded with protection against competition from others. Economic growth barely kept pace with population growth, and the proportion falling below the Indian poverty line grew from 50 per cent at Independence to 62 per cent in 1966.

In the mid-70s India began a slow re-ordering of its economy. Exclusion and self-sufficiency were replaced with reliance on the country's advantage in labour-intensive industry. Growth started to accelerate in the 80s and poverty to decline. But this expansion was fuelled with borrowed money, resulting in a profound crisis at the beginning of the 90s, whereupon in 1991 the government embarked on a reform aimed at putting its finances in order, welcoming trade and foreign investments and encouraging competition and enterprise. Tariff levels, which had averaged no less than 87 per cent, were lowered to 27. The economy was freed from numerous restrictions by three consecutive governments, even though the governments represented different party constellations.

Although a massive process of reform still remains to be accomplished before India becomes a genuine market economy, great results have already been achieved through more productive use of the country's resources. Since the reform started, India has received a steady stream of investments from abroad, and growth has been running at between 5 and 7 per cent annually. The proportion of inhabitants below the Indian poverty line has now fallen to about 35 per cent, fastest during the years 1993–99. Without this reduction, something like 300 million more Indians would have been poor today. Population growth has fallen by 30 per cent since the end of the 60s and average life expectancy has doubled from about 30 after Independence to about 60 today.[18] Half the poor households of India today own a clock and one-third have a radio.

Developments have varied, however, depending on the extent of reform in the various states of India. Large parts of the countryside, which is where the poor live, have not had the benefit of any major liberalisation measures, and poverty has remained stable. At the same time the southern states in particular – Andhra Pradesh, Karnataka and Tamil Nadu – have made very swift progress with liberalisation. Growth in these states has been above the national average, sometimes approaching an incredible 15 per cent annually, and it is these states which have attracted most investments, both from abroad and from the rest of India. The economy has experienced an IT miracle which among other things has resulted in the software sector growing by 50 per cent annually. In Andhra Pradesh, Microsoft opened its first development centre outside the USA. Economic growth has also left its mark on social development. On average the reforming states have succeeded best with medical care and education, and have achieved the fastest reductions of infant mortality and illiteracy. Girls, who hardly ever received any education at all, are now catching up with boys in terms of school attendance. In several of the states (Andhra

18. Berg & Karlsson 2000, chap. 4.

Pradesh, Maharashtra) poverty has declined by about 40 per cent since the end of the 70s, while in non-liberalised states like Bihar and Uttar Pradesh it has hardly diminished at all.[19]

The Indian caste system – a form of apartheid – which divides, assesses and treats people according to the family they come from, has been officially abolished but has proved very persistent. Locally, not least, people of lower caste are treated as an inferior form of humans with fewer rights than others. But now the system slowly is breaking up, with an unprejudiced market hiring the best workers instead of people from the right families. In more and more places "untouchables" are for the first time taking part in village council meetings. Instead of strengthening the caste system, the government is launching anti-discrimination campaigns. The President himself is an untouchable.

19. Bajpai & Sachs 1999.

Global inequality

This is all very well, many critics of globalisation will argue, but even if the majority are better off, gaps have widened and wealthy people and countries have improved their lot more rapidly than others. So inequality has grown. They point to such facts as the per capita GDP of the 20 richest countries having been 15 times greater than that of the 20 poorest countries 40 years ago and now having grown about 30 times greater.

There are two reasons why this objection to globalisation does not hold water. Firstly, even if this were true it would not matter very much. If everyone is coming to be better off, what does it matter that the improvement comes faster for some than for others? Surely the important thing is for everyone to be as well off as possible, not that others are better off than oneself? Only those who consider wealth a greater problem than poverty can find a problem in some becoming millionaires while others grow wealthier from their own starting points. It is better to be poor in the inegalitarian USA (with a poverty level of about 7,800 USD per year) than to be equal in countries like Rwanda (average income about 220 USD monthly), Bangladesh (about 350 USD) or Uzbekistan (about 700 USD). Often the reason why gaps have widened in certain reforming countries, such as China, is that the towns and cities have grown faster than the countryside, but given the unheard-of poverty reduction this has entailed in both town and country, can anyone wish that this development had never happened?

The poor do not always experience poverty. Many concepts of poverty are relative, which is to say that, instead of measuring how poor someone is, they say how poor that person is in relation to others. One poverty concept frequently used, e.g. by the UNDP, rates a person as poor if they have less than half the median wage in the country where they live. This means that a person regarded as "loaded" when living in a poor country like Nepal is considered as poor as a church mouse when living in the affluent USA. These relative figures, consequently, cannot be compared internationally. Those who are rated poor in the USA are not always living in circumstances which we would term poverty. Thus 72 per cent of poor American families have one or more cars, 50 per cent have air conditioning, 72 per cent have a washing machine, 20 per cent have a dishwasher, 60 per cent have a microwave, 93 per cent have colour TV and 60 per cent a video, and 41 per cent own their homes (the poverty reference is to regular income only, real estate is not included in the income level).[20]

Secondly, the allegation of increased inequality is wrong. The notion of global inequalities having increased is based above all on figures from the UN Development Programme, UNDP, not least its *Human Development* report from 1999. But the problem with these figures is that they are not adjusted for purchasing power, i.e. for what people can actually buy for their money. Without that adjustment the figures mainly show the level of a country's official exchange rate and what its currency is worth on the international market, which is a poor yardstick of poverty. Poor people's actual living standard, needless to say, hinges far more on the cost of their food, clothing and housing than on what they would get for their money when holidaying in Europe. The odd thing is that the UNDP itself uses purchasing power-adjusted figures in its Human Development Index (HDI),

20. Cox & Alm 1999, pp. 14 ff.

which is its universal yardstick of living standards. It only resorts to the unadjusted figures in order to prove a thesis of inequality.

In one report, three researchers at the Norwegian Institute for Foreign Affairs have investigated global inequality by means of figures adjusted for purchasing power. Their data show that, contrary to intuition, inequality between countries has been continuously *declining* ever since the beginning of the 1970s. This decline was especially rapid between 1993 and 1998, when globalisation really gathered speed.[21] Thus the past 30 years have witnessed a global equalisation. Comparing just the richest and poorest tenths, inequality has increased, suggesting that a small group has lagged behind (we shall be returning to see which countries and why), but a study of all countries clearly points to a general growth of equality. If, for example, we compare the richest and poorest fifth or the richest and poorest third, we find the differences diminishing. Economists usually measure the degree of inequality by means of the "gini coefficient". If that is zero, complete equality prevails (everyone owns the same amount), if it is one there is total inequality (with one person owning everything). The gini coefficient for the whole world declined from 0.6 in 1968 to 0.52 in 1997, a reduction of more than 10 per cent.

Since equality between the rich and poor *in* these countries appears to have been roughly constant during this time (having increased in half and diminished in half), then global equality, quite contrary to popular supposition, is increasing. The 1998/99 World Bank report reviews among other things the difference in incomes going to the richest and poorest 20 per cent in the developing countries. The review shows, of course, that the difference is very great, but it also shows that the difference is diminishing in all continents! The real

21. Melchoir, Telle & Wiig, 2000. This development towards greater equality will be even faster in coming decades, with the world's work force growing older and thus earning more equally; see Larsson 2001a.

Global inequality is declining

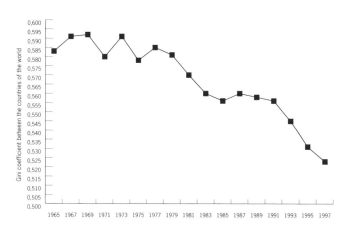

Source: Melchoir, Telle & Wiig, 2000.

exception is post-communist Eastern Europe, where inequality has grown fastest in the countries where reform has been slowest.[22]

Further doubt is cast on the 1999 UNDP report, which contradict this finding, because the UNDP omitted its own statistics for the years when inequality declined fastest, 1995–97. Furthermore, their own welfare statistics, in the Human Development Index, HDI, point to an *even faster* reduction of inequality in the world than is indicated by the Norwegian report. HDI adds together various aspects of welfare – the income, education standard and life expectancy of the population. This index ranges from 0, representing the profoundest misery, to 1, representing complete welfare. This HDI has increased in all groups of countries over the past 40 years, but

22. World Bank 2000d.

fastest of all in the poorest countries. In the OECD countries HDI rose from 0.8 to 0.91 between 1960 and 1993, and in the developing countries it rose faster still, from 0.26 to 0.56.

Standard of living rising everywhere

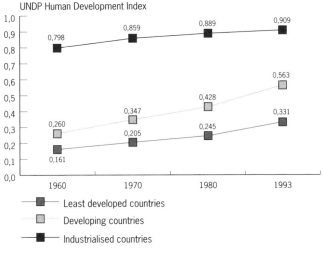

UNDP Human Development Index

- ■ Least developed countries
- □ Developing countries
- ■ Industrialised countries

Source: UNDP.

One sometimes hears it said that the richest fifth of the world's population are 74 times richer than the poorest. Examining what these respective fifths get for their money, i.e. if we use figures adjusted for purchasing power, then the richest fifth is only 16 times richer than the poorest fifth.[23]

23. Larsson 2001a, p. 11 f.

Reservations

This is not by any means to say that all is well with the world, or even that everything is getting better and better. Last year 3 million people died of AIDS, the highest figure ever, orphaned children being one of the cruel consequences. In several African countries more than 15 per cent of the adult population are suffering from HIV or AIDS. Something like 20 million people are now living as fugitives from oppression, conflicts or natural disasters. Even though forecasts concerning the world's water supply have grown more optimistic, we still risk a huge shortage of pure water, possibly resulting in disease and conflicts. About 20 countries, most of them in Southern Africa, have grown poorer since 1965. Illiteracy, hunger and poverty may be diminishing, but many hundreds of millions of people are still afflicted by them. Armed conflicts are growing fewer, but this is cold comfort to the hundreds of thousands of people who are being murdered, maltreated and tortured.

The remaining problems are made all the more intolerable by our knowing that something can actually be done about them. Underdevelopment which appears to be a natural and inevitable circumstance is considered a tragic fate, but when we realise that it is not at all necessary, then fate becomes a problem which can and should be solved. This phenomenon is not unfamiliar: the same thing happened when the Industrial Revolution started to improve living standards in our part of the world 150 years ago. When misery is everywhere, we can easily become oblivious to it, but when it is visible in contrast to something else, our eyes are opened to it – fortunately, because that spurs our efforts to do something about the problems which remain. But this must not deceive us into thinking that the world has actually grown worse, for it has not.

No one can doubt that enormous problems remain in this world of ours, but the fantastic thing is that the spread of democracy and capitalism has reduced them. Where liberal policies have been allowed to operate longest, they have made poverty and deprivation the exception instead of the rule which they have been otherwise, at all times in history and everywhere in the world. Colossal changes await all of us, but at the same time our eyes have been opened to the political and technical solutions which could be applied to them. And so, all things considered, there is no reason why we should not be optimistic.

II

… and it's no coincidence!

That's capitalism for you!

The growth of world prosperity is not a "miracle" or any of these other mystifying terms we customarily apply to countries which have succeeded economically and socially. No schools are built or incomes generated by sheer luck like a bolt from the blue. These things happen due to people thinking along new lines and working hard to bring their ideas to fruition. But people do that everywhere, and there is no God-given reason why certain people in certain places during certain periods in history should be smarter and more capable than others. The main distinguishing factor is whether the environment permits and encourages ideas and work or puts obstacles in their way and tries to exploit the work to its own ends. That depends on whether people are allowed the liberty and possibility of exploring their way ahead, whether they are allowed to own property, invest in the long term, conclude agreements and trade with others. In short, it depends on whether or not they have capitalism. In the affluent world we have had capitalism in one form or another for a couple of hundred years. That is why we are called "the affluent world", because it is capitalism that has given people the liberty and motive forces to create, produce and trade, thereby generating prosperity.

During the past two decades this system has spread throughout the world, in the process termed globalisation. The communist dictatorships in the east and the military dictatorships of the Third World collapsed, and the walls they had raised against ideas, people and goods collapsed with them. Instead ideas have been disseminated which say that creativity cannot be centralised, that it can only be encouraged by entitling citizens to decide for themselves, to create, to think, to work.

Capitalism means that no one is being subjected to outward coercion. We can refrain from signing contracts or doing business deals if we prefer some other solution. And so the only way of getting rich in a free market is by giving people something they want, so that they will pay for it of their own free will. Both parties have to feel that they benefit, otherwise there won't be any deal. Economics, then, is not a zero sum game. Simplifying rather, the bigger a person's income in a market economy, the more that person has done to offer people what they want. Bill Gates and Madonna earn millions and millions, but they don't pinch the money, they earn it by offering software and music which a lot of people think are worth paying for. In this sense they are essentially "servants". In this kind of situation, firms and individuals will struggle to develop better goods and more efficient ways of providing for our needs. The alternative is for the government to take our resources and then decide which types of behaviour to encourage. The only question is why the government knows better than ourselves what we want and what we consider important in our lives.

Prices and profits in a market economy serve as a signalling system which the worker, the entrepreneur and the investor can navigate by. Those who want to earn good wages or make a good profit have to make their way into those parts of the economy where they can best cater to other people's demands. Excessive taxes and handouts pervert these motive forces completely. Price controls are destructive, because they directly distort the necessary price signals. If the government puts a ceiling on prices – that is, imposes a lower price than the market would have done, as for example in the case of rental flats in central Stockholm locations – a shortage will result. People will hang onto the flats they have the tenancy of, even if they don't need them for the moment, and housing companies will stop building. Result: housing shortage. If instead the government puts a floor to prices – that is, imposes a higher price than the market would have done – this will cause surplus. When the EU pays more for foodstuffs than the market, more people than necessary will go in for farming, resulting in surplus production (to be dumped in the developing countries).

But capitalism also requires people to be allowed to retain the resources they earn and create. If you exert yourself and invest for the long term but someone else appropriates most of the profit, the odds are you will give up. Protection of ownership lies at the very heart of a capitalist economy, not only entitling people to the fruits of their labours but also making them free to use their resources without having to ask the authorities first. Capitalism allows people to explore their own way ahead.

This is not to say that someone in the market is necessarily smarter than a bureaucrat, but he is in direct touch with the market and, through the movement of prices, has direct feedback on supply and demand. A centraliser can never collect all this information from all fields, nor is he anywhere near as motivated to be guided by it. And even if one person in the market is no smarter than a bureaucrat, a million people together certainly are! One million different attempts are generally wiser than a single, centralised solution. If the government decides that all resources are to be committed to a certain kind of collective farming and this fails, the whole of society will be economically affected and, if the worst comes to the worst, will starve. If one group of people go in for the same type of farming, e.g. in enterprise form, they alone will suffer the adverse effects if the enterprise fails. A society needs this kind of experimentation and new solutions in order to develop, but at the same time the risks entailed have to be limited, so that the whole edifice of society will not be jeopardised by a few people's mistakes. Therein lies the excellence of individual decision-making and individual responsibility. Personal responsibility, not least, is of the essence. A politician or bureaucrat handling huge sums of money for things like infrastructure investments or campaigning to host the next Olympics is not under the same pressure as entrepreneurs and investors to make rational decisions. If things go wrong and expenditure exceeds income, it isn't the politician who foots the bill.

People who own their property act on a long-term basis, in the knowledge that they will harvest the fruits of their actions. This is the kernel of a capitalist economy – people saving part of what they already have, so as to create more value for the future. This is the same process as when we devote some of our time and energy today to getting a good education which will pay bigger dividends in the long run ("human capital"). In the economy this means that, instead of living from hand to mouth we set aside part of what we have and are rewarded with interest or profits by whoever can use the money more efficiently than we can ourselves. This saving and investment elevates the economy to progressively higher levels. It also finances new machinery and organisational structures to make the workforce more productive.

Organisation is important, because through voluntary co-operation people can produce more than they would by doing everything single-handed. It may take a single craftsman a week to produce a chair, but if he is best at the structure itself and joins forces with someone who can paint and someone who is good at sewing chair cushions, together they can perhaps turn out one chair a day. Given modern machinery they can make a hundred chairs a day. This augments the value of their labour.

Technical progress enabled new machines to manufacture old types of goods less expensively, placing new inventions and goods at people's disposal. As a result of this ongoing improvement of productivity through the division of labour and technical advances, one hour's labour today is worth about 25 times more than it was in the mid-19th century. Employees, consequently, now receive about 25 times as much as they did then, in the form of better pay, better working conditions and shorter working hours. When a person's labour grows more valuable, more firms want to buy it, and to get hold of manpower they then have to raise wages and improve the work situation. If instead wages are increased more rapidly than productivity, through legislation or collective agreements, then jobs will have to go, because the workers' input is not worth what the employer is forced to pay for it. Alternatively one can do as the politicians did for a long time in Sweden – obliterate pay rises by accelerating inflation, so that everyone can keep their jobs. If so, pay hikes will of course be a chimera. Growth and productivity alone are capable of raising real wages in the long run.

All political and economic systems need rules, and this includes even the most liberal capitalism, which presupposes rules defining legitimate ownership, rules on the writing of contracts, the resolution of disputes and many other matters. These rules are needed in order for the market economy to be workable. But there are also rules which prevent the market economy from working – detailed regulations deciding what use people can make of their property and making it difficult to start up a certain kind of activity, owing to the need for licences and permits or restrictive rules on pricing and business transactions. These regulations mainly serve to give more power over the economy to public authorities which are not themselves a part of it and which have not risked their own money. They add up to a heavy burden on the creators of our prosperity. In Sweden alone, entrepreneurs have about 20,000 rules to keep tabs on. Little wonder, then, that more people do not translate their good ideas into entrepreneurial activity.

These rules are also harmful in another way. Impediments to necessary activity result in a large part of a firm's time being devoted to circumventing the rules – time which could otherwise be devoted to production. If this is too difficult, people join the informal economy instead, thereby depriving themselves of legal protection for their business dealings. Many firms will use their resources to coax politicians into adapting the rules to their needs – resources which could otherwise have been used for investment. Many will be tempted to take shortcuts, and bureaucrats will oblige in return for generous bribes, especially in poor countries where salaries are low and regulatory systems more or less chaotic. The commonest way of corrupting a nation through and through is by stipulating permits and controls for production, for imports, for exports, for investments. More than two and a half millennia ago, the Oriental teacher Lao-tse declared: "The more laws that are made, the more numerous thieves and bandits become."

Economic freedom reduces corruption

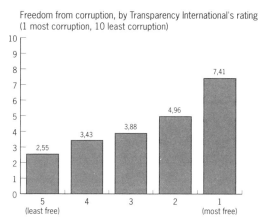

Freedom from corruption, by Transparency International's rating
(1 most corruption, 10 least corruption)

The countries of the world, divided into fifths by degrees of economic freedom.
Source: Gwartney & Lawson et al., 2001.

For restoring honest rules and incorruptible officials, there is no better way than substantial deregulation. Amartya Sen finds in the struggle against corruption a perfectly adequate reason for developing countries to deregulate their economies, even if no other economic benefits were to accrue from so doing.[24]

---

24. Sen 1999, p. 276.

Growth – a blessing

All experience indicates that it is in liberal régimes that wealth is created and development sustained. Politics and economics are not exact sciences. We cannot perform laboratory experiments in order to ascertain which systems work and which do not, but no social phenomenon comes closer than capitalism to achieving this very thing. There are a number of instances of a similar population, with similar preconditions and sharing the same language and norms, being subjected to two different systems, one a market economy and the other a centrally controlled command economy. Thus with Germany divided into capitalist West and communist East, there was talk of an economic miracle in the western part, which in the end had to foot the entire bill for reunification with the ramshackle eastern part, even though the latter was the wealthiest among its Eastern European peers. The same thing happened with capitalist South Korea and communist North Korea. The former was numbered among the Asian tigers, convincing the world that developing countries *can* develop. Whereas in the 1960s it was as poor as Bangladesh, today, with the world's tenth largest economy, it is almost as affluent as a Western European country. The North Korean economy, by contrast, underwent a total collapse, and the country is now afflicted with mass starvation. One can also see the difference between Taiwan, a market economy, which has experienced one of the swiftest economic developments in history, and communist mainland China, which suffered starvation and misery until it saw fit to start opening up its markets.

The same comparison is visible all over the world. The greater the degree of economic liberalism in a country, the more chance that country has of attaining higher prosperity, faster growth, a higher standard of living and higher average life expectancy. People in the economically freest countries are nearly ten times as rich as those in the least free, and they are living more than twenty years longer!

Economic freedom brings prosperity

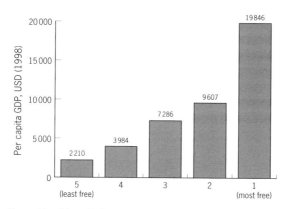

The countries of the world, divided into fifths by degrees of economic freedom.
Source: Gwartney & Lawson et al., 2001.[25]

---

25. These charts, of course, do not distinguish between cause and effect. They could be compatible with countries first growing rich and then starting to liberalise the economy. This is a material factor, but looking at the countries concealed by these figures, one finds that the relation mainly operates in the contrary direction, i.e. that liberalisation measures are accompanied by growth. Nothing I have to say here should be taken to imply that history, culture and other factors make no difference to national development. On the contrary, I believe, for example, that people's ideas and convictions are of momentous import for economic development, but I have concentrated here on the political factors, which of course also impact people's motive forces.

Economic freedom brings growth

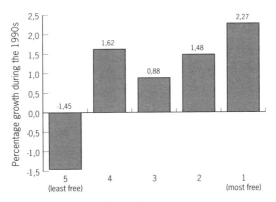

The countries of the world, divided into fifths by degrees of economic freedom.
Source: Gwartney & Lawson et al., 2001.

Economic freedom raises living standards

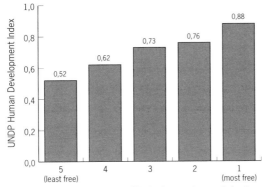

The countries of the world, divided into fifths by degrees of economic freedom.
Source: Gwartney & Lawson et al., 2001.

Economic freedom increases average life expectancy

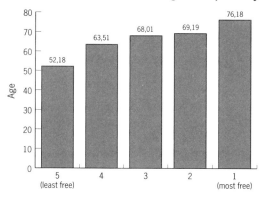

The countries of the world, divided into fifths by degrees of economic freedom.
Source: Gwartney & Lawson et al., 2001.

The economic development of the past two centuries has no counterpart prior to the breakthrough of the market economy in the 19th century. Historically, the normal state of affairs was for people to be more or less destitute, surviving from one day to the next. The medieval European was often chronically undernourished and worked, in his or her one and only article of clothing, in houses which were so filthy and verminous that, in the words of a historian: "From a health point of view the only thing to be said in their favour was that they burnt down very easily!"[26] After the 16th century, when different parts of the world, very slowly and tentatively, began trading with each other, we do find examples of growth, but it was marginal in the extreme.

---

26. Buer, cit. Rand 197, p. 114.

Poverty in the 18th century was much the same on every continent. According to highly uncertain estimates, Europe was only 20 per cent wealthier than the rest of the world. Then, 180 years ago, in about 1820, Europe, as a result of the Industrial Revolution, began moving further ahead. But poverty remained appalling. Per capita income in the very richest European countries was between 1,000 and 1,500 dollars – roughly the same level as in present-day Bolivia or Kazakhstan. Even if all incomes had been perfectly equally distributed, this would still have been insufficient for more than a state of abject misery, with neither clean water nor daily bread and with little more than one garment or so per person. About 75 per cent of the world's population lived in extreme poverty. These are levels which today are scarcely to be seen anywhere in the world: only the very poorest countries – Mali, Zambia and Nigeria, for example – come anywhere near them. During the 200 years since then, per capita incomes have multiplied several times over, worldwide. Global growth during the 320 years between 1500 and 1820 has been estimated at a mere thirtieth of what the world has experienced since then.[27] Since then, incomes in Europe have multiplied more than ten times over. Asia too has put on speed during the past half-century and, the path to prosperity being already known, has trodden it still faster. Living standards today, compared with 1950, are eight times higher in Japan and six times higher in China.

Increased investments and the urge to devise better, more efficient solutions to old problems enable us to produce more, and growth accelerates. This generates new ideas and machinery, enabling the workforce to produce more. GDP – gross domestic product – is a measure of the value of all goods and services produced in a country. Investigating this value per inhabitant of a country – *per capita*, "per head" – we can roughly gauge that country's wealth. Growth – our

27. Maddison, 1995.

producing more goods and services – may not sound the most exciting thing on earth in everybody's ears, and certain radical circles have even come to disdain it, branding those who do care about it as "economistic" or "growth fanatics". This may be partly a healthy reaction to some people having begin to see high GDP as an end in itself, but growth, quite simply, means that production grows, and prosperity and opportunities with it. In our affluent world it may be the prerequisite for starting to save, to consume more, to invest in welfare or, quite simply, to work less for the same payment. In the developing countries it can mean the difference between life and death, development and stagnation, for it is growth that can provide scope for healthy foodstuffs and pure drinking water.[28]

For everyday living in India, growth since the 1980s has meant mud huts being superseded by brick buildings and muddy paths being paved and asphalted. Radios have become widespread, and 40 per cent of the population now have access to television. Electricity has become everyman's property and the dark alleys now have street lighting. Those alleys no longer reek of garbage, and hotbeds of infection are removed by proper drainage. Even the poor can afford clothing and footwear. As the clearest example of what growth implies, the Indian woman no longer washes half her sari at a time. Time was when she had to, because she only possessed one and thus had to wash it while still wearing it.

---

28. The view of growth as an end in itself is absurd. That way, the important thing would be just producing as much as possible. That kind of growth is easily created by the state taking everyone's money and starting up an enormous output of things which people don't want. As for example with steel and munitions in the Soviet Union. Growth has to take place on people's terms, i.e. by producing things which people are demanding. That is why, fundamentally, it is only in a market economy, where demand impacts on prices and production, that growth can really take place in fields where people benefit.

Incomes and living standards go hand in hand

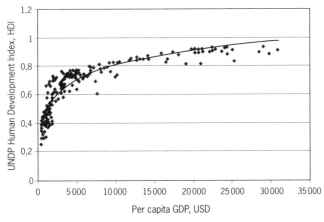

Source: Melchoir, Telle & Wiig, 2000, p. 96.

Growth also means opportunities and power for people. It means that, instead of resorting to the local usurer and getting into debt for a life-time, the ordinary Indian can turn to a bank instead. People can look for jobs in different places, with different entrepreneurs, which eman-cipates the poor from the power of life and death which the village landlord once had over them. Although India has had democratic elections, they do not make all that much difference so long as the poor are completely at the beck and call of the local élite, because then they still have to vote as they are told. Parents in the poor part of the world do not send their children out to work because they like doing it, but because they need the money to feed the family. Growth gives them better incomes and improves the return on education, which means they can send their children to school instead. This also gives the individual greater opportunity within the family. A law against wife beating can be ineffective if the woman is economically dependent on her husband for survival, because in that case she will neither report him nor leave him. When the economy grows and more production materialises, the woman has a chance of getting a job away from home. She becomes less dependent on the husband's caprices.

"In my mother's day women had to grin and bear it. I wouldn't have any of it. I can speak my mind. Life isn't just meant to be sacrifice, you also have to be able to enjoy it. That, I think, is the great change that is happening in Japan. People no longer want to work and work. Today they also want to have time for a good life and a little enjoyment."
29-year-old Japanese Eriklo, who instead of following in her parents' footsteps and working on the land became an advertising artist. [29]

It is sometimes argued that growth only benefits the rich, while the poor of society lag behind. This is a curious notion. Why should poor people benefit less than others from society growing richer? Two World Bank economists, David Dollar and Aart Kraay, studied 40 years' income statistics from 80 countries to see whether this was really true. Their studies show that growth benefits the poor just as much as the rich. With 1 per cent growth the poor increase their income on average by 1 per cent, with 10 per cent growth they raise it, on average, by 10 per cent. Not always and not everywhere – there are exceptions and variations – but on average. This finding tallies with a long line of other surveys, whereas studies suggesting the contrary are very hard to find.[30]

29. Berg & Karlsson 2000, p. 245.

30. Dollar & Kraay 2000a. For a balanced review of the debate on this report, see Vlachos 2000. Reports corroborating these findings include Gallup, Radelet & Warner 1998, suggesting that in proportional terms the poor actually benefit more from growth than other groups.

Growth benefits the poor

Correlation between prosperity and incomes of the poor
in 80 studied countries

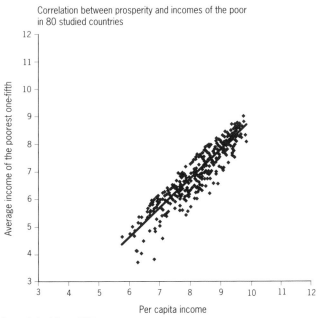

Source: Dollar & Kraay, 2000a.

This makes growth the best cure for poverty. Some economists have spoken of a "trickle-down" effect, in the sense of some taking the lead and getting rich first, after which parts of this wealth trickle down to the poor, as a result of the rich demanding their labour. This thesis rather reminds one of the image of the poor man getting the crumbs that fall from the rich man's table, but this is a completely mistaken picture of the true effect of growth. On the contrary, what happens is that the poor derive benefit from growth to roughly the same extent

Growth benefits the poor

Correlation between economic growth and incomes
of the poor in 80 studied countries

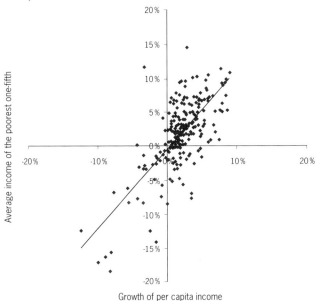

Source: Dollar & Kraay, 2000a.

and at the same speed as the rich. They benefit immediately from the
value of their labour increasing and from the goods they buy becoming cheaper in relation to their income.

No country has ever succeeded in reducing poverty without having
long-term growth. Nor is there any case of the opposite, i.e. of a
country having had long-term sustainable growth which has not been
of benefit to the poor population. Still more interestingly, there is no
instance of a country having had steady levels of growth in the long

term without opening up its markets. The World Bank's latest *World Development Report* contains a good deal of rhetoric about growth not being everything and not being sufficient for development – influenced, no doubt, by the growth of the anti-globalisation movement. But at the same time the tables in the report show that, the higher a country's growth has been in the past twenty years, the faster it has reduced poverty, infant mortality and illiteracy. In the countries at the bottom of the growth league, illiteracy had actually increased. It is possible that growth in itself is not sufficient to bring good development for everyone, but growth is manifestly necessary.

If we have 3 per cent growth per annum, this means that the economy, our capital and our incomes double every 23 years. If growth is twice as fast, these things double about every 12 years. This is an unparalleled growth of prosperity, compared with which even vigorous government measures for the redistribution of incomes take on a puny aspect. And not just puny, but downright dangerous, because high taxes to finance these measures can jeopardise growth. If so, great long-term benefits for everyone are sacrificed in favour of small immediate gains for a few.

A society's economy is above all improved by people saving, investing and working. High taxes on work, savings and capital are therefore, in the words of John Stuart Mill: "to impose a penalty on people for having worked harder and saved more than their neighbours." That means punishing what is most beneficial to society. Or, as somebody has put it: "Fines are a kind of tax for doing wrong, tax is a kind of fine for doing right." We have alcohol taxes to reduce consumption of alcohol, tobacco taxes to reduce smoking and environmental taxes to reduce pollution. So where do we expect the taxation of endeavour, work and saving to get us? It results in many people not exerting themselves top work, invest and hatch new ideas, because most of the proceeds will go to the government. It leads to firms devoting more and more time to tax evasion, time which they could have devoted to constructive work. It leads to people spending more time on things they are not good at. The surgeon stays at home and redecorates the living room instead of doing what he is best at – saving life – because that way he avoids having to pay tax on his own work and pay tax on the painter's wages.[31]

In a dynamic market economy there is also social mobility. Someone who is poor today will not necessarily be poor tomorrow. In the absence of fixed privileges and high taxes, there are great possibilities of raising one's standard of living through one's own exertions, education and thrift. Four-fifths of America's millionaires have made their money themselves, as opposed to just coming into it.

The poorest one-fifth in a capitalist economy like America's earn, it is true, only 3.6 per cent of the country's GDP, a share which does not appear to increase. But by viewing income gaps in these static terms one forgets that there is always mobility within the various groups – upward mobility. Partly because wages rise with higher education and longer working experience. Only 5.1 per cent of the Americans belonging to the poorest one-fifth in 1975 still did so in 1991. In the meantime nearly 30 per cent of them had moved up into the wealthiest one-fifth and altogether 60 per cent of them had arrived in one of the wealthiest two-fifths. By 1991 the people belonging in 1975 to the poorest fifth had raised their annual income (which at that time was only 1,263 dollars in 1997 prices) by no less than 27,745 dollars, which in absolute figures is more than six times the increase obtained by the wealthiest one-fifth.

So the best cure for poverty is having a chance of doing something about it. On average, those falling below the poverty line in the USA

---

31. See Åsa Hansson's Ph.D. thesis *Limits of Tax Policy*, suggesting that if the pressure of taxation rises by one percentage unit in a developed industrial nation, annual growth declines by roughly 0.23 percentage unit. The digest of research presented in Leufstedt & Voltaire 1998 suggests that a growth of the public sector by 10 percentage units reduces growth by about 1.5 percentage units.

only stay there for 4.2 months. Only 4 per cent of America's population are long-term poor, i.e. remain poor for over two years. Meanwhile the poorest fifth is replenished with new people – students and immigrants – who then climb up the ladder of wealth.[32]

32. Cox & Alm 1999, chap. 4. Some have argued that this social mobility is greater in a more egalitarian country, like Sweden, despite heavier pressure of taxation, but this is probably due to a confusion of concepts. It is easier to enter a new income band in Sweden, because pay differentials are so small here, but on the other hand it is more difficult to raise one's earnings in shillings and pence.

Freedom or equality?
Why choose?

Many believe that liberalisation and economic growth imply a growth of inequality in a society. Once again I would like to point out that this is not the crux of the matter. The important thing should be how well situated you are, not how well situated you are in relation to others. The important thing is for as many people as possible to be better off, and this is not a bad result merely because some people improve their lot still faster than others. But there are several reasons why equality is worth aiming for. For one thing, it is appealing that people should not get off to tremendously unequal starts in life. It is important that everyone should have similar opportunities – not so important that it is worth reducing everyone's chances in order to make them as equal as possible, but still important enough for great social inequality to be a problem. This, then, is an important objection to scrutinise.

Another reason is that equality actually stimulates growth, quite contrary to what is often claimed. True, in a very poor society some degree of inequality may be necessary in order for anyone at all to be able to start saving and investing, but many studies have shown that, on average, societies with a high degree of equality achieve, on average, greater economic growth than unequal societies, especially if the inequality concerns land ownership. One reason for this connection is that governments with greater equality can be expected to have greater stability and less political turbulence. Inequality can lead to conflicts, or demands for higher taxes and more distributive policy, which are threats to growth.

But a more important reason is that people must have a certain measure of basic assets – land, for example, in an undeveloped economy, and education in a modern one – to be able to work efficiently and develop society. What matters, then, is a degree of equality in terms of assets, and not what is usually meant in the political debate, e.g. equality of incomes and profits. Thus the important thing in a developing country which has ancient, unfair feudal structures and where a small élite owns the land is land reforms, so that more people will have a share of the land and will thus be able to participate in the economy. The important thing is for the whole population to obtain education and all of them to have good opportunities of borrowing money if they have ideas for business projects. No one must be discriminated against or marginalized, or prevented by licensing requirements, prohibitions and privileges from competing for positions and incomes. This kind of equality spurs the dynamic of the economy, whereas a reallocation of incomes if anything reduces it, because then education, work and the introduction of new ideas become less profitable.

Simplifying matters somewhat, it is equality of opportunity that matters, not equality of results. The important thing is for everyone to have certain basic opportunities and then be at liberty to explore their way forward and achieve different results. These are two sides of the same coin: people have the opportunity of working and exploring their way ahead, and the right to make a profit out of the enterprise if it does well. This results in a society which encourages social mobility and rewards initiative and effort, and consequently also achieves greater prosperity. Thus it is not income differences in themselves that are dangerous for development, but the discrimination and privileges which cause the difference in incomes in undemocratic states. This is corroborated by the connection between equality and growth being clear in non-democratic states but not demonstrable in modern, liberal ones.[33]

But can the opposite also apply, namely that increased growth leads to greater inequality, as is widely maintained? Economists sometimes refer to "Kuznet's inverted U-curve", which is based on an article by the economist Simon Kuznet, published in 1955, arguing that economic growth in a society initially leads to greater inequality and only after some time leads to a reduction of inequality. Many have accepted this thesis as truth and it is sometimes used to discredit the idea of growth, or at least to demand a national distributive policy. Kuznet himself did not draw any such drastic conclusions. On the contrary, he declared that his article was based on "perhaps 5 per cent empirical information and 95 per cent speculation", adding that "so long as it is recognized as a collection of hunches calling for further investigation rather than a set of fully tested conclusions, little harm and much good may result".[34]

If we follow Kuznet's recommendation and investigate what has happened since the 1950s, we can see that his preliminary conclusion is not universally valid. True, it can happen that growth initially leads to inequality, but this is not a general connection. There are countries which have had high growth leading to a reduction of income differences, e.g. Indonesia, Malaysia, Taiwan, South Korea and Mauritius, and there are countries like China, Thailand, Pakistan and Brazil where growth has entailed greater income differences. Similarly, things have moved in different directions in countries with low or negative growth. Equality has increased in Cuba, Colombia and Morocco, while diminishing in Kenya, Ethiopia and Mexico during the 80s and Russia during the 90s. Distribution hinges on other

---

33. Concerning equality of assets versus equality of income, see Deininger & Olinto 2000, for the connection with democracy, see Deininger & Squire 1998.

34. Kuznet 1955, p. 26.

aspects, such as initial position and domestic policy. The World Bank sums up the state of affairs by saying:

> *The available statistics do not indicate a stable relation between growth and inequality. On average, inequality within countries has neither diminished nor increased during the past 30 years.*[35]

Economic growth does not increase inequality

Correlation between economic growth and inequality in 80 studied countries

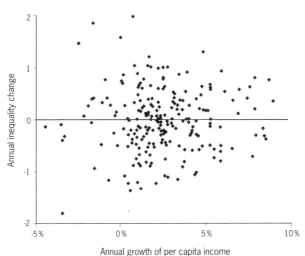

Source: Dollar & Kraay. 2000a.

---

35. World Bank 2000c. The data refuting Kuznet are presented in Deininger & Squire 1998, pp. 259–287. For a review of the research, see Bigsten & Levin 2000.

Studying equality in 70 countries, the economist G. W. Scully found that incomes were *more evenly distributed* in countries with a liberal economy, open markets and property rights. This was above all because the middle class had more and the upper class less in free than in unfree economies. The share of national income going to the richest fifth of the population was 25 per cent lower in "freest" economies than in "least free" economies. The proportion going to the poorest fifth in a society was unaffected by how free the economy was, but their actual incomes were far greater in liberal economies.[36]

Economic freedom increases equality

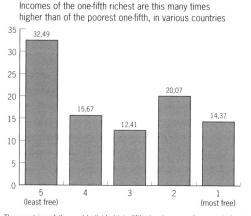

Incomes of the one-fifth richest are this many times higher than of the poorest one-fifth, in various countries

The countries of the world, divided into fifths by degrees of economic freedom.
Source: Gwartney & Lawson et al., 2000.

36. Scully 1992.

Thus, quite contrary to the popular supposition, a higher degree of economic liberalism appears to mean more economic equality. But this tells us nothing about the effect of changes in equality. Perhaps rapid liberalisation programmes and changes of system can have a negative impact on equality? But not even this seems to fit. The Swedish economist Niclas Berggren has investigated how a growth of economic freedom affects economic equality. In countries which have liberalised their economies since 1985, equality has *increased*, while stagnating or diminishing in countries which have refrained from liberalisation. Equality is growing fastest in poor developing countries which are quickly reforming their economies. Berggren's findings indicate that there are above all two aspects which increase equality in a society: freedom of international trade and freedom of international movements of capital – the two most "globalising" reforms.[37]

This pattern is corroborated by a different classification of countries, namely one measuring how "globalised" they are. A.T. Kearny and Foreign Policy have tried to devise a "globalisation index", an estimate of how much a country's inhabitants shop, invest, communicate and travel across its boundaries. The globalised countries, one finds, are not at all more unequal. On the contrary:

The general pattern of higher globalization and greater income equality holds for most countries, both in mature economies and emerging markets.[38]

---

37. Niclas Berggren 1999.

38. "Measuring Globalization", *Foreign Policy*, Jan./Feb. 2001. The most globalised country in the world according to this index is little Singapore, just ahead of the Netherlands and Sweden. A country like the USA only comes twelfth. But this is partly an illusion, the USA being so big as to accommodate far more long-distance travel, trade and communication within its frontiers than small countries.

Liberals and socialists both usually say that individual liberty and economic equality are each other's opposites, thus explaining why they oppose one of these widely appreciated values. They may be right in the sense of choosing to focus on one value or the other in their policy-making, but it is not true to say that the two values are contradictory. On the contrary, there is much to suggest that equality of liberty also confers economic equality. Rights of ownership, freedom of enterprise, free trade and reduced inflation confer both growth and equality.

Property rights – for the sake of the poor

That economic freedom is not an enemy of equality comes as a surprise to everyone who has been told that capitalism is the ideology of the rich and the privileged. In fact the opposite applies. The free market is the antithesis of societies of privilege. In a market economy the only way of retaining a good economic position is by improving your production and offering people good products or services. It is in the regulated economies, with their distribution of privileges and monopolies to favoured groups, that the prevailing conditions are cemented. Those who have the right contacts, can afford to pay bribes and have the time and knowledge to plough through bulky volumes of regulations can start up business enterprises and engage in trade. The poor never have a chance, not even of starting rudimentary businesses like a bakery or a corner shop. In a capitalist society anyone with ideas and willpower is at liberty to try their luck, even if they are not the favourites of the rulers.

Globalisation is especially important from this point of view, because it disturbs power relations and emancipates people from the local potentates. Free trade enables consumers to buy goods and choose solutions from others instead of the local monopolists, free movements of capital also enable poor people with good ideas to finance business ideas and projects. Freedom of establishment means that the village's one and only employer has to offer higher wages and better working conditions in order to attract labour, because otherwise the workers can go elsewhere.

The left often portrays liberalism as the ideology of the rich, because it stands up for rights of ownership. But defending private property is not the same as cementing the prevailing property conditions. Empirical facts tell us that it is not mainly the rich who benefit from the protection of property rights. On the contrary, it may be the most vulnerable citizens who have most to lose in a society without stable rights of ownership, because then it is the people with most political power and contacts who manage best and lay hold on resources. Where there is private property, resources and incomes are channelled mainly to those who are productive and who offer services in the market and the workplace, and underprivileged groups then have a much better chance of asserting themselves than in a system governed by power and graft. Besides, it is they who have most to gain from goods becoming progressively cheaper in relation to incomes, which competition based on rights of ownership helps to make them. Above all, property rights provide an opportunity of foresight and personal initiative, spurring growth and distributing the fruits of it equally, on average, between rich and poor. Thus the introduction of safeguards for private property in a society has a distributive effect as favourable to the poor as commitment to universal education. Nor are things made worse by ownership safeguards apparently also being the reform most conducive to growth.[39]

The Peruvian economist Hernando de Soto has done more than anyone else to show how poor people lose by the absence of property rights. In his revolutionary book *The Mystery of Capital* he turns the view of the world's poor upside down. The problem is not that they are helpless or unpropertied, but that they have no rights of ownership. In fact they are people with great powers of initiative who save large parts of their income which they then spend on improving their land and their homes. After many years spent travelling and researching, he roughly estimates that poor people in the Third World and

---

39. Cf. Dollar & Kraay 2000b and 2000a. Concerning the importance of property rights for economic development, see Rosenberg & Birdzell Jr 1991.

in former communist states have real estate (buildings and the land they stand on) worth about 9.3 billion dollars more than is officially registered. This is a huge sum, almost equalling the combined value of all companies listed on the stock exchanges of the affluent countries – New York, Nasdaq, Toronto, Tokyo, London, Frankfurt, Paris, Milan – and a dozen more besides. But the problem is that the governments do not accept these rights of ownership without tortuous bureaucratic processes. People in the Third World occupy common lands, build simple houses in shanty towns which they are constantly improving, and establish small corner shops, just as poor people in the western world were doing a couple of hundred years ago. The trouble is that in developing countries today it is practically impossible to register this as property. De Soto illustrates these problems through an ambitious experiment. Together with a number of colleagues he travelled the world, attempting to register property. The results are horrifying.

Obtaining legal title to a house built on public land in Peru required 207 different administrative steps at 52 different public offices. Anyone wishing to do something as simple as driving a taxi or starting a private bus service legally could expect 26 months of red tape first. In Haiti people can only settle on a common by leasing the land for five years and then buying it. But just getting a leasehold permit involved 65 steps, taking over two years. Buying the freehold then took far longer. In the Philippines the same thing could take over 13 years. Legally registering a plot of land in the Egyptian desert required permits from 31 authorities, which could take between 5 and 14 years, and doing the same for agricultural land took between 6 and 11 years.

Getting a legal licence for a factory with two sewing machines in the shanty towns of Lima occupied 289 six-hour days of travelling to the authorities, queuing up to see the right people, filling in forms and waiting for an answer, added to which the process cost a total of

1,231 dollars – more than thirty times the minimum monthly wage.

To people without big resources or powerful contacts, these are insuperable barriers. And so poor people are forced to live and run micro-businesses in the informal sector, outside the law. Consequently they have no legal protection and do not dare to invest for the long term, even if they can. Their property is not included in a uniform system of ownership which follows transactions and indicates one owner. Without clarity as to who owns what, how transactions are to proceed, who is responsible for payments and services to the address, the property remains "dead capital". Properties cannot be mortgaged, which would otherwise provide capital for financing the children's education or investments and expansion of the business. Thus the commonest way for small entrepreneurs in affluent countries to obtain capital is cut off in developing countries. Without a registered address and the possibility of having one's creditworthiness investigated, it is often impossible to get a phone or water and electricity supply, and the property cannot even be sold.

Nor can the entrepreneurs expand their business by selling shares in it. Owners of micro-businesses, being forced to work in the informal sector, always have to beware of bureaucrats and the police, or else pay heavy bribes. So they have to keep the business small and hidden, and are thus debarred from economies of scale. Nor do they dare to advertise or to broaden their customer base excessively. They venture to sell to the nearest precincts, but no more. Big deals can only be concluded with members of the family and with people one trusts.

De Soto maintains that between 50 and 75 per cent of citizens in the developing countries work outside the protection of the law, and that roughly 80 per cent of homes and land are not registered in the name of their present owners. In one country he visited the urban authority itself had established an illegal settlement on common land so that its employees would have somewhere to live. So the great majority of the population have assets which they are not allowed to make full use of. In the absence of rights of ownership they cannot use their property as a basis of expansion, which was the western world's path to prosperity. Only an élite in the developing countries have contacts permitting them to engage in modern economic activity. Capitalism without property rights becomes capitalism for the élite only. Millions of capable people with powers of initiative who could be the entrepreneurs of the future become entrapped by poverty.[40]

This is one of the reasons why Russia's economy has not developed during the 90s. Although communism has fallen, the Russian government has still not introduced a uniform system of private rights of land ownership. Land is generally deemed to be basically owned by the government and is just lent or leased to the farmers, with the result that investment is pointless and sale or mortgage unthinkable. Fewer than 300,000 out of a total of some 10 million Russian farmers have anything resembling title to their land. The government imposes severe restrictions on what people can do with land which really belongs to them. Land socialism, of course, inhibits any number of investment opportunities, but because land is often the basis of borrowing, it also impedes the development of a modern credit system. Instead transactions find their way into the informal market. Russia is sometimes portrayed as a kind of hypercapitalism. By all reasonable definitions of capitalism, this is nonsense. Russian land socialism, coupled with a formidable welter of business regulations and trade controls, leads the Heritage Foundation to find it only the 127th freest economy out of 155 investigated, and in Economic Freedom of the World's corresponding table it comes 117th out of 123, after countries like Syria and Rwanda.[41]

---

40. de Soto 2000.

41. Gwartney, Lawson, Park & Skipton 2001, O'Driscoll Jr, Holmes & Kirkpatrick 2001.

Economic freedom reduces poverty

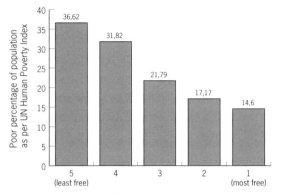

The countries of the world, divided into fifths by degrees of economic freedom.
Source: Gwartney & Lawson et al., 2001.

Regulation of agriculture is another important cause of inequality. Through price regulations and delivery requirements, among other things, many developing countries have tried to benefit the urban population at the farmers' expense. This is part of an attempt to force industrialisation into being, by taxing and regulating agriculture in such a way that its surplus is transferred to industry. The problem is that this has had the effect of shattering agriculture, depriving it of resources which would have been needed in order to streamline food production and actually generate a surplus. In many African and Latin American countries this has created a vicious circle, with heavy migration from the impoverished countryside to the towns and cities. But there is no great demand for industrial goods, because the countryside remains poor, and so unemployment and poverty increase in the towns, and homelessness, crime and prostitution with them. The property which the poor themselves acquire and save up for is not recognised and is not registered. As a result, demand for agricultural produce does not gather speed, and so urbanisation continues. Nor is foreign demand to be counted on, with the affluent countries constructing high tariff barriers against agricultural produce.[42]

There are several types of anti-liberal policy by which the poor are especially hard hit. One of them is inflation, which ruins the value of money. By rapidly increasing money supply, the government obliterates the small monetary assets of the poor, while the rich who own registered land, properties and businesses get off more lightly. Reducing inflation, and above all avoiding the kind of hyperinflation with which many Third World countries have been afflicted, is one of the most important things that can be done to help the less well-to-do, according to the World Bank report by Dollar and Kraay mentioned earlier. One classic example of hyperinflation was Germany's during the 1920s, which ruined the middle class and made people receptive to Hitler's policies. An extreme instance of the opposite occurred at the end of 1989, when Argentina quickly reduced inflation and, in little over a year, reduced the proportion of poor people in great-Buenos Aires from 35 to 23 per cent.

Another connection indicated by Dollar and Kraay's findings is that public spending seems to harm not only growth but also, and above all, a country's poorest inhabitants. This does not ring true to those who believe that public spending is the same as taking from the rich and giving to the poor. In fact the opposite frequently applies. In poor, undemocratic countries especially, it is the élite, the leader, his relatives and friends and powerful corporations that are allowed to dip into the till, while the bill is paid by those without influence in the palaces of the capital city. Oversized military establishments pre-empt the lion's share of resources. The rulers prefer to invest in prestigious international airports, universities and city hospitals rather than in

---

42. Gunnarsson & Rojas 1997, pp. 50 ff.

roads, schools and local hospitals which would really help people. In undemocratic countries, moreover, public medical care and education are often directed to staunch supporters of the régime and to the most comfortably off. This goes to show how wrong many left-wing intellectuals were in the 60s and 70s when they declared that democratic rights and liberties did not matter all that much in the developing countries, because what they first needed to invest in was welfare policy. Without democracy, not even the welfare policy which actually exists will benefit the great mass of the population.

One problem is that inefficient systems of government cannot make the best possible use of money. "I've heard rumours about assistance for the poor, but no one seems to know where it is," as a poor Indonesian put it in the course of conversation. Presumably the money went into a local bigwig's pockets. The same problem exists in India, where bureaucracy and corruption have turned poor relief into black holes. Paying the poor a 1 dollar subsidy through the big programme of food subsidisation has cost the Indian government 4 dollars and 30 cents. It is of course a straight loss to the poor, their supplies being taxed so heavily in order for them to claw back a far smaller amount in the form of aid.[43]

Capitalism is not a perfect system, and it is not good for everyone all the time. Critics of globalisation are good at pointing out individual bad instances – a factory that has closed down, a wage that has been reduced. These things may very well be true. But by concentrating solely on individual instances one is liable to completely obscure the general realisation of how a political or economical system generally works and what fantastic values it confers on the great majority compared with other alternatives. There are seamy sides and problems to be found in all political and economic systems, but this can be no cause for rejecting all solutions. Hunting down negative examples of

43. Berg & Karlsson 2000, pp. 93 f, quotation from World Bank 2000a, p. 85.

what can happen in a market economy is easy enough. By that method water or fire can be proved to be bad things, because some people drown and some get burned to death, but this isn't the full picture.

This way one completely ignores the freedom and independence which capitalism confers on people who have never experienced anything but oppression. One also disregards the calm and steady progress which is the basic rule of a society with a market economy. There is nothing wrong with identifying problems and mishaps in a predominantly successful system if one does so with the constructive intent of rectifying or alleviating them. But if at the same time one condemns the system as such, then one begs the question: what political and economic system could manage things better? And what, in history and in the world around us, suggests that it could?

The East Asian miracle

To gauge the impact of politics on development, it may be enlightening to compare the continents presenting the big contrast in postwar history, namely the growth miracle of East Asia and the disastrous track record of Africa. Zambia in 1964 was nearly twice as wealthy as South Korea. Today South Korea has almost a European standard of living and is roughly 27 times wealthier than Zambia. The Taiwanese used to be about as poor as the population of the Congo. Today they are as rich as the Spaniards, while the Congo has almost marked time. How could things go so well for Asia and so badly for Africa?

The number one success story among developing economies during the post-war era has been East Asia, and especially Southeast Asia. The end of the Second World War found Japan's economy in ruins and the countries it had recently been occupying destitute, starving and wretched. The rest of the world expected these countries to be torn apart by corruption, crime and guerrilla warfare. But since the 1960s these "miracle economies" have had an annual growth rate of between 5 and 7 per cent and their incomes have doubled every decade. Savings, investments and exports have been very large, and the countries have quickly been industrialised. Former colonies like Singapore and Hong Kong have even overtaken the former British colonial power in terms of prosperity.

In nearly all these countries, rapid development has been accompanied by a preservation, or even augmentation, of economic equality. And this despite the absence of a distributive policy. Poverty has rapidly declined. In Indonesia the proportion living in extreme poverty has fallen from 58 to 15 per cent, and in Malaysia from 37 to 5 per cent. Between 1960 and 1990, average life expectancy in the East Asian countries rose from 56 to 71. In the long term the process also led to the democratisation of countries like Taiwan, South Korea and Thailand – and now Indonesia as well.

These are the states which have proved that it is perfectly possible for developing countries to industrialise and develop. They also showed that this can only happen in a basically capitalist, outgoing economy, not in a secluded command economy. Recently many economists have pointed out that the miracle economies also had a great deal of government control, inferring that they are in fact a counter-argument to the idea of liberalism alone creating development. The first of these statements is correct. In particular the first states in the region to develop – Japan, South Korea and Taiwan – had a great deal of government intervention (the subsequent miracles, Indonesia, Malaysia and Thailand, got their economies moving with a more liberal policy). The state governed investments, regulated the banks, invested in and protected chosen industries, and had a whole battery of possible interventions in its arsenal. But there was nothing unique about this: developing countries in all continents have done the same. The World Bank, in its broad evaluation of the miracles, observes:

> *Other economies attempted similar interventions without success, and om avarge they used them more pervasively.* [44]

The East Asian countries differed from others by committing themselves to establishing and protecting rights of ownership, creating a code for the protection of enterprise and competition, and having a stable monetary policy and low inflation. They went in for universal education, resulting in a skilled population capable of developing the country. Because they concentrated on junior education, leaving

---

44. World Bank 1993, p. 6, see also Gunnarsson & Rojas 1997.

higher education to the privately funded market, policy assumed an egalitarian profile, ensuring that higher education establishments were attuned to the needs of the economy.

The East Asian states introduced land reforms which deprived old élites of the land and privileges which they had pirated. This enabled the entire population to participate in the economy. Farmers could now dispose relatively freely of their surplus, saving and investing as they saw fit. This gave them an interest in making agriculture more efficient. The increased yield kept these countries supplied with food while releasing manpower for industry, which in turn encountered rising demand as rural earnings improved. These states have been more interested in creating job opportunities than in stipulating minimum wages and regulating the labour market. This has provided work for most people, and wages have then risen with productivity. Because wages could also be lowered in a recession (at the same time as the goods people buy became cheaper), many of these countries have coped with crises more smoothly and with lower unemployment than others.

In other developing countries enterprise is hamstrung by regulations, and licences and permits are needed in order to start up business. East Asian states, by contrast, have had a notable freedom of enterprise. Individual citizens with ideas have been able to start up firms with a minimum of red tape, and to work untrammelled by detailed controls and price regulations. Hong Kong went furthest. There one could just start a business and then inform the authorities afterwards in order to obtain a permit. This has been hugely important, not only opening the field to initiative but also as an effective antidote to the corruption which often flourishes in the shade of permit procedures.

Although many of the East Asian countries have steered credits and subsidies into the enterprise sector, in doing so they have been less swayed than other developing countries by ties of friendship, the viewpoints of vested interests or the existence of showcase projects. On the contrary, they have taken a relatively independent line towards vested interests and focused their attention on achievement and the exigencies of the market. Prices in the economy have been far more market driven than in other developing countries. These countries have not had price controls and have not distorted world market prices, and so investments have occurred where they have been most likely to succeed. The aim has been to invest in the sectors where a country is most efficient and has advantages compared with other countries. Many of those in the debate who demand that the government intervene and govern investments feel that it must reduce the tempo, retain old solutions and protect businesses. This is the exact opposite of the Asian governments, who regarded ability to withstand international competition as crucial for businesses. The Japanese government drove big corporations bankrupt because they did not have sufficient profit potential, and South Korea was quite unsentimental about shutting down firms which were unable to produce for an open market. This absence of sentimentality has also been applied to the government itself. Whenever subsidies and expenditure have looked like threatening economic stability, the government has quickly scaled down its commitments, thereby evading budgetary crises and inflation.

Above all, these countries have been fiercely committed to integration with the international economy. They are among the world's most export-oriented economies, and have welcomed huge investments by foreign companies. The bigger trade has bulked in the GDP of countries in this region, the faster their economic growth has been. Most of them have had tariff barriers against imports, but the same goes for the rest of Asia, Africa and South America. The East Asian countries are different in that they applied this policy to a lesser extent than other developing countries and dropped it much earlier. While the others were busily pursuing self-sufficiency and avoiding trade, the East Asian countries committed themselves to internalisation. In the 1960s they began encouraging exports, partly by abolishing permit requirements and completely exempting exporters and their suppliers from import duties. Tariffs on capital goods have been low. According to the index of openness constructed by Harvard economists Jeffrey Sachs and Andrew Warner, these countries were among the first developing countries to open up their economies by reducing tariffs, abolishing quotas, freeing exports and making their currencies convertible. The economies of Taiwan, Thailand and Malaysia are rated "open" since 1963 at the latest, Japan's since 1964, South Korea's since 1968 and Indonesia's since 1970. Hong Kong has pursued a more liberal trade policy than any other country in the world.[45] The same revolution did not occur in Latin America until the beginning of the 1990s and has yet to come in Africa.

Far from being an example of the viability of regulation and state control, the East Asian miracle shows that a market-based economy affirming enterprise and openness can create development.

---

45. Sachs & Warner 1995, pp. 26–32, 72–95.

The African morass

The painful contrast to this development is found in Africa, especially south of Sahara. There we find most countries whose per capita GDP has actually decreased since the mid-60s. There we have the world's heaviest concentration of poverty, ill health, undernourishment, illiteracy and child labour. Unlike the rest of the world, over the past 30 years this continent has grown accustomed to a declining standard of living and growing distress. There are certain naturally dictated factors which help to account for this. The tropical climate causes parasitical diseases to flourish, the soil is less fertile and natural disasters are commoner than in our part of the world. One-third of the population live in countries which are completely landlocked, which makes it far more difficult for them to connect with international markets and trade movements. The curious frontier definitions and discriminatory policies of the old colonial powers have contributed towards a severe ethnic and linguistic fragmentation within states. A large part of the continent is being torn apart by wars and conflicts.

But other regions with both nature and culture against them have managed far better than Africa. Even factors like war and famine have political causes – no democracy has ever been afflicted by famine, and no two democracies have ever made war on each other, which shows that to a great extent it is a country's institutions and politics which determine the possibilities of development. In this perspective Africa stands out above all through its far higher degree, compared with other continents, of political oppression, corruption, command economy and protectionism. The African countries have inherited a hierarchic, repressive political structure from the colonial powers, and have used it to oppress other ethnic groups and the countryside, and for the violation of fundamental rights.

The African leaders have been intent on avoiding the policy of the old colonial powers and also the risk of becoming commercially dependent on them, and so they have tried to build self-sufficient economies with draconian tariffs and with nationalisation and detailed control of industry. The economy has been governed by price and exchange controls, and public expenditure has at times run riot. The urban élites have systematically exploited the countryside. Instead of creating markets, countries established purchasing monopolies which paid wretched prices, and they introduced government distribution of foodstuffs. This way the government confiscated the entire agricultural surplus, thereby impoverishing the farmers and abolishing the traders' occupation. Production fell and farmers were driven into the informal market. This impeded plans for industrialisation and posed a threat to society when the economic downturn set in during the 1970s. After trying to borrow their way out of the crisis, many African states were in free fall by the mid-1980s. Structures collapsed, people starved, there were no medicines and machinery simply stopped when spare parts were missing and batteries went flat and could not be replaced. The fall has stopped since then, but has not yet been followed by an upturn. Between 1990 and 1998 Southern Africa's combined GDP declined by 0.6 per cent.

The cause of Africa's hunger and sufferings is not the desert and drought but political oppressors who have systematically shattered the countries' potential and opportunities for the population.

Instead of becoming "dependent" on trade, these states have become dependent on development aid. Africa south of Sahara has received more development assistance per capita than any other region in the world. Where some states are concerned, the annual development assistance equals twice their own incomes. But instead of going to people in distress, the money has often been used to sustain rogue régimes which have exploited their people. Many western donors declared that these countries were not ripe for democracy and individual rights, and that they should rely on planning the economy and reducing their dependence on trade. The result has not been long coming. Potential business fields have been shattered and whereas in the 1960s Africa had 5 per cent of the world's trade, today it has only 1 per cent.

Africa has been afflicted with long-lived leaders like Mugabe in Zimbabwe, Aarap Moi in Kenya and Mobutu in Zaire who have clung to power with the support of development aid from the western world. Someone has spoken of "vampire states", machineries of state which are not interested in stimulating creativity and growth, only in feathering their own nests with the productive resources of society – in actual fact like an army of occupation. Often the leaders, and the clique surrounding them, have seized property by means of direct expropriation and by massive peculation of government funds. Mobutu is understood to have amassed a fortune of about 4 billion dollars while his country was bleeding to death.

Anyone believing hierarchy to be the same as efficiency should study some of these countries. If anything, chaos prevails within their public authorities. The bureaucracy often ignores routine matters, officials disregard orders from superiors and not infrequently do the opposite of what they are told to. The courts are seldom impartial and do not protect contracts or rights of ownership. Corruption is amazingly widespread, paralysing whole states. Officials demand bribes in order for people to be allowed to work and trade, which makes it hard for businesses and impossible for the poor to do so. Often it is ties of friendship and kinship, not merits, that decide within the administration or the economy. Arbitrary rule and corruption have deterred enterprises, and many of these countries are receiving no foreign investments at all. Africa has been marginalized – on that point the anti-globalisation movement is perfectly right – but the reason is that the African countries have not participated in globalisation and have instead been subjected to socialism, gangster rule and protectionism. To the peoples of Africa, globalisation has meant little more than their leaders flying off to conferences in other countries.[46]

Some countries in recent years have succeeded in balancing their national budgets, but these are only marginal changes. Challenging strong vested interests, taking vigorous action against corruption, reducing the apparatus of government and opening the economy to competition have proved more difficult. A bare majority of the countries south of Sahara have reasonably democratic régimes, and these countries have the world's least liberal economic systems. Estimating the amount of economic freedom in the region, the Heritage Foundation finds that six countries cannot be measured, owing to war and domestic turbulence. Of the 42 remaining, not one can be classed as economically "free", only 12 were "mostly free", 29 were "mostly unfree" and 2 were economically "repressed".[47]

Zimbabwe is one of the African countries which have gone against the trend of the past decade in favour of globalisation and liberalisation. Under Mugabe the country has closed its frontiers to goods and services from other countries and raised inflation. Recently things have gone completely off the rails, with large-scale expropriation of property, suppression of freedom of expression and acts of terror

---

46. Sachs & Warner 1997, pp. 335–376, Goldsmith 1998. A confused interpretation considers Africa *more* integrated than other continents with the world economy, because exports from the African countries are unusually large in proportion to GDP. This, however, is due, not to their being unusually outgoing but simply to the native economy being so extraordinarily weak and small.

47. O'Driscoll Jr, Holmes & Kirkpatrick 2001.

against the opposition. And Zimbabwe's extreme poverty increased during the 90s by nearly ten percentage units – about three million people. Nigeria is another example. This huge country, despite a very big potential of natural resources and agricultural land, has remained abysmally poor because of a very strictly regulated and corrupt economy. On the advice of the IMF, among others, certain structural reforms were inaugurated at the end of the 1980s, but their unpopularity led the Nigerian government to drop them at the beginning of the 1990s. Regulations were reintroduced, the credit and exchange market was abolished and interest rates were controlled. Inflation and unemployment resulted. Between 1992 and 1996 the proportion of the extremely poor rose from 43 to an incredible 66 per cent of the national population. Nigeria today accounts for a quarter of all extreme poverty in Southern Africa. Per capita income today is lower than it was thirty years ago, and health and education standards have fallen.

The economists Jeffrey Sachs and Andrew Warner have studied the growth which different political reforms have brought in various African countries. On the basis of various country studies they have attempted to calculate what growth the continent would have had if it had gone in completely for the East Asian policy of open markets, freedom of enterprise, protection of property rights and a high level of saving. They maintain that, despite its poor natural conditions, Africa would then have been capable of achieving an average per capita growth of about 4.3 per cent annually between 1965 and 1990. That would almost have tripled the population's incomes. Of course, this figure has to be taken with a generous pinch of salt, but however wide the margin of error may be, the figure remains shockingly high compared with Africa's actual growth during the years in question – a mere 0.8 per cent per annum.

Studying the good exceptions in Africa – countries which have gone in for free trade and more open economies – it seems plausible that a liberal policy could have been so successful. The cattle farmers of Botswana were swift to realise that it was in their interest to campaign for more open markets, and this resulted in large parts of the economy already becoming exposed to competition by the end of the 1970s. Through its association with the EU the country's exports to the Union are exempt from duties and quotas. Since Independence in 1966, Botswana has been the good exception in a continent which has always been dominated by dictatorships. This has helped to make it one of the least corrupt nations in Africa, on a level with European countries. Botswana's economic growth is also reminiscent of that of the East Asian countries, with annual levels of more than 10 per cent between 1970 and 1990. Another state which committed itself to free trade early on is little Mauritius. Through reduced military expenditure, protection of property rights, reduced taxes, a free exchange market and increased competition, the country has achieved growth rates of the order of 5 per cent. Today nearly everyone has access to clean water, and education and health care are expanding. If countries like Mauritius and Botswana can, why should not the rest of Africa be able to? These countries are not distinguished by any difference in human quality. People in other African countries are also inventive and enterprising, but they are forced to use those powers to evade corruption and regulations and to cope with working in the informal sector.

Another interesting African country is Ghana, which liberalised markets and reduced taxes during the 1990s. In particular, agriculture has been deregulated, and tariffs, price controls and subsidies have been abolished. Production has risen fast, which above all has benefited cocoa farmers, but because they have now been able to invest and to afford repairs, goods and services, everyone capable of assisting in these respects has also benefited from the farming boom. Extreme poverty in Ghana fell during the 1990s from 35.7 to 29.4 per cent of the population, and the country recently introduced a democratic power transfer. Uganda has developed on similar lines and is one of the countries which have been liberalised fastest in the past decade. Trade there has been quickly liberated, price controls abolished, taxes lowered and inflation reduced, at the same time as the first steps have been taken towards protecting property rights and deregulating financial markets. This, coupled with extensive development assistance, has given an annual growth of more than 5 per cent, at the same time as inequality has diminished. In only six years, extreme poverty in Uganda fell from 55.6 to 44 per cent. A relatively high degree of openness and the information work of independent organisations have made this the first country in Africa where the spread of HIV/AIDS in the towns and cities has begun to diminish.

Examples like these of African "lion economies" (the counterpart of Asian tigers and dragons) have shown, despite setbacks, that poverty is not a dictate of nature. Slowly, very slowly, certain states south of Sahara are beginning to use their resources more efficiently and to give their citizens greater economic liberties. The democracies are growing in number and urbanisation is breaking up old tribal loyalties which have hitherto stood in the way of equality before the law. Competition is reducing corruption, because rulers no longer have the same power to confer and withhold permits and privileges. Interest in foreign investments is another motive force, because companies shun investment in corrupt economies. The controlled economies are becoming a little frayed at the edges. The proportion of national budgets south of the Sahara devoted to health and medical care increased, albeit marginally, during the 90s.

Africa has an incredibly long way to go, but, contrary to what some maintain, it can be done. From being in free fall, many African countries have been stabilised, albeit at an extremely low level. It will take determined democratic and liberal reforms to move things forward, and the implementation of those reforms will require democratic leaders with the courage to put the people's interests before those of their friends and the bureaucracies. Given the grim starting point, it is unlikely, but not impossible, for the 21st century to be Africa's century.

III

Free trade is fair trade

Both benefit

Following demonstrations against the Seattle meeting of the World Trade Organisation by tens of thousands of people at the end of 1999, the benefit of free trade has once again begun to be questioned in the course of debate. Voices have been raised calling for countries to be self-sufficient, or saying that the developing countries should "protect" themselves with tariffs until their industries have become fully fledged, or that trade must "be given new rules". Often this criticism is summed up in the view that we are to have "fair trade" instead of "free trade". But in my opinion, free trade is by nature fair trade, because it is based on voluntary cooperation and exchange. Free trade means you, not the government, deciding where you are to buy your goods, without extra cost being imposed on the goods merely because they happen to cross a frontier. Tariffs, which impose a tax on the product when it crosses the frontier, and quotas, which limit the number of goods of a particular kind which are allowed to enter the country, are direct restrictions of citizens' freedom to decide their consumption for themselves. Freedom from these things, free trade, gives us freedom of choice and gives everyone the opportunity of raising their living standard.

It may seem odd that the world's prosperity can be augmented by swapping things with each other, but every time you go shopping you realise, subconsciously, how exchange augments wealth. You pay a dollar for a bottle of milk because you would rather have the milk than your dollar. The shop sells it at that price because they would rather have your dollar than keep the milk. Both parties are satisfied with the deal, otherwise it would never have taken place. Both of you emerge from the transaction feeling that you have made a good exchange, your needs have been better provided for.

Trade results in the person who is best at fabricating bicycles doing just that, the person who is best at milking cows doing so, and the person who is best at manufacturing television sets doing that. Then they exchange, so as to get what they want. Through free trade we can consume goods and services which we could never have produced ourselves. The possibility of free choice means that we can choose the best and cheapest goods possible. It gives us access to goods which we cannot procure by ourselves. In a Swedish shop we can buy bananas and pineapples, even though we cannot grow them ourselves. Even on northern latitudes, fresh green vegetables are on sale all winter, and even people in landlocked countries can buy salmon from Norway. Free trade results in goods and services being produced by whoever is best at producing them and then being sold to whoever wants to buy them. That's really all there is to it.

But in fact the argument for free trade is even stronger. Perhaps most people are aware that you can make money out of trade so long as you produce something better than everyone else, but much of the criticism of free trade is based on the absence of an equal negotiating situation. Certain countries and enterprises are more advanced than others, and can perhaps do everything more efficiently than weaker trading partners. But the fact is that you gain by trade even if you manufacture things less well than others could. The important thing is to do what you are best at relatively speaking, not to be better than everyone else at doing it.

Imagine two people. One of them, Julia, is highly trained, an outstanding surgeon, and also pretty good at housework and baking. The other is John, who has not trained for any particular occupation and, moreover, is not quite as good at housework as Julia. John would like to do something simple which he can learn easily, in the home, and then use it in exchange for things which are more difficult to produce,

109

such as surgery and medical care. But why should Julia agree to any such exchange when she is also better at housework? For the simple reason that she profits by concentrating on what she does best of all. Even if she is twice as good at housework as John, she is a thousand times better at surgery than he is. So she produces the greatest value by devoting her limited time to surgery and then using part of her earnings from that source to buy bread and get someone to do the housework. By concentrating on what she is best at, she has still more resources left over, and can thus afford to buy other goods and services which she wants.

All those who do not want free trade because it takes place "on unequal terms" and is based on "unequal circumstances" would urge John to shut himself off and not do business with Julia. But the fact is that he would profit handsomely by free trade, because then he can concentrate on what he, relatively speaking, does best and exchange it for what he needs and what he himself would be even worse at producing, e.g. bicycles or medical care. Economists usually term this "comparative advantages". John does not need to be absolutely best at his kind of production, it is enough for him to be best at it in relative terms – producing it better than other things he needs – in order for it to pay him to concentrate on that particular thing instead of trying to produce everything he needs by himself. He concentrates on the area in which he has a comparative advantage.

There need not even be any difference of training or education – different degrees of industry or good luck will suffice. Imagine the two people in our example fetching up on a desert island where they must have a fish and a loaf in order to survive. To achieve this, Julia has to spend 2 hours baking and 1 hour fishing. John needs 2.5 hours to bake and 5 hours to fish. So Julia is best at both jobs. But she still gains by swapping with John, because then she can devote her time to what she is absolutely best at – fishing. She can then catch three fish in her 3 hours, while John in the course of his 7.5 hours can bake three loaves. They then exchange the surplus, getting one and a half of each. Thus without working harder or longer, John and Julia have increased their daily output from two fish and two loaves to three fish and three loaves. Either they can opt for this higher output level and have a really good tuck-in, or else they can make do with the old quantities and have more time off instead. If they were able to trade with other islands in the vicinity, they would be able to trade off their surplus, for example, for clothing or tools which those islands are better at producing.

Of course, this is a greatly simplified example, but it still shows how specialisation works in more complicated cases as well. The comparative advantages are just as important between countries as between individuals. In the above examples, John and Julia can be replaced with Sweden and Norway, and the fish and loaves with mobile phones, clothing, tractors or medicine. The principle that it is a good idea to concentrate on what one is relatively best at still applies. This need not be due to naturally given factors, such as Sweden having iron ore and the Arab countries having oil. A country can acquire comparative advantages by chance. Computer corporations in Silicon Valley or fashion tycoons in the north of Italy are happy there, not because nature smiles on them but because they can make use of the contacts, the knowledge and the manpower which, for one reason or another, have begun to accumulate there.

The simple examples given above expose the hollowness of the argument that countries should be self-sufficient and produce for their own populations. When we have free trade, to produce for others is to produce for yourself. It is by producing and exporting what we are best at that we acquire resources for importing what we need. Many developing countries in South America, Africa and elsewhere believed after the Second World War that self-sufficiency was the right policy. Cheered on by the western world, they were going to produce "for use and not for profit". This has meant trying to do everything themselves, at huge expense. The East Asian countries did the opposite. They made what they were best at and exported it, and in return were able to purchase, at lower cost, what they themselves needed. South Korea's first export commodities included wigs and chipboard, Hong Kong did well out of plastic flowers and cheap toys. Hardly things which a benevolent despot would decide people needed, but by exporting these things they acquired economic scope for catering to their own needs.[48]

---

48. The commonest criticism against free trade is that certain tariffs and quotas are needed for the protection of particular industries. It is less common for anyone today to believe in self-sufficiency as a policy, but the belief lives on in groups more critical of civilisation, such as the Green political parties. Advocates also include the French anti-globalist Attac movement. Its chairman, Bernard Cassen, makes self-sufficiency an argument against reducing tariffs for developing countries: "I'm very surprised by the argument that poor countries, underdeveloped countries, must have more market access to the developed ones. What does that mean, in reality? That means that you expect underdeveloped countries to export. To export what? To export commodities that they need for their own internal market … we must revert to self-centred economies, and not to export-led economies that have proved a real failure." Cassen 2000.

Free trade brings prosperity

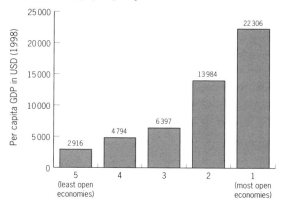

The countries of the world, divided into fifths by degrees of economic freedom.
Source: Gwartney & Lawson et al. 2001.

Free trade brings growth

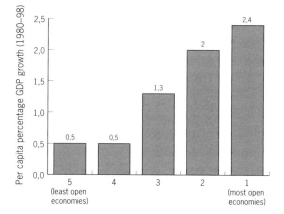

The countries of the world, divided into fifths by degrees of economic freedom.
Source: Gwartney & Lawson et al. 2001.

Important imports

This at the same time reveal another myth about trade, namely that exports, selling to other countries, are a good thing but imports, buying from other countries, are a bad thing. Many believe, like the old national "mercantilist" economists of the 18th century, that a country waxes powerful by selling much but buying little. All experience tells us that this is not a stable situation, because Swedish barriers against imports would push up prices in Sweden. In that case Swedish firms would become more nationally preoccupied, selling to the Swedish market at the Swedish market's high prices instead of exporting at low prices. Import barriers also reduce the focus on exports.

The truth is, as we can see from the above, that we get richest by exporting what we make best, so as to be able to import things we make less well. Otherwise we will have to do everything ourselves and refrain from specialisation. We can make a pile of money by just selling, but our standard of living will not rise until we use that money to buy things which we would not have had otherwise. One of the first trade theorists, James Mill, quite rightly argued, in 1821: "The benefit which is derived from exchanging one commodity for another, arises, in all cases, from the commodity *received*, not the commodity given."

The absurdity of the idea that we must avoid cheap imports becomes clear if we apply it across non-national boundaries – for example, if the city of Gothenburg were to try to prevent the importation of goods from elsewhere, on the grounds that it had to protect its markets. But if imports really were negative, it would be logical for one province to prevent its inhabitants from buying from another, Gothenburg people would lose out on buying goods from Stockholm, one city precinct would gain by refusing to buy goods from another city precinct, and it would be good for a family to decide to make everything themselves instead of buying from others. In the event, of course, this would lead to a tremendous loss of welfare. The family would hardly be capable of producing enough to keep body and soul together. When you go to the shop, you "import" food – being able to do so cheaply is a benefit, not a loss. You "export" when you go to work and create goods or services. I presume that you and the great majority of other people would prefer to "import" so cheaply that you could afford to "export" a little less.

Trade is not a zero sum game in which one party loses what the other party gains. On the contrary, there would be no exchange if both parties did not feel that they benefited. The really interesting yardstick is not the balance of trade (where a "surplus" means that we are exporting more than we are importing) but the quantity of trade, both exports and imports are gains.

"Nothing, however, can be more absurd than this whole doctrine of the balance of trade, upon which, not only these restraints, but almost all the other regulations of commerce are founded. When two places trade with one another, this doctrine supposes that, if the balance be even, neither of them either loses or gains; but if it leans in any degree to one side, that one of them loses and the other gains in proportion to its declension from the exact equilibrium. Both suppositions are false. A trade which is forced by means of bounties and monopolies may be, and commonly is disadvantageous to the country in whose favour it is meant to be established, as I shall endeavour to shew hereafter. But that trade which, without force or constraint, is naturally and regularly carried on between any two places is always advantageous, though not always equally so, to both."
Adam Smith, 1776 [49]

49. Smith 1981, p. 488 f.

Imports are often feared as a potential cause of unemployment. If we import cheap toys and clothing from China, then toy and garment manufacturers here will have to scale down. In a more internationalist perspective one may ask why jobs and investments are more important in Sweden than in poorer countries – do not those countries need them still more, unable as they are to compensate the unemployed? But this is also a mistaken way of looking at things. By obtaining cheaper goods we save resources in Sweden and can therefore invest in new industries and occupations. This also results in the Chinese having more money to spare and being able to buy mobile phones from Sweden. Besides, most enterprises and producers are dependent on raw materials from and subcontractors in other countries. For the production of telephony systems, for example, the Swedish company Ericsson needs electronic components produced in Asia. So when the EU raises tariff barriers against Asia, allegedly for the protection of European jobs, this means that European companies like Ericsson sustain added costs and therefore sell less, which means they are not able to create so many new jobs.

This means that the world's politicians are acting foolishly when they foregather in Seattle or Qatar to negotiate on the abolition of tariffs within the framework of the World Trade Organisation, WTO. The politicians say that they will consent to reduce a tariff only on condition that other countries do the same. This is fundamentally irrational, because we ourselves benefit by reducing our tariffs and being able to import cheaply, even if the others do not. The best policy is unilateral free trade, i.e. Sweden or the EU dismantling its tariffs and quotas even if other countries retain or perhaps increase theirs. Why should we subject our population to more tariffs and prohibitions merely because other countries do so to their populations? As the 18th century French liberal Frédéric Bastiat explained, there is nothing very clever about tipping boulders into our harbours merely because our neighbours have rocky and inaccessible coastlines which

116

it is hard for our ships to put into. Saying "I'm not going to allow myself to choose from a wider range of good and cheap products unless you do the same" is a sacrifice, not a cunning reprisal.

Even so, there are good arguments in favour of multilateral trade negotiations between lots of countries under WTO auspices. They can make it easier for vested interests to accept free trade reforms. If Sweden unilaterally reduces its tariffs this can meet with fierce resistance from Swedish companies and trade unions which do not want competition. But if other countries reduce their tariffs at the same time, the reform will be supported by businesses and unions in export industry, because they benefit by it. Negotiations can make it easier to introduce tariff reductions and to get other countries to do the same, but they can also make it more difficult. If politicians behave as though tariffs are something important which we will only remove if we get something in return, voters will end up believing them. In this way they will get the impression that tariffs are a good thing which the politicians are selling out, whereas in fact they are something harmful. If trade talks are not combined with strong mobilisation of opinion against tariffs and quotas and for imports, there may come a protectionist backlash, as the collapse of negotiations following the WTO Seattle meeting suggests.[50]

The WTO offers an advantage of a different kind, namely that of establishing an impartial code of rules which ensures that all countries honour their agreements. There was a time when the powerful countries could behave as they liked towards the weaker ones. Many of the world's countries wanted a trade organisation with uniform rules to prevent, above all, unilateral actions by the USA against its trading partners. The USA, on the other hand, only wanted a weaker agreement to begin with, and not an organisation to resolve disputes.

---

50. For this reason Tomas Larsson predicted the collapse of the Seattle meeting in his excellent reportage book *The Race to the Top,* originally published in 1999.

Through the WTO the member states have pledged themselves not to discriminate against foreign enterprises and not to introduce any arbitrary trade barriers, over and above the ones they have already. It was to benefit from this that the poorer countries of the world quickly ratified the 1995 WTO agreement, whereas the EU, the USA and Japan – accustomed to doing as they liked – held fire. This has also led to powerful countries like the USA being defeated in WTO disputes, a thing which could never happen at the United Nations, where they have a veto.

Another advantage of the WTO is that all member states have pledged themselves to give the others "most favoured nation" treatment, i.e. automatic access to all tariff reductions granted to any other country. Formerly the USA and the EU, for example, used to reduce tariffs in relation to each other without a thought of increasing freedom of trade with the rest of the world. Now tariff reductions also have to apply to the poor countries (with the unfortunate exception of regional trade agreements, such as the EU).

But the obstacles to unfair tariffs are not all that great. The WTO has no specific rights to forbid anyone to impose them, it can only entitle the injured party to introduce compensatory trade barriers. This is not an ideal situation, because countries should phase out their tariffs regardless of what others do. It would be better if the losing part had to pay monetary compensation or lower other tariffs to compensate. But the regular procedures are at least an improvement on the old days, when a petty dispute could blossom forth into a full-scale trade war. Now states are at least prevented by their honour from reneging on their agreements, though in a couple of widely noted instances the EU has tried to retain trade barriers condemned by the WTO, as for example with the attempt made for many years to discriminate against Latin American bananas and hormone-treated meat. The EU governments act as though one yardstick should apply to the industrialised nations and another to the developing countries, which in the long term will severely damage the WTO's credibility.

From perception of the benefits of imports it also follows that anti-dumping measures are harmful. Politicians often say that they must protect the people from price dumping by other countries, meaning for example that if Malaysia sells us extremely cheap shoes, priced below production cost or cheaper than they are sold in the Malaysian market, this is "unfair competition". The Malaysian producers are then "dumping" prices, and this is something we have to protect ourselves against. But, as the American economist Murray Rothbard has expressed the matter, you should keep a sharp eye on your wallet when somebody says that they want "fair competition", because that means it is about to be picked. This is true where anti-dumping tariffs are concerned. What they really "protect" us from is cheap shoes, TV sets and foodstuffs. The question is why we should need protection from these things. There need not be anything unfair at all about foreign producers "dumping" their prices. For example, they may be forced to do so in order to penetrate a new market, which must be deemed legitimate. New Swedish firms are allowed to do this, so why not foreign ones? Surely, having different rules for Swedish and foreign enterprises amounts to a greater injustice than dumping? It may also be that the Malaysian shoe manufacturers sell their products more expensively in the home market because they have advantages there which they do not enjoy here, e.g. protective tariff walls.

The USA, pro-free trade by its own profession, is in fact the biggest transgressor when it comes to introducing anti-dumping tariffs. Not only do these tariffs harm the enterprise sectors of other countries, but the American economy loses billions of dollars every year through higher prices and lower efficiency. The use of such tariffs has grown in the past decade. When the WTO and international agreements make protectionism harder to introduce through the front entrance, the USA and the EU let it in the back door, with anti-dumping tariffs.

But if the American government subsidises its shoe company with taxpayers' money, then different rules apply in practice. The American company can then maintain lower prices and knock out our Swedish producers, not by being better but by getting more subsidies from its government. Some people feel we should protect ourselves against this. But why? In practice a policy of this kind means the American government subsidising purchases by Swedish consumers. The Swedish reaction ought to be one of gratitude – coupled with a degree of perplexity over the oddities of American policy.

Free trade brings growth

Free trade is primarily a good thing because it brings freedom: freedom for people to buy what they want from whom they please, but also to sell to whoever wants to buy. Economically this leads to the efficient use of resources and capital. A company, a region or a country specialises where it has comparative advantages and can therefore produce a greater value than otherwise. Capital and labour from older, less competitive sectors are transferred to new, more dynamic ones. This means that a country switching to a more free-trade-friendly policy rises to a higher level of production and prosperity, and can therefore anticipate a substantial acceleration of growth for the first few years. But it also leads to a constant endeavour to improve production, because foreign competition forces firms to be as good and cheap as possible, and this leaves consumers free to choose goods and services from the dealer making them the best offer. More resources are then devoted to production, leading to increased investments and new methods, inventions and products. This is really just the same argument as for competition generally. It simply extends competition to even bigger fields, thus making it more intensive.

One of the most important advantages of free trade is hard to measure, namely the advantage that a country trading a great deal with the rest of the world imports new ideas and new techniques into the bargain. If Sweden applies free trade, this means that our companies are exposed to the world's best ideas in their particular fields. This way, they are compelled to be dynamic themselves and they can borrow other companies' ideas, buy their technology and hire foreign manpower. Openness to new impressions and other people has always been a path to development, while introspectiveness means stagnation. It is no coincidence that the most dynamic regions in history have often been in coastal locations and close to towns and cities, while the ones lagging behind are inaccessible, often in mountain regions.

The world's output today is six times what it was 50 years ago, and world trade is 16 times greater. There is cause to believe that production has been led and driven by trade. Exactly what difference open markets make is hard to tell, but practically no economist denies that the difference is positive. There are huge quantities of empirical fact to show that free trade creates economic development.

One comprehensive and frequently quoted study of the effects of trade is that by Harvard economists Jeffrey Sachs and Andrew Warner.[51] They examine the trade policies of 117 countries between 1970 and 1989. After checking for other factors, the study reveals a statistically significant connection between free trade and growth which they are unable to find, for example, between education and growth. Growth was between 3 and 6 times higher in free trade countries than in protectionist ones. Open developing countries had on average an annual growth rate of 4.49 per cent these two decades, while closed developing countries had only 0.69 per cent. Open industrialised countries had an annul growth of 2.29 per cent, while closed ones had only 0.74 per cent.

It has to be emphasised that this is not a matter of how much countries earn by others being open to their exports, but how much they earn by keeping their own markets open. The results show that the open economies had a faster growth rate than the closed ones *every year* between 1965 and 1989. No free trade country in the study had an average growth rate of less than 1.2 per cent per annum, and no open developing country had a growth rate of less than 2.3 per cent!

---

51. Sachs & Warner 1995.

Free trade and growth during the 1970s and 1980s

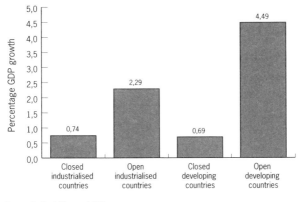

Source: Sachs & Warner, 1995.

in all regions, a country's free trade policy led to an acceleration of growth after a short time, even in Africa. The positive results of free trade were also apparent in the short term. Countries which opened up their economies temporarily and then closed them again showed faster growth during the open period than otherwise.

Nor were slower growth and reduced investments a way for the protectionist economies to purchase more stability. On the contrary, Sachs and Warner showed that closed economies were far more liable than free trade economies to be affected by financial crises and hyper-inflation. Barely 8 per cent of the developing countries judged open from the 70s onwards suffered from crises of this kind during the 80s, whereas more than 80 per cent of the closed economies did so.

Criticism has been levelled at this type of regression analysis, which is based on statistics from numbers of economies and tries to exclude other factors which can affect the outcome, because of the many problems of measurement which they involve. Coping with enormous masses of data is always a problem. Besides, where is one to draw the line between open and closed economies, and how does one distinguish between cause and effect? Then again it is common for countries introducing free trade also to introduce other liberal reforms, such as protection for property rights, reduced inflation and balanced budgets, which makes it hard to separate the effect of one thing from the effect of another.[52] The problems of measurement are real ones, and results of this kind always have to be taken with a pinch of salt, but it remains interesting that, with so very few exceptions, those studies point to great advantages with free trade. All the same, they have to be supplemented with theoretical studies and studies of individual countries before and after trade liberalisation measures, studies which also clearly bring out the advantages of free trade.

The economist Sebastian Edwards maintains that the important thing is not to devise exact, objective measurements but to test any different variables, so as to see whether a pattern emerges. Using eight different yardsticks of openness he has made eighteen calculations based on partly different material and different calculation methods.

---

52. The critics include free traders Srinivasan & Bhagwati 1999. Rodriguez & Rodrik 1999 are leading trade sceptics, but even they point out: "We do not want to leave the reader with the impression that we think trade protection is good for economic growth. We know of no credible evidence – at least for the post-1945 period – that suggests that trade restrictions are systematically associated with higher growth rates ... The effects of trade liberalization may be on balance beneficial on standard comparative-advantage grounds; the evidence provides no strong reason to dispute this."

One of Dani Rodrik's arguments against free trade is that countries with high tariffs, such as China and India, have faster growth than the EU and the USA, which have low tariffs. But he forgets that China and India have achieved these growth figures by liberalising their economies. It is when countries begin reducing their tariffs from high initial levels that they achieve the biggest growth gains, because manpower then switches to occupations in which they have the biggest advantages. The USA and the EU acquired similar impetus when their trade was liberalised. Besides, China and India have such large populations that trade liberalisation *within* the country means free trade on a far bigger scale than is implied by the ordinary regional free trade agreements in the rest of the world.

All but one of the calculations indicated a positive connection between free trade and growth. Edwards estimates that growth has been twice as high in free trade developing countries as in protectionist ones. In a report to the Swedish parliamentary committee Globkom, the economist Håkan Nordström reviews 20 different studies of free trade, all of which clearly show that open, markets give better economic development.[53]

Another attempt to quantify the benefits of trade has been made by the economists Jeffrey Frankel and David Romer. On the basis of their studies they maintain that if a country increases its trade in relation to GDP by 1 per cent, its per capita income can be expected to rise by between 0.5 and 2 per cent. This means that if a country augments its trade by 10 percentage units, this raises the incomes of the poor by between 5 and 20 per cent. These are of course averages, not universal figures, but if by way of experiment we were to work out what this actually means to the poor of the world, we would find that a 10 per cent growth of trade in relation to GDP in a country like Nigeria would mean 25 million people being able to escape from poverty. In a country like India it could mean ten times that number being raised out of extreme poverty. This is a hypothesis, not a prediction, but it conveys something of the explosive potential inherent in free commercial exchange.[54]

There is a clear connection between greater free trade and growth, and poverty reduction. We can see the differences between countries in similar circumstances which have introduced, or refrained from introducing, liberalisation measures and open markets. We see this difference between liberalising Vietnam and non-liberalising Burma, between Bangladesh and Pakistan, between Costa Rica and Honduras, between Uganda and Kenya, and so on.

53. Edwards 1997, Nordström 2000.

54. Frankel & Romer 1999.

But there does not seem to be any strong and unambiguous connection between increased trade and changes in equality – except, possibly, a slightly positive connection. Certain groups lose out by free trade, but they do not represent the poor more often than the rich. Changes in equality depend above all on policy generally. Results in trade-liberalising countries varied during the 90s: in China, inequality has increased, in Costa Rica and Vietnam it has remained constant, and in countries like Ghana and Thailand it has diminished.

> After many years of communist planned economy and deepest poverty, Vietnam since the end of the 1980s has introduced free trade reforms and measures of domestic liberalisation. This has made possible a heavy growth of exports of such labour-intensive products as shoes, and of rice, which is produced by poor farmers. This has resulted in rapid growth and a uniquely swift reduction of poverty. Whereas 75 per cent of the population in 1988 were living in extreme poverty, by 1993 this figure had fallen to 58 per cent, and ten years later had altogether been reduced by nearly half, to 37 per cent. 98 per cent of the poorest Vietnamese households increased their incomes during the 1990s.[55]

One seldom observed aspect of Sachs and Warner's findings is that they show open poor economies to have grown faster than open affluent ones. It may seem natural for poor countries to have higher growth than affluent ones, because they have more latent resources to harness and can benefit from the existence of wealthier nations to which they can export and from which they can import capital and more advanced technology, whereas affluent countries do not have

---

55. Dollar & Kraay 2001.

that advantage. But economists have not found any such general connection previously. The reason is simple: the economy in protectionist developing countries can not use these international possibilities, and so grow less rapidly than the affluent countries. But when Sachs and Warner studied the developing countries which had been open to trade and investments, i.e. those most receptive to the influence of the industrial nations, these countries were found to grow more rapidly than the open affluent countries. The poorer they were from the outset, the faster their economies grew once they were opened up. No such connection exists for closed countries, which suggests that free trade is not only the best policy for growth but also the best policy for developing countries to catch up with the industrialised nations. Poor countries, then, grow faster than rich ones, so long as the two are united by flows of trade and capital.

The same results are still clearer for the 1990s. During that decade per capita GDP fell by an average of 1.1 per cent in closed developing countries. In the industrialised countries it rose by 1.9 per cent, but the fastest growth of all – 5 per cent annually on average – occurred in developing countries which had opened their markets and frontiers. It is free-trading developing countries that are developing their economies fastest, more so than the affluent countries. One pair of economists sum up their findings:

> *Thus, the globalizers are catching up with rich countries while the non-globalizers fall further and further behind.*[56]

History shows that economies can grow faster thanks to foreign wealth and technology. From 1780 it took England 58 years to double its wealth. A hundred years later Japan did it in only 34 years, and

---

56. Dollar & Kraay 2001, p. 26.

Free trade and growth during the 1990s

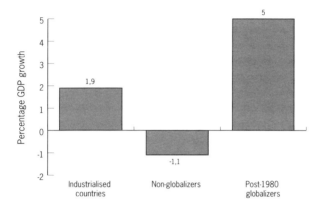

Percentage GDP growth

- Industrialised countries: 1,9
- Non-globalizers: -1,1
- Post-1980 globalizers: 5

Source: Dollar & Kraay, 2001.

another century later it took South Korea only 11 years.[57] The convergence, in terms of wealth, of countries associated with one another is confirmed by many other epochs and groups of countries. During the globalisation of the late 19th century, poorer economies like Ireland and Scandinavia moved closer to the wealthier countries. During the post-war era, poor OECD countries have moved closer to the more affluent ones. Differences between countries have diminished within the EFTA and EU free trade zones. The same result has also been discovered in different parts of such large economies as the USA and Japan. Free trade and mobility, then, make the poor richer and the richer also richer, but the rich do not grow richer as fast as the poor do.[58]

58. This finding is generally confirmed by Been-David & Winters 2000 and by Ades & Glaeser 1999. One argument against free trade bringing growth is that growth was higher during the early post-war decades than it is today, in the age of globalisation. But this is to disregard that growth is quicker when huge tariffs begin to come down and the fact that growth is generally fastest when the starting point is poverty, with any number of opportunities of obtaining a big return on investments, owing to the short-age of capital and disastrous political affairs formerly prevailing – as, for example, after a war. As countries become more fully developed and invested, the economy reverts to a more normal growth curve. Furthermore, the argument cannot in any way explain why, in this case, it is the very countries which go in for free trade that have the fastest growth today, whereas protectionist states are lagging further and further behind.

No end of work

But if free trade is all the time making production more efficient, ought this not to result in a disappearance of job opportunities? When Asians begin manufacturing our cars and South Americans producing our meat, car workers and farmers in Sweden lose their jobs and unemployment rises – so the argument goes. Foreigners, developing countries and machines will compete to produce the things we need, until in the end we will not have any jobs left. If everything we consume today can be produced by half the Swedish labour force in twenty years' time, then surely this means the other half being put out of work? This is the horror scenario depicted in many of the anti-globalisation writings of our time. In the book *The Global Trap*, two German journalists maintain that in the future 80 per cent of the population will not be needed for production. The French writer Vivianne Forrester goes even further in her book *The Economic Horror*, arguing that the great mass of the population will be made unemployed and will therefore be threatened with annihilation in the long term. This is based on an unpleasant view of human nature whereby few people will have qualities causing society to "need" them. Happy to relate, this view is completely misguided.

The notion began to grow popular in the mid-70s, and since then production has been streamlined and internationalised more than ever. And yet, all over the world, far more jobs have been created than have disappeared. In the past few decades the number of gainfully employed people in the world has risen by about 80 million. We have more efficient production than ever before, but also more people at work. Between 1975 and 1998, employment in countries like the

USA, Canada and Australia rose by 50 per cent and in Japan by 25 per cent. Within the EU, where unemployment has gained a stronger hold than in many other places, *more* people found jobs during this period in almost every country. Sweden, Finland and Spain were the only exceptions, but in these countries the employment participation rate has risen since 1998.

It is also interesting to note that it is in the most internationalised economies, with the biggest use of modern technology, that employment has grown fastest. The USA is the clearest instance. Between 1983 and 1985 in the USA, 24 million more job opportunities were created than disappeared. And these were not low-paid, unskilled jobs, as is often alleged in the course of debate. On the contrary, 70 per cent of the new jobs carried a wage above the American median level. Nearly half the new jobs belonged to the most highly skilled, a figure which has risen even more rapidly since 1995.[59]

So allegations of progressively fewer people being needed in production have no empirical foundation. And no wonder, for they are wrong in theory too. It is not the case that only a certain number of jobs exist and that when these can be done by fewer people, more become unemployed. Imagine a pre-industrial economy where most of what people earn is spent on food. Then food production is rationalised, machines begin doing the work of many farmers and foreign competition makes farming more efficient. This results in a lot of people having to leave the agricultural sector. Does this mean there is nothing for them to do, that consumption is constant? No, because it also means more scope for consumption. The money which used to go to labour costs in agriculture can now be used to buy other commodities, such as better clothing, books and industrial goods. The people made redundant in agriculture can then switch to those lines of business instead.

---

59. Rojas 1999.

131

This is not merely conjecture, it is precisely what happened in Sweden with the improvement of agricultural efficiency from the beginning of the 19th century onwards. Before then, about 80 per cent of Sweden's population had been employed on the land. Today the figure is under 3 per cent. But does this mean that 77 per cent of the Swedish population are now unemployed? No, because instead people could start demanding other goods and better services, and manpower went into industry and services in response to that demand.

The idea that the quantity of work to be done being constant, and a job gained by one person always being a job taken from someone else, has resulted in some people wanting jobs to be shared, others wanting to break up machinery, many wanting to raise tariffs and to exclude immigrants. But the whole notion is wrong. By doing a job efficiently, we get a larger total of resources with which to satisfy our needs. The manpower which used to be necessary in order to feed us could then clothe us and provide us with better housing, entertainment, travel, newspapers, telephones and computers. This raises our standard of living.

Interviewed by the Swedish journal *Ordfront*, Susan George, Vice Chairman of the French anti-globalisation organisation Attac, declares that globalisation and international investments do not provide any new jobs at all:

> *Not everything called investment leads to new job opportunities. Eight out of ten investments the world over in the past five years have been concerned with mergers and take-overs, and things like that mostly result in job losses.*[60]

---

60. "Dom kallar oss huliganer", *Ordfront* no. 12/2000.

But it is this very process – a task being done more efficiently, thus enabling jobs to be shed – which enables new industries to grow, providing people with new and better jobs.

"But," perhaps somebody asks, "will it never end? What happens when *all* our needs are being satisfied by a small portion of the workforce?" And when, I wonder, is that supposed to happen? I believe that people will always, for example, be in need of more security, convenience and entertainment. I don't believe we will ever come to think that we are giving our children enough education, that we know enough, that we are doing just the right amount of research or that we are getting enough remedies for our aches and pains. It is hard to see a limit to the quality of housing we would like to have, the quality of food we want to eat, the extent we wish to travel and the quality of entertainment we would like to experience. When our economic scope increases, we will always choose to satisfy new needs, better than ever. If we think we have all that we need, we can demand more leisure instead. Ask yourself whether you could not conceive of two full-time jobs for people to provide you with services and products. Finding the money to employ them, I suspect, is more difficult than hitting on things for them to do. If you, I and everyone else can think of things which we would like two people to do, we have a permanent manpower deficit, with 6 billion people wanting at least 12 billion employees. This is why we will never have too much manpower, no matter how prosperous we become and how efficient our production gets.

Efficiency does of course have a flip side. Sometimes the dynamic market is referred to as "creative destruction", because it is concerned with "destroying" old solutions and industries, but with a creative end in view, namely the transfer of manpower and capital to more productive occupations. This gives a higher standard of living, but at the same time the word "destruction" suggests that not everyone benefits by it. It is of course painful for those who have invested in the old solutions and are axed from less efficient industries. Drivers of horse-drawn cabs lost out on the spread of motorism, and producers of paraffin lamps on the introduction of electricity. In more modern times, manufacturers of typewriters were put out of business by the coming of the computer, and LP records were superseded by CDs.

Painful changes of this kind are happening all the time, as a result of new inventions and methods of production. Some friends of free trade attempt to explain them away by saying that job losses are due above all to technical advances, not to competition from other countries. This is true, but as a defence it rings hollow, because the competition stimulated by free trade helps to accelerate the introduction of new techniques. Unquestionably these changes can cause enormous problems and traumas for those affected, especially if a new job is hard to find. The very fear of the risks this involves causes certain out and out conservative ideologists to reject the capitalist system entirely. A modern society based on a market economy does indeed present new risks and problems, and of course it is very stressful to be in danger of losing one's job and having to go on the dole, with the reduction of living standard and impairment of self-esteem which this implies. But it still cannot be compared with the stress in past ages of perhaps not being able to earn one's daily bread or of drought or flood completely obliterating one's livelihood. It cannot be compared with the anxiety of the present-day Ethiopian farmer, whose life may depend on the coming of rain and on the health of his livestock.

Above all, it is foolish to counter the problems which adjustments entail by trying to prevent the adjustments, because all in all we lose by doing so and incur a lower standard of living. The whole point of trade and development is to direct resources to the point where they are used most efficiently. A Chinese proverb has it: "When the wind of change begins to blow, some people build windbreaks while others build windmills." Stopping change is as foolish as it would have been to obstruct agricultural advances two centuries ago to protect the 80

134

per cent of the population employed on the land at that time. And changes are hard to stop anyway, because the commonest cause of structural change in different branches of economic activity is the changing tastes of consumers. It is a better idea to use the economic gains to alleviate the consequences for those affected.

There is a lot we can do to make changes proceed as smoothly as possible. We should not try to prop up old industries by means of subsidies or tariff walls. Enterprise and financial markets should be free enough for people to invest in the new industries. Wages should be flexible and taxes low, so that people will be drawn to the new and more productive sectors and the labour market should be free. Schools and further education opportunities must be good enough for people to acquire the skills which the new jobs require. Social safety nets must provide transitional security, without preventing people from entering new jobs.

But these problems are seldom as widespread as our newspaper reading can suggest. It is easy to report that 300 people lost their jobs in a car factory owing to Japanese competition. It is less easy and less dramatic to report on all the thousands of jobs which have been created because we have been able to use old resources more efficiently, and it is less easy to report on how much Swedish consumers have gained by a wider selection, better quality and lower prices resulting from this competition. Hardly any of the world's consumers are aware that they have gained between 100 and 200 billion dollars annually through liberalisation measures resulting from Uruguay Round negotiations, but the difference is visible in our refrigerators, in home electronics and in our wallets. Costs affecting a small group on an isolated occasion are easier to see and observe, while benefits applying to nearly everyone creep up on us without our giving them a thought.

A review of more than 50 surveys of adjustment following openness reforms in different countries clearly shows these changes to be milder than the debate on them indicates. For every dollar of adjustment costs, roughly 20 dollars are harvested in the form of welfare gains. A study of 13 cases of trade liberalisation in different countries showed industrial employment to have already *increased* one year after the liberalisation in all countries but one. One reason why changes are less painful in poor countries is that the old jobs mostly offered poor wages and bad working conditions. The people who are usually most vulnerable – those without any specific training – find new work more easily than those with special skills. Because these countries have comparative advantages in labour-intensive sectors, this on average leads to a rapid rise in wages for the manpower concerned. Broad-based liberalisation measures also have the effect of cheapening the goods they need.

Costs are also small compared to benefits in affluent countries introducing trade liberalisation measures. The sectors badly affected by competition and new breakthroughs of technology go through something resembling an ordinary recession. The number of people retiring or leaving of their own free will is often so great as to swallow the job-shedding necessitated by openness reforms, and so large part of the economy can be made more efficient simply by the job market entrants opting for more modern sectors than the leavers. If the changes contribute towards a high, stable level of growth, they can even subdue painful restructuring problems, which are always greatest during downturns. Unemployment, moreover, usually lasts for only a short time, whereas the positive effects on the economy keep on growing. The process, in other words, turns out to be more creative than destructive.[61]

The problems ought to be greatest in the USA, with its constant economic transformation, but the job market there is more like the Hydra in the legend of Hercules. Every time he cut off one of its heads, two new ones appeared. For every two jobs that disappeared in

---

61. Mausz & Tarr 1999.

the USA during the 90s, three new ones were created. This increases the individual person's chances: there is no better safeguard against unemployment than the prospect of a new job. The notion of having to chop and change between different jobs all one's life appears, moreover, to be exaggerated, especially as firms are exerting themselves more and more to train employees for new tasks. The average length of time for which an American stays in a particular job *increased* between 1983 and 1995 from 3.5 years to 3.8. Nor is it true, as many people believe, that more and more jobs are being created in the USA because wages have fallen since the 1970s. A growing proportion of wages have been paid in non-monetary forms, e.g. health insurance, shares, personal savings contributions, day nursery places etc., to avoid taxation. If benefits of this new kind are included in wages, then American wages have gone on rising with productivity. The proportion of consumption among poor Americans which is devoted to food, clothing and housing has fallen since the 70s from 52 to 37 per cent, which clearly shows that they have money to spare for more than the bare necessities of life.[62]

One of the most drastic trade liberalisations in modern history has been carried out by one of Sweden's neighbours, Estonia. Soon after the country gained its independence from the Soviet Union, in 1992, the Estonian government decided to abolish all tariffs in one fell swoop. The average tariff level is now 0.0. The measure proved an unqualified success. The Estonian economy has been rapidly restructured on a competitive basis, but, with the labour market deregulated, this has entailed a relatively low level of unemployment. Western Europe, which in 1990 accounted for only 1 per cent of Estonia's international trade, today accounts for two-thirds of it. The country is attracting large direct investments and can harvest an annual growth

62. Cox & Alm 1999, pp. 65 ff. and chap. 1.

rate of something like 5 per cent. Average life expectancy has grown and infant mortality has fallen, in contrast to those former communist states which have reformed slowly. The change to a liberal system has made Estonia one of the EU's most promising candidate countries. Unfortunately, EU membership will mean Estonia having to adjust to EU protectionism. Instead of having no tariffs at all, the country will have to introduce 10,794 different tariff levels, which among other things will raise food prices appreciably. In addition, Estonia will have to introduce various quotas, subsidies and anti-dumping measures.[63]

---

63. Åslund 2000, Sally 2000.

Freedom of movement – for people as well

Even if a world in which we are free to buy and sell goods and services across national frontiers is a long way off, this is what many people are aiming for. The world's politicians meet regularly in an attempt to extent free trade, albeit far too slowly. As regards the mobility of human beings, the politicians, unfortunately, meet regularly to do everything in their power to reduce it. This has been a very conspicuous aim of the affluent European states ever since the 1970s. At the same time as the Schengen Agreement gives us free mobility within the Union the EU governments are trying to prevent outsiders from penetrating the Union's boundaries. The result is very high walls against the outside and stricter controls on the internal movement of persons.

Citizens of about 120 countries need visas in order to visit the EU. A visa is hard to come by, especially if you are being persecuted. The EU even requires private airlines, on pain of heavy fines, to play customs officials and weed out people who may be carrying false passports and visas. Employees who cannot assess these cases are placed under an obligation to weed people out. As a result the great majority cannot even come to the EU in order to seek asylum – assuming it would have been granted if they had been allowed in! More than two-thirds of those arriving at Stockholm/Arlanda Airport without a valid passport or visa during the past two years have been allowed to settle in Sweden, either as refugees or for humanitarian reasons. That emergency exit is now being closed.[64]

---

64. Hedström & Stenberg 2001.

This stricter policy is causing the rest of the world to attract attention in the most tragic way possible. A port official opening a container in Dover finds 58 Chinese refugees who have died from heat and suffocation after trying to hide from the immigration officials. Africans are found dead on the south coast of Spain, having drowned in the attempt to cross the Mediterranean by swimming or in unseaworthy craft. The big tragedies attract attention, but they have their lesser daily counterparts. Someone has estimated that every day more than ten people die on the borders of the EU. If, through visa requirements and barriers, people are prevented from entering the Union legally, they are forced into drastic and dangerous ways of doing so illegally. Often they fall into the clutches of unscrupulous refugee smugglers who levy exorbitant payment but do not think twice about risking their lives.

When the EU tries to prevent outsiders from coming here, by means of progressively tougher action and stricter controls, refugees are forced to take even bigger risks. If people go through this in order to come to Europe, the EU politicians should seriously reconsider whether they have correctly assessed the refugees' need for protection. The obvious vision must be for each individual to decide his own need or interest in fleeing or migrating to another country, unimpeded by borders and prohibitions.

The same goes for so-called "economic refugees", i.e. people who wish to leave economic deprivation behind them and come to a country where they have the chance of creating a better life. There can be no genuine economic globalisation so long as people are not allowed to cross national boundaries in search of employment. Something like a million Swedes did so a hundred years ago, when they emigrated to America to create a better existence there. People with the same intentions are being prevented from coming to Sweden today – unless, of course, they happen to be star athletes or "foreign experts". The western world rightly castigated the communist states for not allowing their citizens to emigrate. But now that they are permitted to do so, we are forbidding them to enter our countries.

There is no "concession" or "generosity" about opening up our frontiers to refugees and immigrants, any more than there is about opening them up to imports. Greater immigration can be a precondition for our still having a viable economy and security of welfare one generation from now, especially in a sparsely populated country like Sweden. The EU countries are greatly troubled by falling birth rates and ageing population. UNFPA, the United Nations Population Fund, has estimated that to keep the EU population at its present level until 2050, we could do with 1.6 million immigrants annually. And in order to maintain a steady ratio between working and retired populations, the EU would need to take in 13.5 million immigrants *every year*.

It is a profound error to regard immigrants as a burden on a country. They represent a manpower and consumption increment leading to growth in the Swedish market. In the course of a lifetime, even those getting off to a poor start in Sweden generally put more back into society – and the national treasury – than they get out of it.[65] If large numbers of immigrants become permanently dependent on handouts, this gives us cause, not so much to change their characters as to seriously reform our social security systems and labour market regulations. In a healthy economy, moreover, low starting wages need not mean a general reduction of real earnings, because they keep down the prices of the goods and service we consume.

Openness to immigration and emigration is also important for the sake of a living society. This way, people with different starting points and values can address our longstanding problems and come up with creative solutions to them. Immigrants can utilise what is viable in

---

65. Se Österberg 2000, Rankka 2000, "A continent on the move", *The Economist*, 6 May 2000.

our Swedish culture and combine it with traditions of their own, and we native Swedes can do likewise. It is no coincidence that the USA, the most dynamic society in history, was built by immigrants. President Roosevelt once opened a speech by saying: "My fellow immigrants." Even today, the USA is receiving far more immigrants than all other countries, thereby avoiding the EU's problem of an ageing population. In this way the USA is constantly renewing itself and laying the foundations of continued global leadership – economic, cultural and scientific.

IV

The development of the developing countries

An unequal distribution – of capitalism

Twenty per cent of the world's population are consuming over 80 per cent of the earth's resources, and the other 80 per cent are consuming less than 20 per cent. Critics of globalisation never tire of reminding us of this injustice. It is less often one has a proper analysis of the reason for this state of affairs. The critics make it sound as though the poor are poor *because* the rich are rich, as if the 20 per cent had stolen those resources from the 80 per cent. This is wrong. Natural resources were of course stolen in the age of imperialism, but those thefts have played a negligible part in the prosperity of the western world and the poverty of the poor. Even though colonialism did great harm in places, this in itself does not account for differences between North and South. The affluent world has grown fastest *since* losing its colonies. Several of the world's richest countries – such as Switzerland, Sweden and our neighbouring countries – never had any colonies of importance. Others, such as the USA, Canada, Australia, New Zealand, Hong Kong and Singapore, were colonies themselves. On the other hand, several of the world's least developed countries – Afghanistan, Liberia, Nepal and Tibet, for example – have never been colonies.

It is not the countries with abundant raw materials that have grown fastest, and often they are held back, because natural assets give rise to internal conflicts. No, the main reason for the 20 per cent consuming 80 per cent of resources is that they *produce* 80 per cent of resources. The 80 per cent consume only 20 per cent because they only produce 20 per cent of resources. It is this latter problem we ought to tackle, the inadequate creative and productive capacity of the poor countries of the world, instead of waxing indignant over the affluent world producing so much. The problem is that many people are poor, not that certain people are rich.

Critics of capitalism point out that per capita GDP is more than 30 times greater in the world's 20 richest countries than in the 20 poorest. They are right in saying that this inequality is due to capitalism, but not in the sense they believe. The difference is due to certain countries having opted for the path of capitalism, and their inhabitants having been able to achieve fantastic prosperity, while those choosing to impede people from ownership, trade and production have lagged behind. Factors such as climate and natural disasters are not unimportant, but most of the gap can still be put down to certain countries having opted for liberalisation and others for control. The 20 economically most liberal countries in the world have a per capita GDP about 29 times greater than the 20 economically least liberal. If, then, we are in earnest about closing the North-South divide, we should hope with all our hearts that the South will also gain access to a free economy and open markets. Developing countries which have had these things in recent decades have not only grown faster than other developing countries but have grown faster than the affluent countries too.

The world's inequality is due to capitalism. Not to capitalism having made certain groups poor, but to its making its practitioners wealthy. *The uneven distribution of wealth in the world is above all due to the uneven distribution of capitalism.*

Some argue that capital and corporations only make their way into the affluent countries, leaving the poor ones in the lurch, while others maintain that they only make their way into poor countries with low production costs, causing the affluent countries to lose ground. The truth seems to be that they make their way into both. Trade and investment flows in the past two decades have come to be more and more evenly distributed between those economies which are relative-

145

ly open to the rest of the world. It is the really closed economies which, for obvious reasons, are not getting investments and trade, and what is more, the differences between these countries are increasing. Clearly then, instead of globalisation marginalizing certain regions, it is the regions standing aside from globalisation which become marginalized.[66]

A quarter of direct international investments – that is to say, the acquisition and foundation of enterprises, real estate and land – between 1988 and 1998 went to developing countries. Since the beginning of the 80s, investment flows from industrialised to developing countries have risen from 10 billion to 200 billion dollars annually. 85 per cent of direct investments in developing countries go to a mere 10 countries, often the most liberalising. But since these investments have been growing by 12 per cent annually in the past three decades, this also means tremendous increases for countries not included among the top ten.

During the past ten years, private investors have channelled a trillion dollars – one thousand billion dollars – from the affluent world to the poor countries in direct investments. This is roughly ten times as much as in earlier decades, and it also happens to be rather more than the sum total of assistance given by all affluent countries to all developing countries *during the past fifty years*. These investments, of course, do not have the same poverty focus as international development assistance, but on the other hand they probably have a greater positive long-term impact, because they develop the country's productive forces instead of, like traditional development assistance, underpinning centralising structures and powers.

The affluent OECD countries accounted for 80 per cent of world GDP in 1975, a share which has fallen to 70 per cent today. As has

---

66. Low, Olarrega & Suarez 1998. Many states are closed to some extent. 131 out of 161 developing countries still have regulations opposing direct foreign investments.

already been mentioned, poor countries opting for economic liberalisation and free trade have had *faster* growth than the affluent countries in recent decades. Free trade and liberalism, it seems, are a way for developing countries not only to get richer but even to catch up on the wealthier countries. As UN Secretary-general Kofi Annan said at the UNCTAD Conference in Bangkok on 12th February 2000, soon after the demonstrations against the WTO:

> *The main losers in today's very unequal world are not those who are too much exposed to globalisation. They are those who have been left out.*

Africa is the most prominent example. Isolation and regulation cause poor countries to remain poor countries.

The white man's shame

Although the western world has paid lip service to free trade, it has not done very much to aid the process. On the contrary, its highest barriers have been raised against the developing countries, and this policy lives on. In the big rounds of free trade negotiations, tariffs and quotas for the western world's export products have been steadily reduced, but in the areas of greatest importance to the developing countries, such as textiles and agricultural produce, liberalisation measures have failed to materialise. The tariff reductions of the Uruguay Round were smallest for the least developed countries. Asia and Latin America gained relatively little. Africa nothing at all.

Today western duties on export commodities from the developing countries are 30 per cent above the global average. The iron curtain between East and West has been replaced with a customs curtain between North and South. This is not just an act of omission, it is a deliberate attempt to keep poor states out of the running. They may sell us things which we are unable to produce ourselves, but heaven help them if they put us out of business by doing something which we can, but doing it cheaper and better. The western world, for example, maintains low tariffs on cotton, higher ones on textiles and the highest of all on machinery. Duties on processed products from the developing countries are no less than four times higher than on corresponding goods from industrialised countries.

It is goods of the very kind which the Third World could produce that are worst hit by protectionism – labour-intensive industrial goods and services, such as toys, electronics, transport services, textiles and garments. If the duties are between 10 and 30 per cent of the value of the goods, it takes a substantial difference in quality and price for those goods to get into our markets at all. The western countries have pledged themselves to remove their textile quotas by 2005, but even if that pledge is honoured – which is uncertain – textile tariffs will remain averaging about 12 per cent. So the developing countries would be the principal beneficiaries of increased global free trade in manufacturing industry. In one study, estimating that the world economy would gain about 70 billion dollars a year from a 40 per cent tariff reduction, it was argued that some 75 per cent of the total gains would be harvested by the developing countries.[67] This equals the total amount of international development assistance to the developing countries, and it is almost three times the monthly income of all the world's extremely poor taken together. So the breakdown of the WTO talks is a tragedy for the people of those countries.

The most startling protectionism on the part of the affluent countries concerns agricultural produce, world trade in which is growing far more slowly than trade in other commodities. This is due to the policy of the affluent countries. Most of them are determined at all costs to maintain a large-scale agricultural industry of their own, even if they have no comparative advantages in this sector. And so they subsidise their own farmers and exclude those of other countries by means of trade barriers.

There is no easier way of squandering money than through an advanced agricultural policy. Affluent countries are drenching farmers with money through protectionism, subsidies and export grants. The total cost of agricultural policy in the 29 affluent OECD countries burdens taxpayers and consumers with a staggering 360 billion dollars. For that money one could, with plenty of change left over, send all the 56 million cows of these countries

67. Hertel & Martin 1999.

round the world on first class air tickets once every year. Alternatively, the cows could make do with flying business class round the world and in return receive 2,800 dollars pocket money each to spend in tax-free shops during their stopovers in the USA, the EU and Asia.[68]

The European Union's CAP – which, believe it or not, means Common Agricultural Policy, not Crazy Agricultural Policy – involves quotas on foodstuffs and tariffs of about 100 per cent, e.g. on sugar and dairy produce. Here again the EU wishes to exclude processed products which can compete with European ones. Tariffs on basic foodstuffs average only half of those on upgraded foodstuffs. Coffee and cocoa, which we do not produce ourselves, can slip in without any serious customs mark-ups. Meanwhile EU tariffs on meat are several hundred per cent. The hollowness of self-appointed solidarity movements like the French Attac is exposed by their defence of such tariffs against the Third World.[69]

Not only, however, is the EU excluding foreign products, but production and transport by European farmers are being subsidised to a fantastic degree, by something like half the EU budget. Since these grants are paid according to acreage and head of livestock, this is mainly a subsidisation of the wealthiest and of large-scale operations

---

68. Ronnie Horesh: "Trade and Agriculture: the Unimportance of Being Rational".

69. Attac Chairman Bernard Cassen maintains that "every country or group of countries has the absolute right to protect its agriculture," Cassen 2001a. In the international platform defining its essential issues, Attac declares its intention of combating the forces within the EU which are conducting a "free trade crusade" and among other things are seeking to "dismantle the common agricultural policy". This fact, however, is apparently so embarrassing to Swedish Attac adherents that they endeavour to conceal it. In the Swedish translation of this very section in Bim Clinell's adulatory book *Attac: gräsrötternas revolt mot marknaden*, 2000 (pp. 75–78, translated by Margareta Kruse), this section is travestied into merely complaining abut those who "are pushing development towards new fields of deregulation," without any mention of the CAP.

– it is often said that the foremost recipient of grants is the British royal family. The grants give rise to a huge surplus of foodstuffs which has to be disposed of. This the EU does partly by paying farmers *not* to grow anything. Worse still, through export subsidies the EU dumps its surplus on the world market, so that poor countries are unable to compete. This means that the CAP not only prevents Third World farms from selling to us, it knocks them out in their own countries. This is no ordinary price dumping by a systematic undermining of the very type of industry in which the developing countries have comparative advantages and which most of them must start to expand before other sectors can be developed. The CAP is estimated to cause the developing countries a welfare loss in the region of 20 billion dollar *annually*, which is twice Kenya's entire GDP.[70]

The EU's trade policy is irrational and shameful. It protects a small circle of lobbying enterprises and farmers who ignore the fact that their walls are condemning people in other continents to poverty and death. This is a moral disaster. The cynicism of the policy is made all the more apparent by the realisation that the EU as a whole gains nothing by it either. The Swedish government's calculations suggest that a Swedish household with two children could gain about 250 dollars a year by being spared the EU's duties on garments, and no less than 1,200 a year if all agricultural policy were abolished.[71] European taxpayers pay millions of dollars in tax every year for their shops to have a smaller selection of food at higher prices. EU governments subsidise agriculture to the tune of about 90 billion dollars a year and the manufacture of basic industrial products by about the same amount. All cracks through which goods from the developing countries could sneak in are promptly plugged with anti-dumping tariffs

70. Anderson, Hoekman & Strutt 1999.

71. Francois, Glismann & Spinanger 2000, Pagrotsky 1999.

and technical stipulations, e.g. concerning packaging and hygiene – stipulations exclusively tailored to EU enterprises.

On the basis of statistics from the European Commission, the French economist Patrick Messerlin has estimated the cost of all EU trade barriers, including tariffs, quotas, export subsidies, anti-dumping measures and so on. His findings indicate a total annual loss of no less than 5 or 7 per cent of the EU's GDP. In other words, completely free trade would mean the EU being able to add nearly three Swedens to its prosperity *every year*. Messerlin maintains that roughly 3 per cent of jobs in the sectors he has investigated have been rescued by protectionism. Each job costs about 200 thousand dollars per annum, which is roughly ten times the average wage in these industries. For that money every tariff-protected worker could receive an annual Rolls Royce instead; it would not cost us more, and it would not be done at the expense of the world's poor.[72] "Either a branch of enterprise is profitable, in which case it needs no tariff protection; or else it is unprofitable, in which case it deserves no tariff protection," as the Swedish economist Eli F. Heckscher once put it. With tariff protection and subsidies, manpower and capital which could have developed the EU's competitive strength linger on in sectors where there is no comparative advantage. Thus the EU ties the developing countries to poverty, not for the benefit of the European people but for the sake of a narrow, vociferous vested interest.

It is of course hard to quantify the loss which the developing countries sustain as a result of protectionism, but many people try to. UNCTAD, the United Nations Trade and Development Programme, claims that with greater access to the market of the affluent countries, exports from the developing countries would grow by something like 700 billion dollars annually. The British Labour government's white paper on globalisation issues asserts that a 50 per cent reduction of

---

72. Messerlin 2001.

import duties in industrialised and developing countries would lead to a growth of prosperity in the developing countries by something like 150 billion dollars. This is three times as much as global development assistance.[73]

73. "White Man's Shame", *The Economist* 25th September 1999, Short, 2000.

The case of Latin America

One traditional fear concerning trade between North and South is that it would make the Third World dependent on selling raw materials to affluent countries in the North. If the developing countries were to practise free trade, they would never succeed in getting industrialised and selling other products. Many therefore took the view that they should go in for "import substitution", with the government building up native industry behind high tariff walls and expanding it by starting to manufacture goods which would otherwise have to be imported. The aim was a kind of self-sufficiency – being able to fend for oneself instead of specialising and making oneself dependent on world trade. This "dependency theory" rapidly gained ground after the Second World War, partly in the west. This is why western observers in the 1960s expected North Korea, a closed economy, to outdistance export-oriented South Korea, and Mao's China to have far better prospects than pro-trade Taiwan. Import substitution was practised, for example, by India and Africa, but the whole idea was modelled on post-war Latin America.[74]

It was not surprising that politicians in Chile, Brazil and Argentina, for example, fell for the dependency school. Since the mid-19th century the region had experienced an economic upturn through the export of a few central raw materials, such as coffee, bananas, sugar, cotton, copper. But this still did not bring any broad-based national development, because the countries concerned were typical societies

---

74. The description of Latin American conditions is based on Gunnarsson & Rojas 1997.

of privilege. A small, protected landlord class owned enormous tracts of land, at the same time as there was a surplus of destitute, unskilled workers who were often paid in kind, with goods from the estates. In this way the tiny élite hogged the profits but did not invest them. They had no need of labour-saving machinery, because there was a superabundance of labour, and they did not need to improve crop yields, because they had vast acreages at their disposal. If new lands were needed, they were simply stolen from the native population. Agriculture did not develop and no demand was created for manufactured goods, because incomes did not grow. Within the élite, technology and organising ability were conspicuous by their absence. Low education, discrimination and trade regulations made it impossible for the labour force to start up small businesses. The Latin American economies remained dependent on exports of a few raw materials. When, in about 1930, the international economy collapsed and the affluent countries reintroduced protectionism, this came as a death blow to the states of Latin America. Suddenly everything which had built up their economies had vanished.

What this example shows is that trade does not of itself necessarily create dynamic development in an oppressive society. If a country is static and characterised by enormous privileges and discrimination, there is little chance of trade solving all these problems. In order for that to happen, the population must acquire liberty and the opportunity of economic participation. Land reforms would have been needed, to put an end to centuries of feudalism, coupled with a commitment to education and free markets. But these were not the conclusions drawn by the rulers of Latin America and the academics who developed the school of dependence. History, they argued, showed that trade was pernicious and that countries should go in for self-sufficiency and internal industrialisation. They pointed to the wrong villain of the piece. The Latin American countries retained privileges and national intervention, but tried to abolish trade.

The policy which they then proceeded to apply was a textbook example of protectionism – and of economic suicide. The government paid heavy grants to a native industry protected by sky-high tariff walls. During the 1950s strict import prohibitions and quotas were introduced and tariffs averaged between 100 and 200 per cent. Because consumers were unable to buy goods from other countries, the native industries were able to raise their output quickly and generate high growth. Since, however, they were under no pressure from competition, they did not develop technically or organisationally. Instead an already outmoded and inefficient industry was heavily expanded. Home market prices being higher than those on the world market, the companies became less interested in exporting. The economy became more and more politicised when the government attempted to direct manpower, prices and production in favour of industrialisation. Governmental power over the economy grew steadily – in Argentina even the circuses were nationalised. Firms therefore began devoting more resources and energy to currying favour with those in power than to streamlining their production. Strong interest groups were formed which campaigned for benefits or to obtain compensation for benefits granted to others. Distribution was governed more and more by the political struggle and less and less by market transactions.

Those who did not occupy a strong position and were not members of powerful coalitions – Indians, rural workers, small entrepreneurs and the shanty town populations – lagged further and further behind. Tariffs took the bread out of their mouths, and when inflation was made to finance government spending, this obliterated their small savings. The profile of a society of privilege was accentuated, and the already big inequalities escalated to appalling levels. Luxury palaces were built, simultaneously with the sprawling of slums. Some were born with golden spoons in their mouths, others as starving street children. Rio de Janeiro has been described as a bit of Paris surrounded by a bit of Ethiopia. The wealthiest 10 per cent in Brazil began cornering more than half the country's GDP (as compared with roughly a quarter in the USA and a fifth in Sweden). At the same time the ruling classes diverted discontent by pointing to outside enemies, by trying to assert that there was absolutely nothing wrong with their own policy and that the fault lay entirely with foreigners and the USA.

Poor consumers were forced to pay exorbitant prices in shops, at the same time as big industrialists grew richer and richer behind the tariff walls. A car in the 1960s cost more than three times as much in Chile as on the world market, with the result that only the rich could buy one. Price rises also afflicted industry, which for example needed lorries for all its transport operations. Because foreign companies were not allowed to sell to the market if they were not located within the tariff barriers, the governments managed to attract some of them. But western companies did not bring new methods, instead they quickly adjusted to the national policy. Instead of going in for specialisation and efficiency improvements, they became jacks of all trades, manu-facturing everything conceivable which people could not buy from abroad. Whole departments concentrated on bureaucracy in order to obtain start-up permits, cheap credits, special prices and public con-tracts. Keeping well in with the establishment became the path to profit for companies, making them an unsavoury political power fac-tor. Introspection prevented them from obtaining economies of scale by expanding their markets, and the lack of competition meant that they never developed their technology and organisation.

In this way Latin American industry became more and more anti-quated in relation to the rest of the world. Having failed to cope with international competition, it became more and more dependent on privileges and tariffs, which in turn caused it to lag still further behind. Paradoxically enough, exports of the old raw materials beca-me more and more important as a means of financing the growing imports of machinery and semi-manufactured goods which industry needed. Because, however, the government took these resources away from agriculture and exports, these sectors were hampered more and more. The possibility of developing and investing in the only industries capable of withstanding international competition were annihilated. Millions of people left the land for the city slums. In the end the exploitative economy could not sustain the antiquated industrial sector. Massive loans during the 1970s merely postponed the inevitable, but the backlash was all the stronger in 1982, when Mexico suspended payments and a debt crisis of unique proportions became a present reality. In three years the region's per capita income plunged by 15 per cent, and the 1980s brought a long succession of financial crises and hyperinflation. It was only after liberalisation and free trade reforms, inaugurated towards the end of the decade, that these countries came back into the ring and were able to raise their growth. Since then inequality has begun to diminish slowly, but the burden of debt continues to make these countries vulnerable. The peoples of Latin America are still footing the bill for the society of privilege and protectionism.

On the trade route

The possibility of breaking free from dependence on raw materials lies in free trade rather than protectionism. Instead of a shield behind which industry could grow strong, the tariff walls became a shield from competition which made them less efficient and innovative. The developing countries which have switched fastest from exporting raw materials to exporting upgraded products are those which have themselves had the most open economies, above all the Asian countries. Sachs and Warner's major survey of the effects of trade shows that protectionist countries have transformed their economic structure very slowly, whereas free trade countries have moved more in the direction of industrial production.[75] This is clean contrary to what the advocates of the dependency theory contended. Some of them have learned from their mistakes. The sociologist Fernando Henrique Cardoso, who once made a powerful contribution towards the development of the dependency theory, is today (2001) President of Brazil and as such is trying to introduce measures to liberalise trade! Now it is developing countries which in trade negotiations are demanding that the affluent markets be opened up to their exports.

Free trade has greater possibilities than ever of bringing dynamic development in exporting developing countries. A hundred years ago globalisation above all meant the west collecting raw materials from developing countries and bringing them here for processing. This did little to disseminate new technology and new opportunities. Production and processing could not be established in these countries,

---

75. Sachs & Warner 1995, pp. 52–55.

because sending a spare part or important personnel there could take months. But today a factory almost anywhere on earth can receive and dispatch deliveries to any destination within a week and a half and can be reached instantly by phone, fax or e-mail. This means enormous opportunities for basing activities even on what used to be the periphery of the world economy and still keeping in permanent touch with the rest of the world. Even the very core of production can be relocated to poor countries if they have comparative advantages in the sector concerned, which means fantastic opportunities for those who have not had the good fortune of being born in an affluent country.

The above applies not only to manufacturing but also to the service sector. Thanks to satellite communication and the Internet, many foreign companies can place parts of their administrative routines in countries like India, where local inhabitants can be hired for the remote management of things like wage routines, invoicing, ticket reservations and customer services for European and American corporations. And as India is "on the other side of the globe", the companies never sleep. They can even manage the surveillance of office blocks, with the aid of satellite imaging. This is a kind of labour-intensive services where developing countries have obvious comparative advantages. They get employment and higher wages, at the same time as the services are made cheaper to their customers in the industrialised countries.

Exports of industrial goods by the developing countries have risen rapidly in the past 30 years, thanks to improved communications and global free trade reforms. The dependency theory was proved wrong by events. Today manufactured products account for roughly three quarters of exports from the developing countries, as against a quarter in 1965. The share of raw material exports is diminishing all the time. Whereas at the beginning of the 1970s the developing countries accounted for only 7 per cent of global exports of manufactured goods, today they provide over a quarter.

160

The developing countries export more manufactured goods

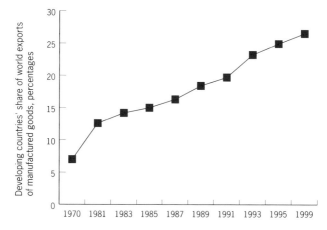

Source: Ghose, 2000, and Overseas Development Institute, 1995.

Mexico is a case in point. Long regarded as dependent on rudimentary exports to the USA, its position has changed rapidly, parallel to its conversion to a policy of free trade. As recently as 1980 only 0.7 per cent of its exports were processed. By 1990 this had risen to 3.7 per cent, and in 1995, after the NAFTA agreement had abolished tariffs between Mexico and the USA, it had risen to 19.3 per cent. The country's having advanced, in six short years, from the world's 26th to its 8th largest exporter can be termed a bonus in this connection, and helps to account for the country's growth running at about 5 per cent annually since 1996.[76]

Critics sometimes complain that labour-intensive industries once

---

76. Lukas 2000, p. 11.

emigrated to Japan because wages there were low and, when wages rose, moved on to South Korea and Taiwan. When production costs rose in those countries they moved to Malaysia and Thailand, for example, and today they are beginning to relocate in China and Vietnam. This, the critics believe, is an example of the ruthlessness of capital – leaving countries in the lurch for paying higher wages. As soon as a country's growth and prosperity get started, it is deserted by companies and investors. But this process is more a case of constantly raising the level of upgrading in production. When a country is poor, it is best at the simplest and least skilled jobs. But when it grows richer, its production more efficient and its population more skilled, they do better out of more qualified, technology-intensive production, and eventually out of knowledge-intensive production. Step by step the economy goes on developing, while poorer countries, relatively speaking, become better performers in more labour-intensive industry. Mexicans are exporting fewer raw materials and more manufactured goods, while Americans are moving more and more from manufactured goods to computer programming and consulting services. In this way the world economy is growing more and more efficient, and at the same time making room for more and more regions and countries. This is why East Asian economies have been likened to a flock of geese. From their different positions in the flock, they have all moved forward to better positions, step by step.

"Let them keep their tariffs"

There are critics of free trade, especially in the churches and in development assistance organisations, whose standpoint is the inverse of traditional protectionism. They perceive the absurdity of us in the affluent world preventing developing countries, by means of tariffs, from exporting to us, but at the same time they feel that the developing countries should beware of buying things from us and should therefore protect their markets with tariffs until they have become affluent enough. Often they make it sound as if we are doing people in developing countries a service by not arguing against their politicians' protectionism. We must "let them keep their tariffs."

This may seem reasonable – if they are poor they must be allowed to derive earnings from exports, but not made to lose them through imports which can put their own industries out of business. Their industry needs "infant industry tariffs" and cannot be exposed to competition until it is competitive. But as we have now seen, it is open countries whose industry develops fastest. Tariffs forced consumers to buy from their own companies, with the result that the latter grew richer. But, not being exposed to competition, they were under no pressure to improve their efficiency and realign their production, or to lower the prices of their goods. This policy, accordingly, enabled the élite to enrich themselves while the great mass of the people were forced to pay more for their everyday necessities, not being able to get them anywhere else. To say that the poor gain by just exporting and not importing is to forget that they are consumers as well as producers. "Letting the developing countries keep their tariffs," then, is tantamount to "letting the developing countries forbid their citizens to buy from a wide variety of goods."

The belief that politicians know better than the market and investors which enterprises can become competitive in the long run is sheer superstition. On the contrary, this protective policy is a way of dismantling market mechanisms which exist to separate failed projects from successful ones. There are few good examples of successful governmental industrial initiatives, and any number of examples of expensive flops: India's failed industrial sector, Brazil's attempt to create an IT industry, the automotive industries of the South American countries and Suharto's protection of the Indonesian motor industry (headed by his son). Japan's department of industry, MITI, is sometimes referred to as a planning success, and it did relatively well, but mainly by responding to signals from the market. By contrast, its efforts to create new industries independently of the market were less successful. MITI invested billions, for example, in breed reactors, a fifth generation computer and a remote-controlled oil rig, all of which projects were expensive failures. Happily – for the Japanese – MITI also failed to throttle certain sectors, as for example in the early 50s, when they attempted to phase out the small car producers and prevent Sony from importing transistor technology.[77] Nearer home, we have failures like the Anglo-French Concorde and Swedish digital television.

The grim fact is that political leaders in many cases have not even tried to make an objective assessment of what can be profitable, but base their decisions on lobbying and corruption, or just prestige. Tariff walls, which were supposed to afford temporary protection for viable enterprises, instead gave permanent protection to inefficient corporations. What was intended as a forcing house of development became a lush climate for corridor politics and slush money. Even if in theory this might occasionally be a successful policy, how do we

---

77. Bartlett 1997.

know that it is in this particular field the policy will be realised, or to this particular field that the policy will be combined, once the political battle is joined? One question one may ask is why poor states should devote their puny resources to reckless mammoth industrial projects when there are other things they could do which are certain to bring distinct benefits: economic reforms, a liberal regulatory structure, investments in education and health.

The argument for Third World tariffs also rests on ignorance of a very important fact, namely that developing countries most often trade with other developing countries. Something like 40 per cent of exports from the developing countries go to other developing countries. If, then, poor consumers are forced to pay heavy prices for products from companies in their own country, they will generally be prevented from buying from companies in the neighbouring countries, in which case the producers will also lose by this policy. They may get a monopoly of their own market, but on the other hand they are forbidden to sell to other markets. Developing countries' tariffs against other developing countries today are more than two and a half times higher than the industrialised countries' tariffs against developing countries. Tariffs in the industrialised countries average about 8 per cent, those of the developing countries 21 per cent. Thus more than 70 per cent of the customs dues which developing countries are forced to pay are levied by other developing countries.[78]

This is the main reason why the developing countries, which constitute only a quarter of the global economy, are forced to bear no less than 40 per cent of the global cost of customs dues. One of the greatest benefits the developing countries can derive from free trade is in fact the abolition of the import tariffs which sometimes multiply commodity prices several times over. Those who believe that, because they are friends of tariffs they are friends of the developing countries,

---

78. Hertel & Martin 1999, pp. 4 ff.

fail to realise that they are actually helping a small clique of companies and rulers in the developing countries, to the detriment of the social economy, consumers and business efficiency.

If we truly believe in free trade, then we must abolish our tariffs and quotas within the EU without demanding concessions from others. Forbidding the poor of the world to develop is immoral. Besides, we ourselves stand to benefit from freer imports, even if others do not want to import from us. But this does not mean that it is wise of the Third World to protect its own industries with trade barriers. On the contrary, the best thing for their populations is for their tariffs also to be abolished, tariffs which today amount to 30 per cent or more. Those wanting them to preserve their tariffs may be an inverted, mirror image of traditional protectionists, but a mirror picture can never be more beautiful than the original.

The debt trap

In the debate on globalisation, severe criticism has been levelled at global economic institutions, especially the World Bank, which leads multilateral work for long-term development in the developing countries, and the International Monetary Fund (IMF), which exists to guide and assist national financial systems, especially in times of crisis. Critics maintain that these institutions serve as collectors of debts from developing countries to the affluent world, and that they demand from developing countries a heavy-handed liberal policy which leads to greater poverty. Left-wing groups and churches the world over say that the World Bank and the IMF should be democratised and Third World debts should be written off.

"Democratised" means that all countries should have equal voting rights in these institutions, as opposed to power commensurate with the financial contributions they make. This may sound right, but at the same time these are basically development aid organisations, and countries choosing to channel their development assistance through them expect to have a say in how the money they give is going to be used. All countries could be given equal power over the funds, but that would only result in countries like the USA withdrawing and sending their money through other channels. That would mean the end of the IMF and the World Bank, which in its way, of course, would effectively settle the dispute over them, but hardly in the way most of the critics had envisaged.

The IMF and the World Bank have a great deal on their consciences which a liberal should criticise them for. Criticism ought, for example, to be levelled against many decades' argument in favour of planned economies in the developing countries and against the World Bank's involvement in sterilisation projects which have entitled serious abuses against the persons affected. The same goes for large-scale projects, such as dam construction projects, for which the states assisted require the compulsory relocation of thousands of inhabitants. But the opponents of globalisation do not appear to criticise activities of this kind. Instead they oppose recommendations of low inflation and balanced budgets. But demands of this kind on developing countries are not just demands in general. Instead they are requirements which the institutions make for lending money to countries which have acute financial deficits and are on the verge of bankruptcy. Like all credit providers, they would prefer to be paid back, and so they make demands on policy in order for the country eventually to emerge from its crisis and be capable of repaying what it has borrowed. There is nothing fundamentally wrong with this, and the recommendations (termed structural adjustment programmes) have generally been healthy: a balanced budget, a lower rate of inflation, reduction of excessively high exchange rates, greater competition, open markets, less corruption and more regulation, as well as a reduction of military spending, for example, in favour of things like education and health care. Much work has been devoted to insisting on transparency and insight, and to cleaning up dubious dealings and nepotism between rulers and economic players.

But there are a number of debated cases where recommendations by these institutions have been destructive – for example, the inaction they displayed concerning the Asian crisis. Sharp criticism can be levelled against the demand for contraction in countries which were already entering a profound depression. In September 1997, for instance, tax increases forced on Thailand by the IMF deepened the economic crisis to an alarming degree. In certain cases the IMF has recommended governments to retain excessively high exchange rates, thereby triggering speculation. Constant crisis packages can also lead to investors and governments taking bigger risks than they would do otherwise, because they know that if they get out of their depth the IMF will jump in to save them. From a liberal perspective it is bizarre that tax payers are forced to pay for the mistakes of investors. Other criticism says that the IMF has generally been too interfering instead of issuing general recommendations. Using promises of multi-million payments, IMF bureaucrats have tried to exercise remote control of other countries' policies. It has been rightly criticised for echoing the days of colonialism. We are perfectly right to insist of Third World rulers extending basic democratic rights and liberties to their peoples, but we must not attempt to control the details of their policy-making.

But the foremost lesson taught by a couple of decades of IMF and WB recommendations is the smallness of their impact in the countries receiving the funds. To many governments in real crisis, these loans have been their last chance of avoiding real and drastic economic reforms. In the event they have only needed to promise reforms in order for huge sums of money to be placed at their disposal. This is a perilous double game, with local potentates out to retain as much control and corruption as possible, just implementing minor reforms to keep the IMF envoys happy. With the wisdom of hindsight, Russia's finance minister Boris Fiodorov, for example, maintains that the IMF's grants to Russia have delayed the liberal reforms which that country would otherwise have been obliged to introduce. Instead of pursuing a good policy, his colleagues found it patriotic to raise the biggest possible loans and then to start negotiating about the writing off of debts.

"[The 25 billion dollars which the IMF and the World Bank lent Russia during the 90s] played a vital part in delaying the implementation of a consistent economic strategy and made the authorities less willing to introduce painful but necessary policy changes ... The Russian political élite is now fully convinced that Russia will receive continuous international finance whatever its economic policy."

Andrei Illarionov, Russian liberal economist, today adviser to President Putin.[79]

It is a very dangerous supposition that reforms can be "wangled" from outside by means of economic inducements. In the majority of cases, resource transfers of this kind have had the effect of underpinning a failed system. Assistance, if it is to have any positive effects, must come *after* a pronounced and genuine intention of introducing reforms. When in 1994 the World Bank reviewed 26 different structural adjustment programmes, it found that only 6 of them had led to a serious change of policy. Above all, those in power could not, or would not, reduce and streamline bureaucracy and their own control of the economy. Countries have sometimes tried to meet certain important stipulations, such as budgetary balance, by destructive policies such as increasing taxes and tariffs or printing more money or reduction of the most important public spending, on education and health, instead of subsidies, bureaucracy and the military.

Another problem is that programmes are often too complicated for inefficient governments to implement. When a corrupt machinery of government has to take account of perhaps a hundred different stipulations and guidelines at once, things get difficult, especially as it must at the same time keep track of any number of other aid programmes from individual countries. Also, due to structural adjustment programmes being often quite vaguely written, the IMF does not have a strong negotiating mandate. This makes it easy for governments to delay and torpedo programmes. Breaches of the programmes have led to a cancellation of payments, but, bizarrely, the funding tap has been turned full on again as soon as the politicians have ver-

---

79. Illarionov 2000.

bally promised renewed compliance. This, it seems, can be repeated indefinitely. One analyst maintained that 15 years of structural adjustment programmes in Africa had meant "a minimum increase of openness to the global economy."

The unwillingness of the recipient countries to follow the advice given makes it wrong to brand the IMF's liberalising recommendations as the cause of these countries' profound crises, as many left-wing movements do, especially as the countries actually following the recommendations apparently have done better than those disregarding them. Those complying with them – Uganda and Ghana, for example – have on average had higher growth and thus reduced poverty. States ignoring and opting out of such liberalisation programmes – Nigeria and Zambia, for example – are totally unimpressive, having become bogged down in poverty and inequality of fearful dimensions.[80]

So what about debt cancellation? I believe there are good reasons for it, but also risks involved if we do not go the right way about it. Above all, though, the debate is exaggerated. Critics of the IMF and WB claim that something like 20,000 people die in the developing countries every day because of indebtedness. This figure is worked out by adding up the interest payments which developing countries are forced to make to these institutions and then working out how many human lives could be saved for the same amount of money. Apart from this presupposing that all the money would otherwise go on medicines and food instead of munitions, which is not at all credible, it overlooks another important fact. These debt-ridden countries receive *more* grants and development assistance from the industrialised countries and global institutions every year than they pay in interest. The fact is that the 41 most heavily indebted poor countries

---

80. The analyst is Goldsmith 1998, p 11. Concerning the effect of programmes, see Demery & Squire 1996, and Sachs 1996.

(HIPCs, Highly Indebted Poor Countries) received about twice as much from the western world as they pay every year. So to accuse the western world of causing the deaths of tens of thousands of people in the developing countries every day by collecting interest payments is a dishonest and repugnant play on statistics.[81]

Even so, debt cancellation is right in principle. The opponents say that one should pay one's debts, which of course is true. The only question is why one should be forced to pay other people's debts. Perhaps a dictator borrows masses of money to build up his country's military machine and his own fortune, but then, after political upheavals, a democratic régime takes over and finds itself clutching an armful of IOUs. Is it not more reasonable for the borrowers to bear the risk of the country not being able to pay the money back? Ordinary market institutions have learned from experience and have long since given up advancing money to deeply indebted countries, African ones especially, while political institutions like the IMF and the WB have gone on sending money at every economic crisis. Through a combination of generosity and irrationality they lured many developing countries into the debt trap during the 1980s. Most of those countries have absolutely no chance of paying off their debt, and perpetuation of the debt trap will do no one any good. A country like Tanzania has a foreign debt which is twice as large as its annual export revenues, and debt servicing undermines, for example, the funding of education for the young. Because challenging privilege, slashing subsidies and sacking civil servants are politically hazardous, it is often the long-term investments which suffer when cutbacks are needed.

This is not to say that the kind of unconditional debt cancellation for all countries which many popular movements – the Jubilee 2000 campaign, for example – have advocated is all plain sailing. On the contrary, this can mean the western world financing corrupt régimes

---

81. World Bank 2000a, p. 202.

which use the money to buy arms and consolidate oppression. In that case we have helped to perpetuate unsavoury régimes, which again is not a very moral thing to do. To avoid this, certain demands should be made for democracy and reforms, parallel to debts being cancelled. One of the problems of debt cancellation is that it distorts the flows of development assistance, in favour, not of the poorest or of democracies, but of those who are deepest in debt. In 1997 these countries received four times more development assistance per capita than equally poor but non-indebted countries. The Ivory Coast, for example, received 1,276 times more development assistance per capita than India.

Debt cancellation has been going on, to a greater or lesser extent, since 1979, when, following an UNCTAD meeting, the creditors cancelled debts of 45 countries totalling 6 billion dollars. The problem is that this policy has encouraged the contracting of further debts. Countries which have got rid of their debts have quickly replaced them with new loans. One study has shown that an increase in a country's debt cancellation equalling one per cent of GDP down to 1997 has meant, on average, an 0.34 per cent *increase* in its burden of debt. Then again, the money has not been spent on good investments, and the respites have not been used to improve policy. On the contrary, one finds that debtor countries pursue an inferior policy and implement fewer long-term reforms than other poor countries. One grim guess is that these countries often borrow more instead of prioritising their expenditure, because they count on a future cancellation of debts, and that they put off liberal reforms until they can "sell" them to the IMF and World Bank for the greatest possible cancellation of debts. In September 1996, when the World Bank and IMF launched their initiative aimed at eventually writing off the debts of 41 countries rated "highly indebted", this followed two decades of debt cancellation.[82]

---

82. Easterly 1999.

This is a sign of the policy's ineffectiveness. What we could really do with is a "once and for all" strategy whereby the debts of the poor, reform-oriented governments are written off at the same time as it is convincingly indicated that no more debts will be written off in future, impelling the countries concerned to borrow more. One way would be to cancel all debts now and then refrain from lending any more money. Instead loans, if any, would have to be contracted on the international capital market, from investors who are willing to take the risk and who personally believe that they will get their money back. This, however, does not appear to have been the strategy when the WB and IMF signalled the exemption of 22 countries from two-thirds of their debts. True, this measure is accompanied by various stipulations, such as heavier investment in education and health and measures to combat corruption, but new loans may very well come to be considered after the cancellations, in which case there is a serious risk of debts growing again and a similar cancellation initiative becoming necessary in ten years' time.

Studies of the effect of development assistance point to very mixed results. In many cases assistance has been purely destructive and actually reduced national growth. It has strengthened the central state, enabling it to exploit the countryside and destroy agriculture and potential industries. Development assistance has in many cases helped corrupt dictators to cling onto power. (Castro has amassed a fortune of one billion dollars, but his country's per capita GDP has fallen by 500 dollars to about 1,300.) This is very much true of Swedish development assistance, which has above all favoured socialist dictatorships. Giving assistance without demanding democracy and reforms is tantamount to subsidising dictatorships and stagnation. But development assistance has also proved capable of strengthening economies – if they are already pursuing a successful policy, with property rights, open markets and a stable budgetary and monetary policy. With a policy of this kind in place, assistance can lead to more growth than the economy would have had otherwise. But development assistance is not usually conditional on good policy in the receiving country. Donors often think more in terms of how much they are giving, perhaps in order to calm their consciences, than of the actual effect which the assistance produces. Instead of going to countries with good institutions, assistance goes to those to which the donor is politically close, especially old colonies. This is one reason why assistance through multilateral organisations like the World Bank can achieve better results that national and partite assistance.[83]

---

83. World Bank 1998, Burnside & Dollar 2000.

The right medicine

One common objection to the market economy is that it causes people and enterprises to produce for profit, not for needs. This means, for example, pharmaceutical companies devoting huge resources to research and medicines to do with obesity, baldness and depression, things which westerners can afford to pay for, whereas only a fraction is devoted to attempting to cure tropical diseases afflicting the poorest of the world's inhabitants, such as malaria and tuberculosis. This criticism is understandable. The unfairness exists, but capitalism is not to blame for it. Without capitalism and profit interests, not everyone would have obtained cures for their illnesses – in fact, far fewer would do so than is now the case. If wealthy people in the west demand help for their problems, their resources can be used to research and eventually solve those problems, which are not necessarily at all trivial to the people afflicted with them. Capitalism gives companies economic motives for helping us with medicines and vaccines. Us westerners spending money this way does not make things worse for anyone. This is not money which would otherwise have gone on researching tropical diseases – the pharmaceutical companies simply would not have had these resources otherwise. And, parallel to free trade and the market economy promoting greater prosperity in poorer countries, they too will have progressively greater possibilities of economically governing the purposes of research and production.

Thus it is not a problem for the Third World that more and more diseases have been made curable in the western world. On the contrary, this is something that has proved capable of helping them, and not just because a wealthier world can devote more resources to helping the poor. In many fields the Third World can inexpensively share in the research financed by wealthy western customers. In many cases they pay nothing for it. The Merck Corporation gave free medicine to a project to combat onchocerciasis (river blindness) in eleven African states. As a result they have now rid themselves almost completely of a parasite which formerly affected something like a million people, making thousands blind every year.[84] A current example is that of the Monsanto biotech corporation allowing researchers and companies free use of their technique for developing "golden rice", a strain of rice enriched with iron and beta carotene (pro-vitamin A), which could be the saving of a million people annually in the Third World who are dying of vitamin A deficiency diseases. A number of pharmaceutical companies are lowering the prices of inhibitors for HIV/AIDS in poor countries by up to 95 per cent, on condition that the patents are preserved, so that they can maintain full prices in wealthier countries.

Companies can do this because there are affluent markets with customers who can pay well. They can only do what they have resources for, they cannot simply accept expenditure with no earnings. But this is what many people complaining over efforts by pharmaceutical companies to preserve their patents feel they should do. If patents, e.g. for inhibitors for HIV/AIDS, were abolished altogether, far more poor people in the world would be able to afford them, because they could then be reproduced at very low cost. This might give greater access to a medicine today, but it would drastically reduce availability for the future, because pharmaceutical companies spend huge amounts developing medicines. For every successful preparation there are on average 20 or 30 unsuccessful ones, and producing a new, marketable medicine can cost tens of millions of dollars. The high prices of the few medicines which can be sold are necessary in order to

---

84. World Bank 2000a, pp. 182 f.

finance all this research. If patents disappeared, hardly any company would be able any longer to afford the researching and development of medicines.

So it is not the pharmaceutical companies we have to blame for not enough being done to cure diseases in developing countries. The industrialised countries could, for example, resolve to pay a certain amount for every child in the world vaccinated for malaria or for everyone receiving inhibitors for HIV/AIDS, as the economist Jeffrey Sachs has proposed. If entrepreneurs and NGOs were to do this, business enterprises would have an incentive for commitment. If this is a political task, then surely it would be more reasonable to apportion the costs between everybody instead of putting back-breaking demands on the pharmaceutical companies. But in western politics the resources, it seems, are always cornered by loud-mouthed local interest groups.

Personally I believe we have more to expect from philanthropic capitalists, because capitalism does not force people to maximise their profit at every turn, it enables them to use their property as they themselves see fit. Microsoft's Bill Gates, the very personification of modern capitalism, himself devotes more to the campaign against disease in the developing countries than the American federal administration does. Between November 1999 and 2000, through the 23 billion dollar Bill and Melinda Gates Health Fund, 1.44 billion dollars went to vaccinate children in developing countries for common diseases and on research, for example, into HIV/AIDS, malaria and TB in developing countries. This is a quarter of what all industrialised nations combined devote to combating disease in the developing countries. So the poor and the sick of the world have reason to rejoice in Gates being worth more than 50 billion dollars. Clearly they would stand to gain more from a handful of Gateses than from a second Europe.

V

Race to the top

I'm all for free trade, but …

The affluent countries take a highly protectionist stance against the developing countries, but this is defended above all by vested interests and through lobbying. Less often one sees it being ardently defended in public debate, because wanting to get rich at the Third World's expense is not considered all that legitimate. On the other hand there is a type of protectionism which is closely related but is considered far more presentable in public debate, namely the idea of making trade subject to certain conditions. "We're all for free trade," these people say, and go on to add something like "but not on any terms whatsoever" or "but it needs a different kind of code." If someone starts off by saying "I'm all for free trade, but…" you should listen very carefully to what follows, because if the "but" is strong enough, it means they are not for free trade at all.

This is the way the discussion often goes in Sweden, where free trade is a positively charged concept.[85] In other countries it is often a term of abuse. Never shout it out loud on a Parisian street, or you will risk being pursued by an angry crowd. Certain Swedish globalisation sceptics go so far as to assert that the discussion has nothing to do with "being for or against free trade," because everyone is in favour of

85. The same phenomenon is associated with the concept of "globalisation". When international anti-globalists were staging a demonstration in Prague, it was organised by the umbrella organisation "Initiative against economic globalisation", but the Swedish variant, knowing globalisation to have a positive connotation in Sweden, styled itself "globalisation from Beneath" instead. Bernard Cassen, Chairman of French Attac, says that he has "tried to find a single advantage with globalisation, but in vain" (Cassen 2001b), at the same time as the Swedish Attac movement say that they are not at all opposed to globalisation, they just want different rules for it.

some kind of code for free trade. But the code of free trade, complete with rights of ownership and freedom of enterprise, is intended to facilitate free exchange and cannot in any way be equated with rules, prohibitions and quotas aimed at restricting free exchange. The discussion is *de facto* concerned with being for or against free trade, and you are for it if you want more liberal rules of trade, otherwise you are against it.

A commonly held protectionist view today is that we should not permit trade with countries which have unacceptably bad working conditions or condone child labour or do not do enough to protect the environment. Otherwise we permit other countries to put our firms out of business through inferior social condition ("social dumping") or disregard for the environment ("eco-dumping"). So when drawing up trade agreements with poor countries we must always insist on provisions about the environmental or labour standards, requiring those countries to improve their environmental policy or their working conditions, on pain of our not doing business with them. It is not only unions and companies who join in this chorus, but socially committed movements as well. But to the developing countries the provision idea comes as protection coupled with a neo-colonialist bid to control their policy-making.

"The question is why industrialised countries are suddenly bothering about Third World workers now that we have shown we can compete with them," says, for example, a sceptical Youssef Boutros-Ghali, Egypt's Minister for Trade.[86]

It was following US President Bill Clinton's proposal (in an inter-

---

86. Cit. Greenhouse & Khan 1999. Adherents eagerly point out that the International Confederation of Free Trade Unions favours social clauses, but it does so in spite of vociferous opposition from its members in the South. The other international union organisation, the World Federation of Trade Unions, with 110 million members in 130 different countries, has argued against the inclusion of social clauses in WTO trade agreements.

view by the *Seattle Post Intelligencer* on December 1st, 1999) of this kind of boycott of countries not meeting certain requirements that the WTO talks in Seattle deadlocked at the end of 1999. Swedish trade minister Leif Pagrotsky spoke of "Clinton's great blunder" and the developing countries refused to negotiate under such threats.

Whatever well-heeled demonstrators and presidents in economically powerful countries may believe, low wages and poor environmental conditions in developing countries are not due to stinginess. There are of course exceptions, but generally the problem is that they cannot afford to pay higher wages and have better working conditions, because their productivity is so low. Wages can be raised as labour becomes more valuable, i.e. in step with productivity, and this can only be achieved through increased investments, better infrastructure, more education, new machinery and better organisation. If we force these countries to raise wages before productivity has been improved, this will mean firms and consumers having to pay more for their manpower than it is currently worth, in which case they will be put out of the running by more productive, better-paid workers in the western world. Unemployment among the world's poor would swiftly rise. Economist Paul Krugman has dubbed this a policy for good jobs in theory and no jobs in practice. Jesus Reyes-Heroles, Mexican Ambassador to the United States, has explained:

> *In a poor country like ours the alternative to low-paying jobs isn't high-paying jobs – it's no jobs at all.*[87]

In practice, labour and environmental provisions tell the developing countries: *You are too poor to trade with us, and we are not going to trade with you until you have grown rich.* The problem is that it is only through trade that they can grow richer and in this way, step by step,

---

87. Lukas 2000, p. 11.

improve their living standards and their social conditions. That is Catch 22: they cannot trade until their working conditions and environment protection are of a high standard, but they cannot raise the level of their working conditions and environment protection if they are not allowed to trade with us. Scrutinising the argument underlying trade clauses, one finds it as absurd as insisting that someone immediately improve their dental health, otherwise we'll break their toothbrush. Someone has compared it to the Vietnam war strategy of burning the village in order to save it.

Suppose this idea had been current at the end of the 19th century. In that case Britain and France would have noted that Swedish wages were only a fraction of theirs, that Sweden had a 12 or 13-hour working day and a six-day week, and that Swedes were chronically undernourished. Child labour was widespread in spinning mills, glassworks and match and tobacco factories, and one worker in twenty was under 14 years old. Britain and France, accordingly, would have refused to trade with us and closed their frontiers to Swedish cereals, timber and iron ore. Would Sweden have gained by this? Hardly. On the contrary, it would have robbed us of our earnings and blocked our industrial development. We would have been left with our intolerable living conditions, the children would have stayed in the factories and perhaps to this day we would be eating bark bread when the harvest failed. But that didn't happen. Sweden's trade was allowed to grow uninterruptedly, industrialisation got under way and the economy was revolutionised. In step with growth, slowly but surely, we were able to tackle the abuses. Wages rose, the working day was shortened and children began going to school in the mornings, not to the factory.

If today, as a condition for trading with the developing countries, we require their mining to be as safe as in Sweden, we are making demands which we ourselves did not have to meet when our mining industry was developing. It was only after raising our incomes that we were able to develop the technology and afford the safety equipment we are using today. If we require the developing countries to adopt these things right away, before they can afford them, then their industry will be knocked out and only we in the industrialised countries will be able to afford it. If we prevent poor countries from exporting to us because their working conditions are not good enough, this will result in their export industry being eliminated and their workers instead having to look for jobs in native industry, with lower wages and poorer working conditions as a result. This will not help the world's poor, but it will protect our industry. This, one suspects, is the motive of certain groups in affluent countries for proposing such clauses.

What the adherents of labour and environmental provisions in trade agreements want to do is deny developing countries the chance which Sweden and the other affluent countries were once given. If they sincerely desire to help the developing countries, then surely they should campaign for the west to help them get rid of their problems, for example by sharing our technology and know-how with them instead of ceasing to trade with them? Instead, some of them, such as the American union AFL-CIO, is trying to stop the transfer of modern technology to the Third World! There already exist other venues for tackling the specific issues and helping developing countries to improve their labour and environmental standards, e.g. the United Nations Environmental Programme (UNEP) and the International Labour Organisation (ILO).

In this case, what are we to do about the requirement of respecting patent and intellectual property rights, a requirement which developing countries have to accept in order to be admitted to free trade cooperation within the WTO? Why should we require them to accept patents for a 20-year-period if we do not require them to maintain even a minimum level as regards social conditions? There is a simple reason, namely that infringements of intellectual property rights act as a trade barrier. Few companies would avoid investing in or selling to a country because it is too poor or its wages are too low, but they might well shun a country where they risked having their product ideas stolen. Besides, offences of this kind are easier to proceed against, because the losses can often be quantified in cash terms.

Patents, in my opinion, are important, as a recognition of the creator's right to the created and to payment for it, and, accordingly, because they are generally conducive to a climate of innovation and research. Even so, I don't find the arguments strong enough for patents being included – as they are today with the TRIPS-treaty – in the rules of the WTO. Here again, we should permit trade with everyone, irrespective of the policy they follow. The commercial liberty of the Swedes is not to be infringed because of other countries pursuing a bad policy, and the citizens of other countries are not to be punished more than they are being punished by domestic policy. If the policy of these countries turns businesses away and does not act as a spur to innovation at home, then so much the worse for them, but it is no reason why we should forbid citizens of our country to trade freely with them. It is trade that provides an economic development which will eventually enable the developing countries to acquire wealth and proper codes on intellectual property rights. We must not use trade barriers as a weapon for pushing through the policy we want to see. Instead we should keep our frontiers open and at the same time urge the countries in question to start respecting patents.

Child labour

But are there really no exceptions? Economic conditions so disgusting that we must prohibit trade because of them? One example often quoted in the course of debate is the employment of children. There are today something like 250 million child workers between the ages of 5 and 14. No one can be anything but dismayed at the thought of millions of young people being robbed of their childhood and, in many cases, their health and happiness. But are these children helped by the EU ceasing to trade with the countries where they live? No, the absurdity of such a proposition becomes clear as soon as we realise that the great majority of children are employed in sectors which have nothing whatsoever to do with trade. 70 per cent of child workers are employed in agriculture. Only 5 per cent, about 10 or 15 million children, are employed in export industry, for example on making footballs, sewing garments or knotting carpets. And all available sources indicate that these child export workers are the least badly done by, with the least dangerous working conditions. So the alternatives are worse.

The problem, once again, is that we judge the Third World according to our own material standard of living. The fact is that child employment was widespread in Sweden just a few generations ago. It has existed in all societies. In pre-industrial France, parents were forbidden *not* to send their children to work. Children in a poor country do not become workers because their parents are unkind but because the family needs their earnings in order to survive. So we cannot prohibit child labour in these countries just like that, still less forbid the countries concerned to export things to us, because in that case, pending an improvement in material conditions, the children will be forced into even worse occupations – at the very worst, into crime and prostitution. In 1992 it was revealed that the American Wal-Mart chain was buying garments which had been manufactured by child workers in Bangladesh. Congress then threatened to prohibit imports from countries with child labour. As a result of that threat, many thousands of children were sacked by the Bangladeshi textile industry. A follow-up by international organisations showed that many of the children had moved to more dangerous, less well-paid jobs, and in several cases become prostitutes.[88] A similar boycott of the Nepalese carpet industry, according to UNICEF, resulted in over 5,000 girls being forced into prostitution.

The Swedish NGO Save the Children (Rädda Barnen) is one of the organisations which have tried to instil a degree of moderation and sense into the debate on child labour:

In most cases the Swedish Save the Children says no to boycotts, sanctions and other trade-related measures against the employment of children. Experience has shown that the children who have to leave their jobs as a consequence of such measures risk finding themselves in more difficult situations and more harmful occupations.

Half the child workers work part time, and many do so to finance their schooling. If they were to lose their jobs, as a result of prohibitions or boycotts, a difficult situation would be made even worse. To tackle the problems, we have to distinguish the problems – prostitution and the enslavement of children, for example – which have to be fought by every available means, whereas child labour otherwise can only be counteracted through economic improvements and rising living standards. Save the Children, Sweden, continues:

---

88. Bellamy 1997, p. 23.

General assertions that child labour is a good or bad thing serve little purpose [...] To regard all occupations as equally unacceptable is to simplify a complicated issue and makes it more difficult to concentrate forces against the worst forms of exploitation.[89]

Child labour in Sweden was primarily eliminated, not by prohibitions but by the economy growing to such an extent that parents were enabled to give their children education instead, thereby maximising their incomes in the longer term. In addition, mechanisation made the simplest manual labour less profitable. It was this development which eventually enabled us to prohibit such child labour as remained, not the other way round. The same recipe can reduce child labour in developing countries today. ILO, the International Labour Organisation, has noted that the number of workers aged between 10 and 14 is declining substantially with the growth of the Asian economies. In India the proportion of child workers has fallen from 35 per cent fifty years ago to 12 per cent today. In East and Southeast Asia, child labour is expected to have vanished completely by 2010.[90]

Everyone must have access to education, and that education must give a bigger return. It must be capable of leading to a better-paid job than could have been obtained without schooling. Only then will it become possible, and remunerative, for parents to save their children from work. It is not enough for education to be universally available. Schools also have to be of good quality. In many countries the schools are beneath contempt and children attending them are badly treated, perhaps even subjected to physical violence. This is connected with the schools being public institutions whose teachers are almost unsackable. Part of the solution lies in freedom of choice, enabling

---

89. Rädda Barnen: "Faktablad om barnarbete".

90. Berg & Karlsson 2000, p. 64.

families to take control of schools from staff and national authorities, perhaps through a voucher system, as in Sweden.

It is always open to discussion whether in a particular situation temporary trade sanctions are a feasible way of bringing down an exceptionally cruel dictatorship, for example one which practises apartheid or slavery, makes war or massacres civilians. But in this case the régime is punished in the knowledge that the sanctions can harm the country's population and even, if prolonged, strengthen the position of the rulers. Trade generally tends to make the maintenance of centralisation difficult, because it gives rise to more international contacts and other power centres than the sovereign power. If all countries participate in sanctions against a dictatorship, perhaps some useful purpose can be served in certain cases. Symbolic sanctions, such as the freezing of diplomatic relations and sporting boycotts, can be particularly useful against dictatorships, because they do not harm the population in the same way as a suspension of trade. But the important thing here is that sanctions of this kind should not in any way be mixed up with sanctions resorted to against countries because they are still poor.

The best policy is to bring pressure to bear in other contexts and in political fora, instead of proceeding to dismantle what is perhaps the most effective solution – trade. Our politicians and organisations should never cease criticising other countries if they violate human rights, practise censorship, persecute dissidents or prohibit associations – trade unions, for example. Our giving the populations of other countries a chance to develop by trading freely must never be confused with a benevolent attitude towards their governments. Swedish politicians keeping well in with dictatorial régimes in order for Swedish export enterprises to be able to sell to their countries are in practice legitimising their oppression. If governments are anti-liberal, their oppression should never be passed over in silence. "Injustice anywhere is a threat to justice everywhere", as Martin Luther King put it.

But what about us?

"All right then," certain anti-globalists reply, "it may be good for the developing countries, us trading with them in spite of their being poor, but it's bad for us." For if the developing countries pay lower wages, do not protect their environment and have insufferably long working hours, then their cheap output will eliminate our well-paid jobs, forcing us to lower our standards and our wages. We will have to keep working harder and longer to keep up. Firms and capital quickly migrate to where they can pay the lowest wages and have the worst working conditions. It will be a "race to the bottom". The one with the lowest social standard will win and will corner the investments and export revenues.

Theoretically this seems a tough case to answer. The only trouble is, this thesis has no foundation in reality. The world has not witnessed a deterioration of working conditions or wages in past few decades – on the contrary. And the explanation is simple. Consumers are not above all interested in buying goods from people who are poorly paid, they are above all interested in obtaining products which are as good and cheap as possible. The reason for wages being lower in developing countries is that firms there are less productive, producing less per employee.

If wages rise because productivity does so, there is no problem and consumers have no reason for invariably choosing what has been produced by the cheapest labour. In thirty years, Japanese wages rose from one-tenth of the American level to a level higher than America's. But this did not make Japanese workers less competitive, because their output capacity rose at the same rate.

Firms are not primarily looking for cheap labour. If they were, the world's aggregate production would be concentrated on Nigeria. Wage costs in the OECD countries equal about 5 or 10 per cent of total production costs. The prospect of reducing them marginally is no enticement to relocation. Firms are more interested in getting as much as possible out of the capital they have committed. Wages in poor countries are low because, relatively speaking, manpower there is worth less to business undertakings, due to its being less skilled and having access to less efficient machinery. As investments, educational standards and prosperity rise in the developing countries, wages also go up, and so things will be taking an upward turn in the developing countries rather than a downward one in the industrialised world. This is exactly what empirical facts demonstrate. In 1960 the average Third World worker had about 10 per cent of an American industrial worker's wage. Today this has risen to 30 per cent, in spite of the American wage level also having risen. If competition had kept wages down in affluent countries, the proportion of national income going on wages ought to diminish, but it is not doing so.[91]

The populist American presidential candidate Ross Perot argued rhetorically and skilfully against the NAFTA free trade agreement with Mexico and Canada. If it came into force, the people would hear a "great sucking sound" as all American jobs were vacuumed up by Mexico. Since this particular free trade agreement came into force in 1995, employment in the USA has risen by 10 million job opportunities. The US labour force is the world's best paid. If American firms were solely intent on paying low wages, they ought to leave the country *en masse* for various African countries. And yet 80 per cent of their investments go to high-wage countries, especially countries like the UK, Canada, the Netherlands and Germany, all of which have equivalent or higher social standards and regulatory levels. What firms are

91. Burtless et al 1998, chap 4.

Third World wages are rising

Average wage of a worker in the developing countries,
as a percentage of American factory worker wages

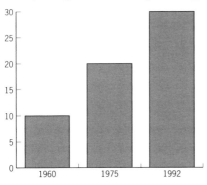

Source: Burtless 1998, chap. 4.

mainly looking for, then, is social and political stability, the rule of law, free markets, good infrastructure and skilled manpower. Countries competing to offer these things can be compared with a race to the top, rather than to the bottom.

It is commonly supposed that we in western Europe and the USA are having to work harder and harder and put in progressively longer hours to cope with competition from the Third World and from increasingly efficient machinery. Some people do indeed work more than is healthy, and there is a widespread feeling of higher demands and faster tempo at work. But this does not stem from Third World competition. Instead it is due to bad employers, mostly in the public sector, who do not care about their personnel, and to highly qualified people who are too preoccupied with their careers and therefore choose to work so hard. This is something we can change, as individuals, employers and employees. The poor have at all times been con-strained to work more than the rich, until now. Now people in high income brackets are working several hours longer than low income earners.

The time we all spend working has diminished with rising prosperity, for the simple reason that growth enables us to do less work for the same payment – if we want to. Compared with the parental generation, most of today's workers go to work later, go home earlier, have longer lunch and coffee breaks, longer vacations and more public holidays. According to American statistics, working hours today are only about half of what they were a hundred years ago and have diminished by 10 per cent since as recently as 1973 – a reduction equalling 23 days per annum. On average, American workers have acquired five extra years' waking leisure since 1973. This is also because we have begun working progressively later in life, are retiring earlier and are living longer. A western worker in 1870 had only two hours off for each hour worked, spread out over a lifetime. By 1950 this had doubled to four hours off, doubling again to the present figure of about eight hours off for each hour worked. Economic development, thanks partly to trade enabling us to specialise, makes it possible for us to reduce our working hours considerably and also to raise our material living standard. We have never taken less time to earn our living.

Even so, it is natural for us in the affluent western world today to talk a lot about stress. This is partly to do with something basically positive, the fantastic growth of options available to us. The pre-industrial Swede, spending all his life in one place and perhaps meeting a hundred people in a lifetime, was unlikely to feel that he did not have time for everything he wanted to do. People spent a lot of their non-working time sleeping. Today we can travel the world, read newspapers, see films from every corner of the globe and meet a hundred people *every day*. We used to go to the letterbox and wait for the

We are working less and less in the course of a lifetime

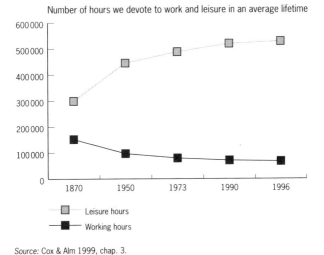

Number of hours we devote to work and leisure in an average lifetime

□ Leisure hours
■ Working hours

Source: Cox & Alm 1999, chap. 3.

Working hours are diminishing

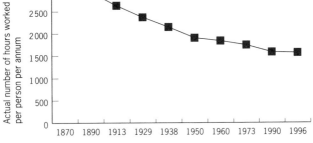

Actual number of hours worked per person per annum

Source: Cox & Alm 1999, chap. 3.

postman. Now the mail is in our in-box, waiting for us. We have acquired a huge entertainment industry which offers an almost infinite number of ways to pass the time if we happen to be at a loose end. No wonder that the result is a certain frustration over not finding time for everything. Compared with the problems people have had in all ages, and which most people in developing countries still have today, this kind of worry can only be termed a luxury.

Stress and burnout at work are real problems, but in many ways these are new words for old phenomena. At the same rate as more and more Swedes are being sicklisted for burnout, fewer seem to be getting sicklisted for neck disorders and mental problems. This matter also has to be viewed in perspective. Every age and place tends to think that its own particular problems are worst. Often this is due to ignorance or to a romanticization of the past. It can be a problem, being so ardent about one's work as to overdo things, but isn't there a bigger problem involved in so many people being bored to death by their work? We must not forget that the big problem still is that so many people have jobs which offer them neither challenges nor development.

The essential point when discussing burnout and capitalism concerns the possibility of getting a hold on one's situation – and which system gives one the best opportunity of doing so. There are problems with employees who work too hard and employers who demand too much or are too vague and indistinct. Individuals can always make mistakes. But capitalism enables people to give priority to what they consider important. They can choose to take things easier if they feel that they are working too much, they can pressure their employer for better conditions, e.g. through the trade union, and the employer can review the work situation. For one's own part one can opt out of certain things so as not to feel permanently at the beck and call of others. You don't have to check your e-mail at the weekend, and there is no law against turning on the answering-machine.

It is flexibility, the possibility of avoiding rigid, uniform solutions, which makes the market economy best for coping with problems. The worst problems are those of people who feel they have least power over their work, those who have no say in when and where the work is to be done. This applies mainly to women's jobs in the Swedish public sector, especially health and education.[92] Bureaucratic and political structures place power far away and allow no flexibility. Decision-making and restructuring take place over the heads of the personnel. Since, traditionally, the employees have had only one employer to turn to, that employer has never needed to worry about their needs and interests. The same monopolisation has perpetuated a low wage level for large groups of women. If people feel stressed from too much responsibility and liberty, they can do something about it. If they suffer from stress due to lack of power, there is nothing they can do about it.

This monopolisation has also resulted in public sector employees being more afraid to speak their minds, propose changes and criticise their employer than employees in the private sector, even though, unlike private sector employees, their right to do so is constitutionally safeguarded under freedom of expression and information. Having no one else to turn to, they are utterly defenceless. It is more than twice as common for people with a national government employer than for those employed in the private sector to feel that they will impair their standing at work if they express critical viewpoints. It is almost twice as common for county council employees to maintain that their ideas are never listened to. No less than 55 per cent of doctors in the public sector maintain that their views are ignored, as against 15 per cent of factory workers. 27 per cent of high school teachers in public schools believe that they risk impairing their position at work if they express criticism, as against 1 per cent of factory workers.[93]

---

92. Most recently confirmed by Sifo in 2001.

93. Aronsson & Gustafsson 1999.

Big is beautiful

In the anti-globalists' world view it is the multinational corporations that are leading the race to the bottom. By moving to developing countries and taking advantage of poor people and substandard legislation, they are making money hand over fist and forcing other governments to adopt ever laxer policies. On these terms, tariffs and barriers to foreign investments become a defence for the national, a protection against a ruthless entrepreneurial power seeking to profiteer at people's expense. The alternative is horrific visions of the enormous multinationals ruling the world, regardless of what people think or want. The fact that 51 out of the world's 100 biggest economies are corporations is repeated like a fateful mantra. The problem, though, is not that corporations are growing but that more national economies are not doing the same. Big corporations are no problem – they can bring important economies of scale – so long as they are exposed to the threat of competition in the event of their turning out products inferior to or more expensive than those of other firms. What we have to fear is not size but monopoly.

Free trade is often said to given businesses more power. But enterprises in a liberal society have no powers of coercion. State power is based on the right of coercion, backed up as a last resort by the police. The power of corporations, for example, to get people to work for them or to pay for their products is based solely on their offering something which people want – employment or products. Even if you have to accept a job in order to survive, the employer has not coerced you or made your situation worse. On the contrary, he has given you a better alternative to an even more desperate situation. Corporations can of course do a great deal of harm – for example, by moving out of a small community – but only because previously they have offered something positive which they are now retracting.

What has happened in the age of globalisation is not that corporations have acquired more power through freer trade; they used to be far more powerful – and still are – in dictatorships and controlled economies. Large, powerful corporations have always been able to deceive the public interest by going in cahoots with the rulers and hobnobbing with them on luncheons and dinners, by obtaining protection through monopolies, tariffs and subsidies the minute they have put in a phone call to the political leaders. What free trade has done has been to expose corporations to competition. It is above all consumers that have been made freer, so that now they can ruthlessly pick and choose even across national boundaries, rejecting those firms which do not come up to scratch.

Historical horror stories of companies *de facto* governing a society always come from regions where there has been no competition. People living in isolation in a small village or a closed country are dependent on the enterprises existing there, and are forced to buy what they offer at the price they demand. This enriches a tiny clique at the consumers' expense. Sometimes capitalism is accused of having created monopolies and trusts, enormous associations of businesses which compete, not by being best but by being biggest and escaping competition. But this is not brought about by capitalism. On the contrary, free trade and competition are the best guarantees of someone else penetrating the market if the dominant enterprise misbehaves. It says much that the first monopolies appeared, not in 19th century Britain, whose policy was almost one of laissez-faire, but in the USA and Germany, which became industrialised later and protected their markets with tariffs. In Sweden too, we have had monopolies of this kind. The sugar monopoly grew powerful by the last turn of the century as a direct consequence of the high duties on sugar. It lives on today because of the EU's sugar tariffs, which make EU sugar prices 160 per cent higher than those of the world market.

Capitalists really have the biggest interest of all in monopolies and exclusive privileges. Introducing a market economy and free trade is one way of taking these things away from them and forcing them to offer the best possible goods and services in return for a share of our resources. Free trade gives enterprises the freedom to offer more consumers what they want, but it does not confer privilege of coercive power on anyone. The freedom of enterprise in a free market economy is the same as the waiter's freedom to offer the menu to the restaurant patron. And it entitles other waiters – foreign ones, even! – to come running up with rival menus. The loser by this process is, if anyone, the waiter who once had a monopoly.

That which many critics of the market call for – firms less intent on profit, markets that are less free, less hectic restructurings and so on – could be seen in Russia of the 90s, where government-owned enterprises were in practice given away, instead of being privatised through an open auction. In many cases this resulted in the management and employees taking over the old firm – free of charge, without having to raise money for the venture through a modernisation of production to yield future profits. Because this would require major structural changes and heavy job losses, which would be troublesome for everyone working there, the whole modernisation of the enterprise sector is being stonewalled and growth is not accelerating. Instead, many of them are helping themselves to corporate resources. Many of these firms were cornered by people with strong political contacts – the oligarchs, as they are called. They have been more concerned with expanding their own spheres of influence and plundering the businesses than with developing them for future profit, as people investing their own money in a project would have an interest in doing. In addition, it is more difficult for outsiders to compete with these old firms, because Russian business is subject to a battery of tariffs, licensing requirements, arbitrary detailed regulations, a very low level of legal safeguards and rampant corruption. After initial liberalisation measures in 1992, the Russian process has if anything moved in the contrary direction. Paradoxically enough, lack of freedom for Russian enterprise leads to enormous freedom for a handful of big corporations with good political protection.[94]

Nothing forces people to accept new products. If they gain ground, it is because people want them. Even the biggest companies survive on customer sufferance and would have to close down tomorrow if they ceased bothering about their customers. Mega-corporation Coca Cola has to adapt the recipe for its drinks to different regions in deference to varying local tastes. McDonald's sells mutton burghers in India, teriyaki burghers in Japan and salmon burghers in Norway. TV mogul Rupert Murdoch has failed to create a broad Asian channel and instead is having to build different channels to suit the local audiences.

Companies in free competition can grow large and increase their sales only by being better than others, and they can only operate in international markets by maintaining superior productivity. Those failing to do so quickly go bust or get taken over by others who can make better use of their capital, buildings, machinery and employees. Capitalism is very tough – on firms offering old-fashioned, poor-quality or expensive goods and services. Fear of old companies growing progressively larger and eventually becoming independent of the markets has absolutely no foundation in reality. Experience from the most capitalist country in the world, the USA, indicates exactly the opposite. Ever since the 1930s, critics of the market have been speaking of the risk of dominion by big corporations. Meanwhile the market share of the 25 biggest corporations has steadily dwindled.

---

94. Illarionov 2000.

Yes, companies get bigger, but they also get more competitors. Freer, more efficient financial markets, causing capital to spread to new entrepreneurs with fresh ideas, have made in progressively easier for small firms to compete with the big corporations. And things have been made easier still by advances in information technology. Between 1980 and 1993 the 500 biggest American firms saw their share of the country's total employment diminish from 16 to 11.3 per cent. Presumably the most important indicator of the weight of the 500 biggest firms is their sales in relation to GDP. This figure fell dramatically, from 59.3 to 36.1 per cent – almost by half in just 13 years. During the same period the average personnel strength of American firms fell from 16.5 to 14.8 persons, and the proportion of the population working in firms with over 250 employees fell from 37 to 29 per cent.[95]

Most things, then, indicate that the dominance of the largest corporations diminishes in a free market, in favour of a host of more flexible undertakings. Half the firms operating internationally in the world today have fewer than 250 employees. Many of the biggest are being knocked out by competitors. Of the companies on the 1980 list of the 500 biggest enterprises in the USA, one-third had disappeared by 1990 and another 40 per cent had gone five years later. In certain capital-intensive industries, such as pharmaceuticals, motor manufacturing and aerospace, size matters more, owing to the cost of developing new products. But big mergers among these companies betoken, not their having power over consumers but their inability to survive otherwise. True, the biggest trademarks are always being imprinted in our minds, but we forget that they are all the time being joined by new ones and are losing old rivals. How many people recall that Nokia, just a few years ago, was a small Finnish firm manufacturing motor tyres and boots?

95. Edwards 2001.

Big corporations are becoming less dominant

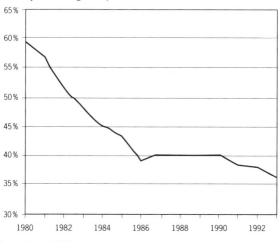

Percentage of American GDP accounted for
by the 500 largest corporations

Source: Edwards 2001.

Companies starting up in other countries would not have a market if
no one wanted to do business with them, and they will not get any
workers if they fail to offer good conditions. Being more productive
than others, they produce cheaper goods, and because, consequently,
their workers are worth more to them, they pay them more and have
better working conditions than other firms. This becomes extraordinarily clear if we compare the conditions of people employed in
American factories and offices in developing countries with people
employed elsewhere in the same country. Critics observe, quite rightly, that employees in developing countries have far worse conditions
than we have in the affluent world, but this is an unfair comparison,
because we have far higher productivity. The interesting comparison,

202

the one which decides whether foreign firms in a developing country are a good thing, is how well off these employees are compared with other workers in the same country. In the poorest developing countries, someone working for an American employer draws no less than eight times the average national wage! In middle income countries, American employers pay three times the national average. Even compared with corresponding, modern jobs in the same country, the multinationals pay about 30 per cent higher wages. Foreign firms in the least developed countries pay their employees, on average, twice as much as the corresponding native firms. Marxists maintain that the multinationals exploit poor workers, but if exploitation means many times greater wages, then surely exploitation is the better alternative?

The same difference applies to working conditions. ILO, the International Labour Organisation, has shown that it is the multinationals, especially in the footwear and garment industries, which are leading the trend towards better workplace and working conditions. Due to the low standard of suppliers' factories in the Third World, the Nike sportswear company has long been vilified by anti-globalists. But the truth is that it is one of the companies offering employees the best of conditions, not out of generosity but with an eye to profit. These companies can pay more because their productivity is higher, and they are more responsive to popular opinion. Nike, consequently, has demanded a higher standard of its suppliers, and native firms have to follow suit.

Zhou Latai, one of China's foremost labour attorneys, who represents injured workers, has pointed out that it is Western consumers who are the principal driving force behind the improvement of working conditions, because they are making Nike, Reebok and others raise standards: "If Nike and Reebok go," Latai points out – and he believes this can happen unless China gets free trade through the WTO – "this pressure evaporates. This is obvious."[96]

---

96. Lukas 2000, p 6.

When multinational corporations accustom workers to better wages and better-lit, cleaner factories without dangerous machinery, they raise the general standard. Native firms then also have to offer better conditions, otherwise no one will work for them. This trend is easiest to quantify in terms of Third World wages, which, as we have already seen, have moved from 10 to 30 per cent of American wages in the past 40 years.

Nike have seen to it that their subcontractors also open up their factories to impartial inspection. Systematic interviews of anonymous employees by the Global Alliance for Workers and Communities show of course that there are complaints, but above all that employees are glad to have got a job in the first place and they consider it to be a good job. At the Indonesian factories, 70 per cent of employees had travelled long distances to get their jobs, three-quarters were satisfied with relations with their superiors and felt that they were free to put forward ideas and suggestions. The later roughly equals the proportion of Swedish national government employees who feel free to communicate viewpoints to their employer, which puts the answers into perspective, even though the situations, of course, are not comparable. At the Vietnamese factories, 85 per cent wanted to go on working for at least another three years, and the same number felt secure with their working conditions and the machinery. At the Thai factories only 3 per cent felt that they were on poor terms with their superiors, and 72 per cent considered themselves well paid. The provision by companies of free medicines, health care, clothing, food and transport for their workers was particularly appreciated.

One of the few western debaters to have actually visited Nike's Asian subcontractors to find out about conditions there is Linda Lim of Michigan University. She found that in Vietnam, where the minimum wage was 134 dollars, Nike workers were getting 670. In Indonesia, where the minimum wage was 241 dollars, Nike's suppliers were paying 720.[97] Once again, it is vital to remember that these conditions are not to be compared with ours in the affluent countries but with the alternatives open to these people. If Nike were to withdraw, on account of boycotts and tariff walls from the western world, the suppliers would have to shut down and the employees would be put out of work or would move to more dangerous jobs with lower, less steady wages, in native industry or agriculture.

Many developing countries have what are called economic "free zones", mainly for export industry (also known as export-processing zones), where firms are allowed to start up with specially advantageous tax conditions and trade regulations. These are accused by anti-globalists of being free zones for slave-driving and inhuman working conditions. There are indeed abuses and scandals in some quarters, and resolute action is needed to prohibit them. Mostly this happens in poor dictatorships, and so instead of freedom having "gone too far" it has not gained a foothold. In her book *No Logo*, which has quickly become popular in anti-capitalist circles, the Canadian activist Naomi Klein claims that Western companies have created terrible working conditions in these zones, but she does not offer any proofs, or a systematic picture of this. She has only heard a few rumours of bad conditions in one Philippine export-processing zone, which she admits having travelled to only because it was one of the worst. When the OECD tried to obtain an overall picture of these zones, the notable thing was that they had multiplied job opportunities for the poor, and that wages there were higher than in the rest of the country. In the great majority of the thousand or so small zones, the same labour legislation applied as elsewhere in the country. In addition, more and more free zones are observing that cheap labour is not the full recipe

97. The surveys can be accessed at http://www.theglobalalliance.org/. Concerning Lim, see Featherstone & Henwood 2001. For Swedish national government employees, see Aronsson & Gustafsson 1999.

for successful competition, and are encouraging firms to invest in and educate their work forces. In the same study the OECD pointed out that there was a positive relation between fundamental rights for the employees (prohibition of slavery and abuses, freedom to negotiate and to form trade unions) and more investments and higher growth.[98]

It is multinationals that, by virtue of their size, are able to finance research and more long-term projects. According to the OECD, these corporations reinvest some 90 per cent of their profits in the country where they operate. Operating as they do in several countries, they serve as channels for know-how, more efficient organisational structures and new technology. Complaining over the existence of multinationals means complaining over better wages, lower prices and greater prosperity. It is these enterprises which are leading the international race to the top. And it is not only in the developing countries that multinationals offer better conditions. Foreign firms in the USA pay about 6 per cent higher wages than native American firms, and they are expanding their personnel strength twice as fast. Foreign businesses account for 12 per cent of R&D investment in the USA and for no less than 40 per cent in the UK.[99]

Of course, this is not to say that all firms behave well, any more than all people do. There are villains among entrepreneurs too, just as in politics or entertainment. We can find instances of companies treating their employees, the population or the environment badly. In the raw materials industry especially, there is a tendency to keep well in with the régime of the country where the enterprise operates, no matter how dictatorial and oppressive it may be. Otherwise the firms in many cases would not be allowed to operate there. But bad behaviour by some is no reason for banning large corporations or prevent-

---

98. OECD 2000.

99. "Foreign Friends", *The Economist* 8th January 2000. OECD 1998.

ing them from investing, any more than we should eject all immigrants because some of them are criminals, or dissolve the police because of police brutality. Instead it is a cause for prosecuting firms if they break the law and for criticising and boycotting those firms which conduct themselves badly.

The big problem generally concerns the régimes granting firms permits, or even inducing them, to behave irresponsibly. There has to be a strict distinction between government and enterprise sector. Governments must establish firm regulatory codes and corporations must produce and trade in the best possible way within those codes. If firms comply with bad regulatory codes, then the main remedy should be a reform of the codes and criticism of the corporation, not impediments to enterprise as such. The solution lies in democratising governments and creating fair laws which indicate that one party's freedom ends where the other party's begins.

The presence of multinational corporations in oppressive governments can very often be an aid to the pursuit of democracy, because these corporations are sensitive to pressure from western consumers, which has a direct impact on sales. It can be easier to influence Nigerian politics by boycotting Shell than by trying to bring pressure to bear on the Nigerian government. This, in fact, is the subtitle of Naomi Klein's book *No Logo*. Klein points out that the big corporations have tried to create a special positive aura for their trademarks through many decades of advertising and goodwill. But by doing so they have also shot themselves in the foot. The trademarks, being their biggest asset, are hugely sensitive to adverse publicity. It can take a company decades to build up a trademark but only a few weeks for activists to demolish it. Really, though, Naomi Klein ought to see this as an argument for capitalism, because this way the corporate giants can be pressured if they behave badly in any respect. Honest Fred on the corner can cheat you because you will never see him again, but the big trademarks, as a matter of survival, have to behave respectably.

They have to turn out good, safe products and treat employees, customers and the environment well so as not to lose their goodwill. Negative attention spells huge losses.[100]

The Economist has also observed that corporate morality is often superior to that of the average government. Most companies formulate guidelines and define requirements for dealing with environmental problems and sexual harassment, even in countries where these expressions do not exist in the local vocabulary. Most companies would instantly fire a board chairman implicated in corruption scandals like Germany's former federal chancellor Helmut Kohl or in sexual escapades and dubious dealings like former US President Bill Clinton. And yet these were heads of state in two of the most democratic and stable of western countries.[101]

---

100. Klein 2000. Klein finds it repugnant that firms exploit people's need of belonging and group identity. But if this is a basic need, then surely it is a good thing that it should be catered to by freely chosen trademarks rather than inherited identities? I would rather see people arguing about whether a Mac or a PC is best than about whether being black or white is best. Surely triviality itself makes it preferable for people to feel superior for having Adidas trainers rather than for being heterosexual?

101. "The world's view of multinationals" *The Economist*, 27th January, 2000. Even a critic like Björn Elmbrant maintains that the world's enterprise is not growing worse "but that continued exploitation is more and more becoming mingled with responsible entrepreneurship." Elmbrant 2000, p. 79.

The Bangladeshi garment industry is a case in point of foreign enterprises channelling knowledge and new ideas which can revolutionise an economy. During the 70s local entrepreneur Noorul Quader established co-operation with the South Korean Daewoo company. Daewoo sold sewing machines to Quader and trained his workers. When his firm started up in Bangladesh, Daewoo assisted him for just over a year longer with marketing and advice on new methods of production, in return for 8 per cent of earnings. 130 skilled workers and two engineers from South Korea inaugurated production in Bangladesh in 1980, and garment exports were accepted by the authorities as an island of free trade in a protectionist economy and Western costumers were allowed to buy them without the normal tariffs. Output almost doubled every year, and in 1987 the company was already selling 2.3 million sweaters, worth 5.3 million dollars. By then 114 of the 130 original workers had already started up garment firms of their own, and all of a sudden, Bangladesh, which until now had not had a single garment export enterprise, had 700 of them. Today there are more than three times that number, making garment manufacturing Bangladesh's biggest industry, accounting for some 60 per cent of the country's exports. The factories have more than 1.2 million employees, about 90 per cent of them women, who have moved in from the impoverished countryside in search of more secure, better-paid jobs. Another five million are employed in industry as a whole. Although working conditions are bad, they have often meant new opportunities of choice and higher wages, even in the traditional occupations, which are now having to exert themselves to attract workers.[102]

---

102. Crook 1993.

"Gold and green forests"

Although multinational corporations and free trade are proving good for development and human rights in the Third World, another objection still remains, namely that the environment is the big loser. Factories in the western world can relocate to poorer countries with no environmental legislation, causing the latter to be afflicted with heavier pollution, added to which, the West has to follow suit and lower its environmental standards in order to stay in business. Anti-globalists are in the habit of corroborating this thesis with the odd example of a factory which has been sited on a particular side of a national boundary so as to be able to pollute there. This is a dismal thesis, implying that people obtaining better opportunities, resources and technology use them to abuse nature. Does there really have to be an antithesis between development and the environment?

This thesis runs into the same problem as the whole idea of racing to the bottom. It doesn't tally with reality. There is no exodus of industry to countries with poor environmental standards, and there is no downward pressure on the world's environment protection. On the contrary. The greater part of American and Swedish investments go to countries with similar environmental stipulations to their own. There has been much talk of American factories moving to Mexico since the NAFTA free trade agreement was signed, but what is less well known is that since free trade was introduced Mexico has tightened up its environmental regulations, following a long history of complete nonchalance of environmental issues. This is part of a global trend. All over the world, economic progress and growth are moving hand in hand with intensified environmental protection. Four researchers who studied these connections noted that "we find a very strong, positive association between our [environmental] indicators and the level of economic development". A country which is too poor cannot afford to bother about the environment at all. Countries usually begin protecting their natural resources when they get the chance of doing so. When they grow richer they start to regulate effluent emissions, and when they have still more resources they also begin regulating air quality.[103]

Prosperity brings more environmental regulations

Correlation between prosperity and environmental regulation in 31 studied countries

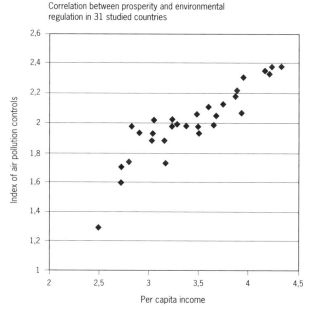

Source: Dasgupta, Mody, Roy & Wheeler, 1995.

103. Dasgupta, Mody, Roy & Wheeler 1995.

There are a number of factors causing environment protection to increase with wealth and development. People who barely know where the next meal is coming from have no possibility of giving priority to a good environment. To abate misery and subdue the pangs of hunger takes priority over any nature conservancy. It is when our standard of living rises that we start attaching importance to the environment and obtaining resources to improve it. Such was the case earlier in Western Europe, and so it is in the developing countries today. This, however, requires people to be able and allowed to mobilise opinion, and to live in a democracy, otherwise their preferences will have no impact. Environment destruction is worst in dictatorships. But it is prosperity, as well as mentality, that makes environment protection easier in a wealthy society. A wealthier country can afford to tackle environmental problems, it can develop the environment-friendly techniques – wastewater and exhaust emission control, for example – and can rectify mistakes made previously.

Global environmental development resembles not so much a race for the bottom as a "Californian effect" race to the top, the reference here being to the State of California's Clean Air Acts, first introduced in the 1970s and tightened up since then. These severe regulations on emissions made rigorous demands on motor manufactures. Many prophets of doom predicted firms and factories moving to other states and California soon being obliged to repeal its regulations. But instead the opposite happened. The other states gradually tightened up their environmental stipulations, the reason being that their companies needed the wealthy Californian market. So car manufactures all over the USA exerted themselves to develop new techniques for reducing emissions. Having done so they could more easily comply with the exacting requirements of other states, whereupon these again ratcheted up their requirements. Anti-globalists usually claim that profit interest and free trade cause business enterprises to entrap politicians in a race for the bottom. The Californian effect implies the opposite: profit interest and free trade enabling politicians to pull business corporations along with them in a race to the top.

This is because environmental protection accounts for a very small proportion of most firms' expenditure. What they are after is a good business environment, with a liberal economy and a skilled workforce, not a bad environment. A review of research in this field show that there are no clear indications of national rules on the environment having led to a diminution of exports or to fewer companies locating in the countries concerned.[104] This finding undermines both the arguments of this kind put forward by companies against environmental regulations and those propounded by environmentalists maintaining that globalisation has to be restrained for environmental reasons.

Incipient signs of the Californian effect's race to the top are present all over the world, because globalisation has caused different countries to absorb new techniques more rapidly, and the new techniques are generally far gentler on the environment. A couple of researchers have investigated steel manufacturing in 50 different countries. They came to the conclusion that countries with more open economies took the lead in introducing cleaner technology, and that their production generated almost one-fifth less emissions than the same production in closed countries. This process is being driven by the multinational corporations, the reason being that they have a lot to gain from uniform production with uniform technology. Because they are restructured more rapidly, they have more modern machinery. And they prefer assimilating the latest, most environment-friendly technology immediately to retro-fitting it, at great expense, when environmental stipulations are tightened up.

Brazil, Mexico and China – the three biggest recipients of foreign investments – present an unambiguous connection, namely: the more

---

104. Jaffe, Peterson, Portney & Stavins 1995.

investments they get, the better control they gain over air pollution. The worst forms of air pollution have diminished in the cities during the period of globalisation. When western companies start up in developing countries, their production is considerably more environment-friendly than the native production, and they are more willing to comply with environmental legislation, not least because they have powerful trade marks to safeguard. Only 30 per cent of Indonesian companies comply with the country's environmental regulations, whereas no fewer than 80 per cent of the multinationals do so. One out of every ten foreign companies maintained a standard clearly superior to that of the regulations. This development could go faster with more open economies, and in particular if the governments of the world could phase out the incomprehensible tariffs on environment-friendly technology.[105]

Sometimes in the course of debate one hears it said that, for environmental reasons, the poor countries of the South must not be allowed to grow as affluent as our countries in the North. For example, in a debate article published by the newspaper *Dagens Nyheter*, Archbishop K. G. Hammar and a group of Church representatives argued:

> *If everyone were to attain the European level of consumption, the environmental effects would be devastating.*[106]

But the studies show this to be colossal misapprehension. On the contrary, it is in the developing countries that we find the gravest, most harmful environmental problems. In our affluent part of the world, more and more people are mindful of environmental problems such

105. Investments and the environment: Wheeler 2000. Steel production: Wheeler, Huq & Martin 1993.

106. Hammar et al., 2000.

as endangered green areas. Every day in the developing countries, over 7,000 people die from air pollution when using wood, dung and agricultural waste in their homes as heating and cooking fuel. No less than 2.8 million people are estimated to die every year from polluted indoor air. These are *supremely real* "devastating environmental effects". Tying people down to that level of development means every year condemning millions to premature death.

Pollution does not increase at all with growth, instead it presents an inverted U-curve. When growth in a very poor country gathers speed and the chimneys begin belching smoke, the environment suffers, but when prosperity has risen high enough, the environmental indicators show an improvement instead: emissions are reduced and air and water present progressively lower concentrations of pollutants. The cities with the worst problems are not Stockholm, New York and Zürich but rather Peking, Mexico City and New Delhi. In addition to the factors already mentioned, this is also due to the economic structure changing from raw-material-intensive to knowledge-intensive production. In a modern economy, heavy, dirty industry is to a great extent superseded by service enterprises. Banks, consulting firms and IT corporations do not have the same environmental impact as old factories.

According to one survey of available environmental data, the turning point generally comes before a country's per capita GDP has reached 8,000 dollars. At 10,000 dollars the researchers found a positive connection between increased growth and better air and water quality.[107] That is roughly the level of prosperity of Argentina, South Korea or Slovenia. In the Nordic countries the level of prosperity is about 20,000 or 30,000 dollars. Here as well, the environment has consistently improved since the 70s, quite contrary to the picture obtainable from the media. In the 70s there was constant reference to smog in American cities, and rightly so, for the air was judged to be

---

107. Grossman & Krueger 1994, Radetzki 2001.

unhealthy for between 100 and 300 days a year. Today it is unhealthy for less than 10 days a year, with the exception of Los Angeles. There the figure is roughly 80 days, but even that represents a 50 per cent reduction in 10 years.[108] The same trend is noticeable in the rest of the affluent world – for example, in Tokyo, where, a few decades ago, doomsters believed that oxygen masks would in future have to be worn all around the city because of the bad air.

Prosperity goes easier on the environment

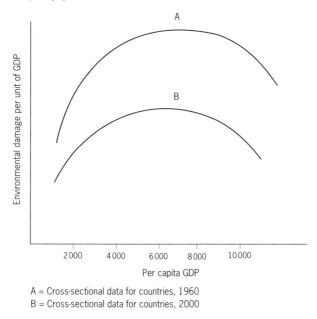

A = Cross-sectional data for countries, 1960
B = Cross-sectional data for countries, 2000

As can be seen, wear and tear on the environment diminishes not only with increased prosperity but at all income levels over time.

Source: World Bank 1992.

Apart from its other positive effects on the developing countries, such as being spared hunger and not having to watch their children die, prosperity beyond a certain critical point can improve the environment. What is more, this turning point is now occurring progressively earlier in the developing countries, because they can learn from more affluent countries' mistakes and use their superior technology. For example, air quality in the enormous cities of China, which are the most heavily polluted in the world, has steadied since the mid-80s and in several cases has slowly improved. This has coincided with uniquely rapid growth.

Some years ago, the Danish statistician and Greenpeace member Bjørn Lomborg headed a survey by about ten students of statistics and facts about the world's environmental problems. To his astonishment he found that what he himself had assumed to be self-evident, namely the steady deterioration of the global environment, did not agree at all with official empirical data. On the contrary, air pollution is diminishing, refuse problems are diminishing, resources are not running out, more people can eat their fill, and people are living longer. Lomborg gathered facts from as many fields as he could find, and published them in the book *The Sceptical Environmentalist : Measuring the Real State of the World*. The picture thus emerging is a very important corrective to the general prophesies of doom that can so easily be imbibed from newspaper headlines.

Lomborg shows that air pollution and emissions have been declining in the developed world during recent decades. Heavy metal emissions have been heavily reduced, nitrogen oxides have diminished by almost 30 per cent and sulphur emissions by about 80 per cent. These problems are still growing in the poor developing countries, but at every level of growth the annual particle density has diminished by 2 per cent in only 14 years. In the developed world, phospho-

108. Moore & Simon 2000, section XIV.

rus emissions into the seas have declined drastically, and coli bacteria concentrations in coastal waters have plummeted, enabling closed bathing points to reopen. (Today we can safely bathe in and eat fish from the inner city of Stockholm. Not many Third World capitals can say the same.)

Lomborg shows that, instead of a large-scale deforestation, the world's forest acreage increased from 40.24 to 43.04 million square kilometres between 1950 and 1994. He declares that there has never been any large-scale tree death due to acid rain. The oft-quoted, but erroneous statement about 40,000 species being exterminated every year is traced by Lomborg to its source – a twenty-year-old estimate which has been circulating in environmentalist circles ever since. The documented cases of extermination during the past 400 years total *just over a thousand species*, of which about 95 per cent are insects, bacteria and viruses. Lomborg declares the refuse problem to be smaller than we imagine. The next hundred years' Danish refuse could be accommodated in a 33-metre-deep pit with an area of 3 sq. km, even without recycling. In addition, Lomborg illustrates how increased prosperity and improved technology can solve the problems which lie ahead of us. All the fresh water consumed in the world today could be produced by a single desalination plant, powered by solar cells and occupying 0.4 per cent of the Sahara Desert.

It is a mistake, then, to believe that growth automatically ruins the environment. And claims that we would need this or that number of globes for the whole world to attain a western standard of consumption are equally untruthful. This claim is usually made by environmentalists, and it is concerned, not so much with emissions and pollution as with resources running out if everyone were to live as we do in the affluent world.

Clearly, certain of the raw materials we use today, in present-day quantities, would not suffice for the whole world if everyone consumed the same things. But that information is just about as interesting as if a prosperous Stone Age man were to say that, if everyone attained his level of consumption, there would not be enough stone, salt and furs to go round. Raw material consumption is not static. With more and more people achieving a high level of prosperity, we start looking round for ways of using other raw materials. Man is all the time improving technology so as to get at raw materials which were previously inaccessible, and we are attaining a prosperity which makes this possible. New innovations make it possible for old raw materials to be put to better use and for rubbish to be turned into new raw materials. A century and a half ago, oil was just something black and sticky which people preferred not to tread on and definitely did not want to find beneath their land. But interest in energy supply led to methods being devised for using it, and today it is one of our prime resources. Sand has never been all that exiting or precious, but today it is a vital raw material in the most powerful means of production of our age, the computer, namely in the form of silicon – which makes up a quarter of the earth's crust and which we use for making computer chips.

There is a simple market mechanism which averts shortages. If a certain raw material comes to be in short supply, its price goes up. This makes everyone more interested in economising on that resource, in finding more of it, in reusing it and in trying to find substitutes for it. Studying raw material prices over the past few decades, we can see that the trend is a falling one and that metals have never been as cheap as they are today. Prices are falling, which suggests that demand does not exceed supply. In relation to wages, i.e. in terms of how long we must work to earn the price of a raw material, natural resources today are half as expensive as they were fifty years ago, and one-fifth as expensive as a hundred years ago. In 1900 the price of electricity was eight times higher, the price of coal seven times higher and the price of oil five times higher than today.[109] The risk of short-

109. Moore & Simon 2000, section XV.

219

age is declining all the time, because new finds and more efficient use keep augmenting the available reserves.

In a world where technology never stops developing, static calculations are uninteresting, and wrong. By simple mathematics Lomborg establishes that if we have a raw material with a hundred years' use remaining, a 1 per cent annual increase in demand and a 2 per cent increase in recycling and/or efficiency, that resource *will never be exhausted*.

If, moreover, shortage do occur, then with efficient technology most substances can be recycled. One-third of the world's steel production, for example, is being reused already. Then again, technology can outstrip the depletion of resources. Not many years ago, everyone was convinced of the impossibility of the whole Chinese population having telephones, because that would require several hundred million telephone operators. But the supply of manpower did not run out, technology developed instead. But then it was declared that nationwide telephony for China was physically impossible, because not all the world's copper would suffice for installing heavy gauge telephone lines all over the country. Before that had time to become a problem, fibre optics and satellites began to supersede copper wire. The price of copper, a commodity which people believed would run out, has fallen continuously and is now only about a tenth of what it was 200 years ago.

People in most ages have worried about important raw materials becoming exhausted. But on the few occasions when this has happened, it has generally affected isolated, poor places, not open, affluent ones. To claim that people in Africa, who are dying by the thousand every day from supremely real shortages, must not be allowed to become as prosperous as ourselves because we can find theoretical risks of shortages occurring, is both stupid and unjust.

The environmental question will not resolve itself. Proper rules are needed for the protection of water, soil and air from destruction.

Systems of environmental charges are needed which will make polluters interested in not damaging the environment for others. Many environmental issues also require international regulation and agreements, which confronts us with entirely new challenges. When talking about the market and the environment, it is important to realise that efforts in this quarter will be facilitated by a freer, growing economy capable of using the best solutions, from both a natural and a human viewpoint, and that in order to meet those challenges it is better to have resources and advanced science than not to have them.*

Very often, environmental improvements are due to the very capitalism which is often blamed for the contrary. The introduction of private property creates owners with long-term interests. A landowner must see to it that there is good soil or forest there tomorrow as well, because otherwise he will have no income later on. If the property is collective or government-owned, no one has any such long-term interest. On the contrary, everyone then has an interest in cornering the resources quickly before someone else does. It was due to their being common lands that the rain forests of the Amazon began to be rapidly exploited in the 60s and 70s and are still being rapidly exploited today. Only about a tenth of the forests are recognised by the governments as privately owned, even though in practice Indians possess and inhabit large parts of them. It is the absence of definite fishing rights which causes (heavily subsidised) fishing fleets to try to vacuum the oceans of fish before someone else does. No wonder, then, that the most large-scale destruction of environment in history has occurred in the communist dictatorships, where all ownership was collective.

---

* To promise someone "gold and green forets" implies that you will produce whatever he or she wants, even if it is practically impossible.

A few years ago a satellite image was taken of the borders of the Sahara, where the desert was spreading. Everywhere the land was parched yellow, after nomads had over-exploited the common lands and then moved on. But in the midst of this desert environment could be seen a small patch of green. This proved to be an area of privately owned land where the owners of the farm were able to prevent over-exploitation and engaged in cattle farming that was profitable in the long term.[110]

Trade and freight are sometimes criticised for destroying the environment, but this can be rectified with more efficient transport and purification techniques, and also environmental charges to make the cost of pollution visible through pricing. But the biggest environmental problems are associated with production and consumption, and there trade can make a positive contribution, even aside from the general effect on growth. Trade leads to a country's resources being utilised as efficiently as possible. Goods are produced in the places which entail least expense and least wear and tear on the environment. This is why the amount of raw materials used for a given product keeps diminishing as process efficiency improves. With modern production processes, 97 per cent less metal is needed for a soft drink can than 30 years ago, due partly to the use of lighter aluminium. A car today contains only half as much metal as 30 years ago. This makes it better for production to take place where the technology exists, instead of everyone trying to have production of their own, with all the consumption of resources which this entails.

If governments really believed in the market economy, they would stop subsidising energy, industry, road construction, fisheries, agriculture, devastation of forests and many other things out of the national treasury. These subsidies have the effect of keeping activities alive

110. The example is quoted in Nordin 1992, p. 154.

which would otherwise not exist or else would have been performed by better methods or in other places. The Worldwatch Institute maintains that taxpayers the world over are forced every year to pay about 650 billion dollars towards environmentally destructive activities. Abolition, the Institute claims, would lead to a global tax reduction of eight per cent. In the USA alone this would mean every family paying 2,000 dollars less tax a year.[111]

EU meat production shows that not only the environment but animals as well are made to suffer by unproductive industries. It is madness to subsidise inefficient livestock management in the EU which has meant cruel conditions for animals with severely cramped transport conditions and, at times, rearing on carcass meal. It would be a better idea to abolish agricultural tariffs and import meat, for example, from South America, where the animals can roam great tracts of land, grazing freely, until they have to be rounded up. But this is prevented today by sky-high tariffs. During the mad cow disease crisis, for example, Swedish McDonald's wanted to avoid the hazards of using EU meat for its hamburgers, but was not permitted to import from South America. The forequarter meat from which the mince is made is excluded by tariffs of several hundred per cent.

111. Roodman 1998.

VI

Irrational, international capital?

The leaderless collective

Critics of capitalism argue that the market machinery may perhaps, after prolonged endeavour elevate a country to the heights of prosperity, only to see everything blown to pieces a month later. They paint the picture of irrational speculators investing wildly and then making off with their capital when the herd mentality changes direction. Nearly 1.5 trillion dollars cross national boundaries every day, they complain, as if this fact were a problem in itself. The Swedish journalist Björn Elmbrant describes the financial market as "a leaderless collective staggering about and tripping over its own feet." [112]

Anxiety about financial markets is easily created. They seem abstract because so few people have any direct contact with them. We only feel their effects, and so it is easy to make a mystery of them. The force involved prompted one of President Clinton's economic advisers to exclaim: "[In the next life] I want to come back as the bond market." Trend-setting left-wing debaters love pointing to patterns of stock market behaviour which seem odd if one cannot understand the reason for them. In this way suspicion is cast on the market. A firm's shareholders, for example, are pleased when it axes jobs. But this does not mean that they love the sight of unemployment. What appeals to them is the greater productivity and reduced expenditure which can result.

But the American stock market generally takes an upward turn when unemployment does so. Is not this a sign of rejoicing in the misfortune of others? No, it is a sign of investors knowing that the Fed (the American equivalent of a central bank) takes rising unemployment as

---

112. Elmbrant 2000, pp. 89 f.

226

a sign of a downturn and a reduced risk of inflation, and therefore lowers the interest rate. What the stock market loves is not unemployment but the economic lubricant which is a lowering of interest rates. This is no stranger than the intrinsically strange phenomenon of the stock market sometimes leaping upwards when the trade cycle indicators point downwards and growth decelerates. Great, they say to themselves: that must mean another interest rate cut on the way at last.

But stock market fluctuations are increasing, no one can deny that. This must at least mean that investors have become less long-termist and are just following the crowd? There may be a grain of truth in this. Of course the market is not perfectly rational in every situation, whatever that would mean. The roller-coaster movement in recent years, especially of Internet consultancy share prices, shows exaggerated hopes and mistaken pricing to be a natural part of a market which is about the future. But it also shows that the exaggerations will not survive indefinitely. Exaggerated hopes cannot make up for lack of real substance in an enterprise.

Part of the reason for the fluctuations is not short-termism but the stock market having become very long-termist. With the old type of industrial enterprise, its future can be easily judged from historical data concerning investments and sales. So valuation of the enterprise was fairly stable. But in new, more research-intensive sectors with less certain sales prospects, long-term sales can be harder to predict. It is less easy now to tell whether the firm is going to boom or bust. How are we to know that firms developing new mobile phones today will also be frontrunners in ten years' time? When we do not know this, every indication regarding future prospects gives rise to rapid changes. The same applies to the entire stock market when it is unclear which way the economy is going to move. Every hint of the future bringing an up- or downturn will impact swiftly.

Imagine, then, what it is like with companies focusing entirely on the future – those engaging in pharmaceutical research, for example.

Possibly they will no longer exist in ten years' time, but perhaps they will find that vaccine for HIV, in which case their shareholders will become millionaires. "Bubbles" can then occur for perfectly rational reasons. Even if a horse is unlikely to win the race, given high enough odds there may be cause to put some money on it. Taking the trade cycles as a whole, though, share price fluctuations do *not* appear to have increased where traditional firms are concerned.

Now, many critics of the market say that they have nothing against national financial markets. "Hypercapitalism" is the problem – capital without boundaries ravaging all over the world without even having to present a passport at the frontier. This, we are told, is a hasty capital which cares more about the next quarter's profits than about long-term development and technical renewal. But the defence of the mobility of capital is a question of freedom. This is not a matter of "the freedom of capital", as the critics complain, because capital is not a person capable of being free or unfree. It is a matter of people's freedom to decide about their own resources, e.g. freedom to invest their pension savings where they themselves believe it is best to do so; pension funds are in fact the most important investors in the international market. Something like 80 per cent of the Swedes own shares, either individually or through funds. They are the market. This is also a question of businesses being at liberty to seek finance from other countries as well. Factories and offices do not build themselves – it takes capital. The notion of this throttling long-term development is contradicted by that development having proceeded hand in hand with more and more research and innovation. This growing freedom has been important for favourable global development in recent years, making it possible for capital to be invested where it yields the biggest return and, accordingly, is used as efficiently as possible.[113]

---

113. For a good introduction to the subject, see Eklund 1999, and for a rather more theoretical approach, Eichengreen & Mussa et al. 1998.

This is easy to understand if we think of narrower boundaries than national frontiers. Suppose you have a thousand dollars you want to put out at interest, and you can only do this within your own precinct. Personally I might choose between investing the money with a bookbinder or a jukebox proprietor. Because I believe in the latter, I lend him the money. With it he can buy a new jukebox and a second-hand pinball game, but because demand for his products isn't all that great, he will only make a small profit on his investment, so he can only pay me 2 per cent interest on my money. But, since the bookbinder would only pay me 1 per cent, the jukebox man need have no fear of my taking my money elsewhere.

If instead I have the whole town to choose from, there will be more people competing for my capital. A guitar factory, enabled by my money to purchase a new grinding machine, could raise its earnings considerably, and is therefore able to pay me twice as much interest as the jukebox proprietor. I earn more this way, but so does the whole economy, because the resources are used more efficiently than with the alternative. This is even more true, of course, if I am allowed to invest my money nationwide or worldwide. In that case all potential investments are compared with each other. Still more firms will then be after my money, and those capable of using it best are prepared to pay most for it. Money, loans and share capital are generally invested where they are expected to yield the biggest return. In this way capital is used efficiently and boosts productivity, which develops the economy where it is invested and gives the biggest return to the investor.

Because one has to compete with everyone else, it may sound as if the wealthiest firms lay hold on all capital, because they can offer most payment. But capital is also obtainable from all the different countries, and so the supply increases. And it is not the wealthiest who bid most, but those who can make most out of the money. The biggest profits, as a rule, are not made in industries where there has already been ample investment, but in new enterprises which have not yet been able to arrange finance for exciting projects. Capital markets are most important of all to those with good ideas but no capital. As we saw earlier, free capital markets appear to augment a society's economic equality. These markets cause people and businesses with a lot of capital to profit by placing the capital in the hands of those who have none but look capable of using it more efficiently. And so they enable small firms to set up in competition with the established ones. The more flexible the market, and the fewer the impediments, the more easily capital flows to those who can make best use of it.

The affluent countries have large quantities of capital while the poor countries of the South are short of it. So free movement of capital means investments moving towards more capital-starved countries with better investment opportunities. The developing countries receive more than a quarter of the world's combined investments in businesses, projects and land. This amounts to an enormous private transfer of capital from industrialised to developing countries. The flow of capital to the developing countries is now running at about 200 billion dollars, net, per annum. This is more than four times the figure a decade ago and fifteen times as much as twenty years ago, thanks to freer capital markets and improved information technology. This is something fantastic for countries which have always been held back by shortage of capital. As mentioned earlier, in ten years the poor countries of the world have obtained a trillion dollars in foreign direct investments – slightly more than all the development assistance they have received, worldwide, in the past 50 years. So the leaderless collective, allegedly staggering about and tripping over its own feet, has been more than five times cleverer than the governments and development aid establishments of the affluent countries at channelling capital to the developing countries.

Progressively larger share of investments to the developing countries

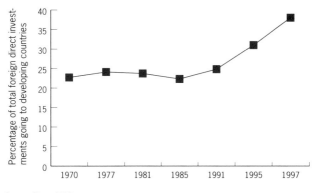

Source: Ghose 2000.

The developing countries get increasingly more capital

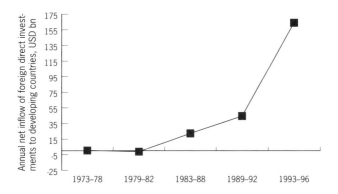

Source: Eichengreen & Mussa et al. 1998

As critics of globalisation point out, only about 5 per cent of all economical transfers comprise real trade in goods and services. The remaining financial trade is concerned with "making money out of money", which, some of the critics maintain, adds nothing of value to the economy. But there is nothing so productive as the financing of production improvements, which provides resources for production and spurs technical progress. An international financial market enlarges the volume of investments. When there are large and efficient financial markets with the ability to buy and sell risks (derivatives), this makes it possible to finance bigger projects and take bigger risks than was previously possible. This is what accounts for the lion's share of turnover in the financial market. With billions of dollars being turned over every day, a very small portion of the money actually changes hands: most of the transactions are due to firms and investors reallocating their investments, so as to guard against risks. It is since this became possible that the developing countries have gained proper access to international flows of capital.

Through access to international finance we can spread our risks, simply by investing in different quarters. If Sweden's economy did badly, then formerly this would have meant not enough money being available for old age pensions. Today there would be enough money to go round, because we are allowed to spread our saving between different countries. Sweden's new premium pension system has enabled me personally – and before this I had neither shares nor trust fund units – to invest part of my future pension in new markets in Latin America and Asia, instead of tying the money up in Sweden. The financial markets also make it possible for households, businesses and even governments to borrow when their incomes are low and repay when they are higher. This becomes a way of alleviating downturns without being forced to cut down on one's consumption as drastically as would otherwise be necessary.

In its Capital Access Index the American Milken Institute has shown that economies develop best when capital is readily available and cheap and is distributed openly and honestly, whereas they manage least well when capital is in short supply and is expensive and arbitrarily distributed. Broad, free financial markets with many players create development, while "government-owned flows of capital concentrated in a few financial institutions and enterprises inhibit growth." Studies have generally shown that the functional development of financial markets in a certain country provides a good indication of that country's growth for coming years. There are studies which have not revealed any connection between freedom from capital regulations and growth in the country concerned, but in those studies no attempt has been made to measure the intensity of the regulations. One survey which tried to do so in 64 industrialised and developing countries and which eliminated the impact of other factors points to a clear average connection between freedom of capital movements and economic growth. That study also indicated that countries with freedom for capital receive far more taxation revenue from businesses. Freedom causes resources to go where they are used most productively, which makes it easier for businesses to start up and facilitates international trade.[114]

---

114. This study, and those conflicting with it, are summarised in Eichengreen & Mussa 1998, p. 19. See also Yago & Goldman 1998.

Regulate more?

The problems associated with the mobility of capital are that it can suddenly flee countries which get into economic difficulties, or that a currency can be subjected to destabilising speculation. Many lenders and investors have no specific knowledge of a particular country's economy, so if large numbers begin to leave it they themselves may take this as indication that something is wrong and follow the tide. Panic and herd mentality set in. The possibility of obtaining continued credit vanishes. Projects have to be discontinued, firms lose all their resources and the economy slams on all the brakes.

One of the reasons for short-term capital transactions growing faster than the market for long-term investments and commodity trade is that the latter is very severely regulated in all states of the world. If these markets were to be properly liberalised, we would get different proportions. Some feel that the level of regulation must be equalised, but in the other direction, by also regulating the financial market by means of controls of different kinds. Malaysia, for example, introduced, as a temporary measure, strict exchange controls during the Asian crisis. But even if this could alleviate the immediate effects, it will cause investors to avoid the country in the future. If they are prevented from leaving the country when they want to, they will demand a higher return for coming there in the first place, and the country will risk a capital shortage. All empirical data show that a free outflow of capital from a country increases its influx of capital. The immediate result in this particular instance was that Malaysia's neighbours – Indonesia, for example – suffered a swifter exodus of capital, due to widespread fears of its following the Malaysian example of controls. In the long term this recoiled against the country itself: much confidence has been lost. One investor in Asian funds recently said of Malaysia that:

A market that used to have up to 18 per cent of weighting in most funds is now totally ignored. [115]

Worse still, closure has coincided with the country rapidly moving towards dictatorship.

One alternative is a more permanent regulation of short-term flows of capital. If quick capital does not get in in the first place, this reduces the risk of the country suffering an exodus of capital later on. Chilean rules have often been looked on as exemplary in this respect, the country having avoided major crises. Chile has insisted on capital entering the country remaining there for a certain length of time and on a certain portion of it being deposited at very low interest with the central bank. This type of regulation seems to work better than alternative controls, but Chile's reason for introducing these rules was that saving was too high and so it did not want to have more capital in the country. This is hardly the situation "afflicting" other developing countries. On the contrary, they need more capital and more investments. But even in capital-rich Chile, this had led to financial problems. Big companies operating internationally have circumvented the controls and got hold of capital anyway, while small businesses have coped less well and have to pay many times more interest.

Besides, the perspective of these rules is excessively short term. Chile was hit by a real economic crisis in 1981–82, with bank failures and a 90 per cent devaluation. That happened at the same time as its capital controls were at their most rigorous, when inflows of capital were prohibited unless the capital remained in the country for at least

---

115. McNulty 2001.

five and a half years. Wise from the crisis, Chile decided to reform and consolidated its chaotic banking sector, which is probably the main reason why it has avoided further crises. (Incidentally, Chile's decision to cancel its capital regulations came at the height of the Asian crisis.)[116]

Capital controls often serve as a means of lulling investors and politicians into a false sense of security. If politics are not stable, the crisis, once revealed, can hit all the harder. Only months before the Asian crisis hit South Korea, local politicians and international investors believed the country's restrictions on the mobility of capital would save it from an exchange crisis. In 1997 the Goldman-Sachs investment corporation judged South Korea's banks and central bank to be in bad shape, but since the country had capital regulations they declared that investors could disregard the risks this implied. The investors took the advice and ignored the risks. The Asian crisis then struck hardest against Indonesia and South Korea – and eventually Russia – which had the stiffest capital regulations in any growth market. (At the same time as those having least regulations – Hong Kong, Singapore and Taiwan – got off lightest.)[117] Brazil too was hard hit; politicians there thought that restrictions against short-term capital would steer them clear of the crisis.

The thing is that, sooner or later, policy mismanaged leads to crisis. And if capital controls make politicians believe that they are free to pursue any policy they like, the odds are that they will aggravate the crisis. In theory, temporary capital controls in a crisis could give the country a respite in which to modernise its banking and finance sector, firm up the budget and liberalise the economy. Often, though, regulations are put to the opposite use, as a way of avoiding painful reforms. One sign of this is that countries with capital regulations

116. Edwards 1999.

117. Micklethwait & Wooldridge 2000, p. 55.

have, on average, bigger budgetary deficits and higher inflation than those without. This is also why liberal economies with freer financial markets emerge from their crises more quickly. We can compare the rapid recovery of many Asian states after the Asian crisis with Latin America's crisis of the early 80s, after which they imposed controls on capital outflows and refrained from liberal reforms. The result was a lost decade of inflation, prolonged unemployment and low growth. Compare Mexico's lightning recovery after the "Tequila crisis" of 1995 with the same country's prolonged depression after the debt crisis of 1982.

Another problem with capital controls is that they are hard to maintain in a world of ever-improving, ever-faster communications. They are in practice an invitation to crime, and a great deal of the investors' time is devoted to circumventing the regulations. The longer a regulation has been in force, the less effective it becomes, because investors then have time to find ways round it. Besides, most regulations have their exceptions, for particularly important or vulnerable enterprises. So in most countries controls become an incentive for corruption, and different people are treated differently by the law.

Tobin tax

One proposed capital regulation which has achieved popularity in recent years is the so-called "Tobin tax", named after the Nobel economics laureate James Tobin, who first suggested it. This is a low tax of 0.05–0.25 per cent on all currency exchange, advocated by the Attac movement among others. The idea is to slow down capital movements and make investors think once again before allowing capital to cross currency exchange boundaries. In this way harmful speculation and major exchange crises could be avoided. Criticism of the Tobin tax has focused on the impossibility of introducing it. In practice all countries have to agree on it, otherwise transactions will go through non-signatory countries. And if it could be introduced, more and more trade would go to the central currencies in order to avoid transactional costs. Perhaps nearly the entire world economy would end up using dollars. But there is a more serious objection to the Tobin tax: even if it were possible to introduce, it would be harmful.

This tax is more harmful to the financial market than regulations by individual countries. The only effect of the latter is to reduce inflow in the country opting for them, whereas a Tobin tax would reduce turnover and the possibility of external financing all over the world, even for countries considering themselves to be in great need of such finance. Obstacles to the movement of capital pen it in where it is already, i.e. in the affluent countries, and the Third World is the loser. The Tobin tax, therefore, is not really a tax on capital but a tariff which makes trade and investments more expensive. Advocates of the Tobin tax claim that it need not have this effect, because it is so low.

For long-term investments the cost will be negligible. But the problem is that an investment is not just one transaction. An investor may perhaps part-finance a project, recoup some of the money in profits, increase the investment if it is successful, transfer earnings to other parts of the operation, add capital, buy components from abroad, and so on and so forth. With every little transaction taxed, the total cost of the Tobin tax will be many times greater than the low cost suggested by the percentage figure on paper, and so it will be more profitable doing business in one's own currency, in one's own region. This will lead to a general reduction of the return on capital, and it will cause capital-starved countries to have less access to capital and, consequently, fewer investments. Interest rates will rise and borrowers will have to pay more for their loans.

The adherents of the Tobin tax say that what they really want to get at is sheer currency speculation. But the idea of there being some hard and fast boundary between useful investments and useless speculation is completely wrong. Derivatives – options, for example – which the critics usually regard as sheer speculation, are necessary in order for investments to work. In a world of changing prices and exchange rates, a firm's forecasting can be completely overturned if it does not have the type of insurance which derivatives afford. Suppose a company extracts a metal and the price of that metal suddenly falls dramatically, earnings fail to materialise and bankruptcy threatens. Instead of devoting a large part of its activity to wondering how markets are going to develop, the firm can buy a right to sell the raw material at a predetermined price later on – a sale option. The purchaser of this option takes over in this way the risk and the responsibility of predicting market developments. The metal company can quietly concentrate on extracting the metal and the risk is willingly taken over instead by people who specialise in observing developments and apportioning the risks – in a word, "speculators".

In a world of rapidly changeable exchange rates, firms encounter the same risk if, for example, the currency in which they are paid quickly depreciates, and it is even more difficult for a metal company to keep track of economic developments in the currency country and exchange risks over a period of several months or years. This makes it more important still to be able to trade in currency derivatives of different kinds, so that a company can, for example, purchase the right to sell the currency it will be receiving at a predetermined price. But it is this very "speculation" that a Tobin tax would prevent. And, just like an ordinary investment, it involves more than one single transaction. If a speculator only took over complete risks, he would be very vulnerable. The speculator must all the time be able to reapportion his risks according to developments, and so as to balance the various assumptions of risk. This is guaranteed by a large second-hand market which enables one to trade in these derivatives almost immediately. This is how the insurance is made as cheap as possible for the company and it can invest in spite of risks. (Just as the second hand market for shares, the stock market, gives people the courage to finance enterprises from the outset by participating as shareholders.)

The structure of the Tobin tax is aimed at this very market. It would result in few speculators being ready to take over risks, and in their demanding much more payment for doing so. The insurance, then, would be much more expensive for companies and investors, with the result that they would not dare or could not afford to invest in countries and currencies with a greater element of risk. Once again, it is the more capital-starved and risk-laden regions – poor developing countries – that would be the losers. Investors would only place their capital where it seemed secure and where they knew the market. During the past decade the developing countries have received over a quarter of all direct foreign investments. This figure would fall dramatically if a Tobin tax were introduced. It would be more difficult for people and businesses in poor countries to obtain loans, and they would be forced to pay higher rates of interest.

The financial market, then, would risk being disrupted by a Tobin tax. But that tax would not be capable of preventing exchange crises. In practice it provides only a low threshold which impedes everyday trading. But above that threshold exchange transactions could suddenly become profitable, in which case there could be drastic fluctuations. The problem of currency speculation and capital exodus would not be averted. When speculators realise that they have a chance of breaking a fixed exchange rate (for example, sterling and the Swedish krona in 1992), they stand to make such enormous amounts of money that a tax of a fraction of the gain would not deter them. If they can make 20 or 50 per cent on an exchange rate, they will not be put off by a tax of 0.05 per cent. The same applies when confidence in a country fails and gigantic losses can be avoided by getting out fast (as in the Asian crisis of 1997). The small tax which is sufficient to disrupt the everyday, healthy functioning of the financial market would not be sufficient to prevent these crises.

Then again, the big turnover in the exchange market reduces the risk of temporary shortages and distorted pricing. A bigger market also reduces the risk of individual players and transactions decisively affecting prices. In this way the free exchange market prevents the occurrence of violent exchange rate fluctuations, something which, paradoxically enough, the Tobin tax could augment by reducing the liquidity of the exchange market. Constant equalisations and adjustments would be replaced by big occasional jolts. Currency market jolts and volatility have not increased since the 1970s, in spite of markets having been liberalised and the volume quadrupled. The fact is that countries with severe capital regulations have far *more erratic* exchange rates than those with fewer restrictions.[118]

But for all these shortcomings, the Tobin tax still has one advantage, namely that it would yield tremendous revenues. The Attac

118. Eichengreen & Mussa 1998, p. 18.

movement counts on 100 billion dollars a year, others say 10–50 billion dollars a year. However, the question is whether this money could ever be collected. Collection would require an immense bureaucracy keeping check of all transactions throughout the world and also with the power to collect the money. We are talking here about transactions taking place in all computers all over the globe, including countries which in practice have neither accounting systems nor an effective administration. In other words, there would have to be some kind of world government, the bureaucracy of which would presumably eat up a large part of the revenues collected. How is this bureaucracy to be governed? By the United Nations, where dictatorships have the same power as democracies? Who would stop it from swerving into an orgy of corruption and expansive power? And who would get the money?

In theory, all the same, the Tobin tax would mean several billion dollars which, for example, could be used to help the Third World. But if we are convinced that a capital transfer of this kind would be a good help, why can we not achieve it by other means? For example, why not abolish the tariffs against these countries, or dismantle the EU's destructive agricultural policy which is holding them back? Why not augment development assistance or introduce a global charge on polluting activity (not all polluting factories can move to a tiny tax haven, whereas all capital can)? Why should we necessarily procure revenue by sabotaging the financial market? Unless that is the true motive!

The Asian crisis

To find out how crises can be prevented, one ought to study earlier crises and their causes. The Asian crisis of 1997/98 is often said to have come like a bolt from the blue, with healthy economies suddenly being hit by speculative assaults and the exodus of capital. It wasn't like that at all. The grain of truth is that these countries would not have suffered an exodus of capital if they had not liberalised movements of capital, because then the capital would never have come to them in the first place. What created the crisis, though, was a combination of factors among which speculation was not the triggering factor but rather the drop that made the already full glass run over.[119]

The economies affected had begun showing clear warning signs, and these grew stronger during 1996 and early 1997. They had received enormous inflows of capital during the 90s, especially through short-term borrowing abroad, encouraged by their governments. For example, the proportion of the debts of Thai banks and institutions borrowed from abroad rose from 5 to 28 per cent between 1990 and 1995. The creation by the central bank and by banking regulations of a high level of interest rates at home made it lucrative to borrow abroad, partly so as to lend at higher rates of interest at home. Governments encouraged these loans with fixed exchange rates and

---

119. Radelet & Sachs 1999, Larsson 2000. Certain aspects of the crisis have been hugely exaggerated by left-wing debaters. Elmbrant 2000, pp. 85 f., claims for example that 50 million Indonesians were plunged into extreme poverty (less than a dollar a day) by it. This is more than four times as many as even temporarily became absolutely poor in the whole of Southeast Asia. Official World Bank figures show the increase in Indonesia to have been less than a million by 1999, and it has declined since then. World Bank 2000a, p. 163.

tax subsidies. At the same time they discriminated against long-term capital. South Korea tried to exclude it completely by prohibiting direct foreign investments and purchases of shares and securities. Short-term loans were the only possible way of raising capital from abroad.

A South Korean bank could borrow dollars or yen for a very short term – money which it would soon have to pay back. Meanwhile it lent this money at a higher rate of interest for long-term investments in South Korea. Thus is counted on all the time being able to renew the foreign loan, otherwise it would suddenly be left without money which it had promised elsewhere. In addition, the capital was channelled through banks and finance companies which were unprepared for such enormous inflows. They were not exposed to competition, and they were often allied with the ruling power and with strong economic interests. So a great deal of the resources, for example, in South Korea, Malaysia, Thailand and Indonesia went to favoured firms and prestige projects. Outsiders had no reason to be apprehensive, because they knew that the ruling powers would never allow their favourites to go to the wall. This applied to the national banks, but also to firms like "chaebols" – South Korea's super-corporations – or the business empire operated by Suharto's acquaintances in Indonesia. Besides, foreign creditors knew for sure that the IMF would intervene and save them from losses if the region as a whole ran into problems. And so the foreigners lent unlimited amounts, resulting in over-investment in low-yield heavy industry and real estate, instead of dynamic enterprises.

All the countries destined to be hit by the crisis had enormous short-term debts in relation to their reserves. At the same time they all had fixed or controlled exchange rates. This created a number of eventually devastating problems. Usually one does not dare to borrow huge sums abroad and then lend them only somewhat more expensively at home if exchange rates are all the time fluctuating somewhat.

One can lose on even very small exchange rate movements unless one is insured against the risk. But with the government professedly guaranteeing a fixed exchange rate, this risk appeared to vanish and everyone was able to borrow like mad. In addition, regulation meant that the local currency was overvalued (by about 20 per cent), not least because the dollar, to which many of these currencies were pegged, rose. This helped to make exporting more difficult. Thai exports, which had risen by 25 per cent in 1995, actually started to decline the following year. In 1996, the year before the crisis which allegedly came like a bolt from the blue, the Thai stock market index lost one-third of its value.

Because exchange rates were higher than the market felt they ought to be, the currencies became a prey to speculators, just like Sweden's fixed exchange rate in 1992. If anyone is prepared to pay more for something than it is worth, speculators are of course keen to cash in on this and harvest the profits. Speculators can borrow fantastic sums of money in local currency and exchange them at the maximum rate in the central bank. As a result the countries affected by the Asian crisis in 1997 were forced to use their currency reserves to defend the excessive exchange rates.

This provided a very rational cause for the exodus of capital. Confidence in the countries' economy and future growth had begun to evaporate. What was worse, so did belief in the ability of their economies to weather a crisis. It was known that they did not have viable legal institutions, such as bankruptcy legislation. Now they had also exhausted the reserves which guarantee foreign loans and the whole of the financial system. If everyone pulled out the reserves would not be sufficient. Individual investors realised that they must recover their capital quickly so as to get it out in time. The notion of the government being able to save all enterprises in difficulty began to wobble. The foremost in getting rid of the local currency were not speculators but native enterprises needing to pay off their loans quickly. When the countries were forced to abandon their exchange rates after huge losses, confidence in them declined still further. Capital fled, loans were not renewed, and firms were suddenly left without finance. The crisis was on.

Undoubtedly, investors influenced one another, and something of a herd mentality ensued, but this was not a matter of blind panic. Countries with healthy economies and solid institutions, like Taiwan, Singapore and Australia, coped well when their neighbours were knocked sideways. And so the term "Asian crisis" is not all that accurate. A conspectus clearly shows that it was national policy that decided how greatly a country was affected by the crisis. Two researchers who studied the course of the crisis summed it up as follows:

We found no evidence of contagion, in which the currency difficulties of one country were transferred to other countries. All of the countries that suffered the most serious financial difficulties did so because each had real economic difficulties, associated in large part with an excessive growth of bank credit and bank loan and insolvency issues.[120]

The effects of the crisis were felt all over the world, but in an integrated world it is natural for events in one quarter to affect others; this is not due to an irrational herd mentality. Shortage of liquidity means that investors have to repatriate capital from other risk-laden countries. Swedish companies and banks, and thus the Swedish economy, are of course affected by one of their most important markets being plunged into a profound crisis. Asian banks in crisis have to withdraw resources from Russia, which makes problems for Brazilian banks and fund operators who have lent money in that direction, and so on. But international effects operate in both directions. Positive events in one country can produce positive effects elsewhere. The previous upturn

120. Yago & Goldman, 1998.

in Latin America and Asia contributed to good times in Europe and the USA. And very possibly it was the subsequently strong economy of the USA that saved the world from depression in connection with the Asian crisis and quickly pulled the Asian economies up again.

Instead of crisis

There are methods for avoiding financial and exchange rate crises, the most essential of them being for a country to have a healthy economic policy. The very first people to move their savings away from a country which subsequently experiences a massive exodus of capital are usually its own citizens, who have a front-seat view and most often know best which economic problems their rulers are attempting to conceal. This suggests that lack of confidence is brought about by real problems, not by ignorance and follow-my-leader. The top priority for crisis avoidance is for the government to have control of its finances and inflation. Galloping budgetary deficits and high inflation were not the problem during the Asian crisis, but they are definitely the commonest and fastest way of ruining confidence in an economy.

The most important long-term commitments for new economies are reforms of legal and financial institutions. Countries should liberalise their domestic financial markets and their trade policy before opening up to foreign capital, otherwise the capital will not be channelled in harmony with the market, and will thus lead to malinvestment. Supervision and regulation of the financial sector have to be reformed and competition permitted. Corruption and nepotism must be weeded out and superseded by the rule of law and capital yield requirements. Given the capacity of ignorance for causing panic in critical situations, much depends on reliable information and the transparency of national and corporate dealings, something which many Asian governments have deliberately obstructed. Credit valuation and bankruptcy laws, which in reality have been lacking in many Asian countries, have to be introduced. The global community could provide effective counselling on the building up of national financial markets. Rules of accounting and capital coverage requirements can be co-ordinated and agreements introduced on the management of financial crises from one instance to another; up till now, such management has been pretty arbitrary.

It is true that the liberalisation of financial markets has sometimes been followed by financial crises. The trouble, however, is not liberalisation as such but the absence of necessary concomitant institutions. The Indo-American economist Jagdish Bhagwati is one of those who have pointed out that liberalisation of capital flows can create problems if it precedes other important reforms. His solution is not capital controls but the countries first creating political stability, free trade and domestic reforms, such as privatisation, before attempting to liberalise their financial markets.[121] In practice, though, liberalisation, which comes easier, has often preceded domestic reforms, which can be a slower process and are often obstructed by vested interests. The IMF is much to blame for deregulations previously having occurred without the necessary preconditions being in place. Two journalists on *The Economist* have compared the IMF's advocates of capital mobility to a keen salesman in a pet shop declaring that a dog is wonderful company, while forgetting to explain that in order to survive it must be fed and taken for walks.[122]

Nowadays the IMF devotes more effort to advice on the creation of good institutions in the long term, and governments have become interested listeners. This is a very important task, but these reforms demand long-term work of a none too glamorous nature. Shouting for capital controls and a Tobin tax, however misguided it may be, can appear easier and more exciting. The rational quick-fix reform in this spirit is the abolition of controlled exchange rates. James Tobin, the

---

121. Bhagwati 1998.

122. Micklethwait & Wooldridge 2000, p. 178.

author of the eponymous tax, has himself pointed to fixed exchange rates as perhaps the principal cause of the Asian crisis.[123]

It is fixed exchange rates that give speculators something to speculate against. As soon as economic problems, a suspicion of devaluation or an inflationary policy occur, the exchange rate is perceived as too high. The market then thinks that the currency is not worth the price which the government has put on it. With a fixed exchange rate, speculators can earn vast amounts by borrowing in the currency and selling it to the central bank. An excessive exchange rate in relation to supply and demand, and to what the currency will be worth after the likely devaluation, amounts to a huge subsidisation of speculation and of exchange crises. Wrong pricing is not compatible with openness to movements of capital, and the only question is whether the prices or the movements of capital are wrong. Speculators selling local currency when the central bank pays over the odds for it is no stranger than thousands of Europeans growing sugar beet when the EU pays over the odds for it.

When the fixed exchange rate is too high, it is already too late, whatever governments may do. Either they defend the exchange rate, at colossal expense, emptying their reserves and raising interest rates as a result, which amounts to a stranglehold on the economy, or else they let the value of their currency fall steeply to the market level, in which case the country's industry is unable to repay big loans which it contracted at the higher exchange rate. Either way, crisis follows. This is what happened in, for example, Sweden and Great Britain in 1992, Mexico 1994, Southeast Asia 1997, Russia 1998 and Brazil in

---

123. Interviewed by Radio Australia on 17th November 1998, Tobin said: "My own feeling is that it's a great mistake for developing economies to try to have fixed exchange rates. ... The three big currencies – the dollar, the yen and the Deutsche Mark (soon to be the Euro) – have floating rates, and we don't have exchange rate crises among them. I don't know why we insist on having fixed exchange rates for Korea and Thailand and so on. But that creates crises ..." See also Tobin 1998.

1999. Since then, most big growth markets have abandoned fixed exchange rates, with a few exceptions, as Turkey and Argentina. No wonder then, that those two countries were hit by crisis in 2001.

In this connection, two analysts of the Asian crisis point out:

> *We are not aware of an example of a significant financial or currency crisis in an emerging market with fully flexible exchange rates.*

By contrast, crisis is a regular concomitant of fixed exchange rates. In another study, two economists point out that practically all fixed exchange rate arrangements, sooner or later, have been hit by exchange rate crises.[124]

---

124. Concerning variable exchange rates, see Radelet & Sachs 1999, p. 13. Fixed exchange rates: Obstfeld & Rogoff 1995.

The dictatorship of the market?

There is one objection to free financial markets which transcends the economic arguments. Critics of globalisation see them as a threat to democracy. With free markets, capital and businesses can quickly move across national boundaries if they are dissatisfied with the policy pursued. Swedish-Finnish enterprises like MeritaNordbanken and StoraEnso are legally based in Helsinki to avoid Swedish double taxation. When Sweden had a heavy budgetary deficit, the country was punished with elevated interest rates. All these things, the critics reason, imply that markets are beginning to steer politics, and they go so far as to speak of a "dictatorship of the market".

This is a mockery of a slogan, relativising the crimes of real dictatorships and attempting to join together two phenomena which are opposites rather than running mates. The first country to introduce a non-convertible currency – that is, one which its citizens were not allowed to exchange for other currencies – was probably the extremely protectionist nazi Germany. The communist governments actually regarded dictatorship as a precondition for the command economy. Shifts of power and a free debate would upset long-term government planning and were only compatible with the liberal market, in which individuals decide for themselves. In contrast, new democracies invariably choose, as one of their first actions, to open up their markets and liberalise the economy.

The converse also applies. In the long run it is hard for dictatorships accepting economic freedom to avoid political liberty as well. In country after country during recent decades, we have seen rulers who have granted their citizens the right to choose goods and invest freely also being forced to give them a free choice of government. This happened to the Southeast Asian and Latin American dictatorships. Mexico's single-party state collapsed a few years after the country had opted for free trade, Suharto's dictatorship collapsed like a house of cards in the wake of the Asian crisis, and now we can see some of the first democratic power shifts to have taken place in Africa, in the very states which have committed themselves to more open markets.

People who grow richer, are better educated and are accustomed to choice, will not acquiesce in others deciding matters on their behalf, and so the market economy often leads to democracy and democracy consolidates the market economy. When groups which were previously excluded acquire a political voice, it becomes less easy for the élite to feather its nest at their expense. This leads to more economic liberalisation measures, which reduce poverty and, consequently, strengthen democracy. A decentralised economic system makes possible the establishment of groups independent of the political power, which in turn is a basis for political pluralism. International surveys of economic freedom have shown that citizens who are entitled to trade internationally are roughly four times likelier to enjoy political democracy than those who do not have this right. This is partly why democratic activists in China want their country to join the World Trade Organisation: that way transparency and decentralisation lie, added to which, a dictatorship which has always acted tyrannically and arbitrarily will be obliged to conform to an impartial international code.

Commenting on the possibility of China opening up its economy, an imprisoned dissident said: "Before the sky was black. Now there is a light. This can be a new beginning."[125]

---

125. In China the advocates of WTO membership are often critics of the régime, reformists and liberals, while the opponents are to be found among the big corporations, the security service and the army. Cit. Pomfret & Laris 1999. Concerning opposition from old forces, see Pomfret 2000.

The 20th century clearly showed that no economic system but capitalism is compatible with democracy. This being so, any talk of a "dictatorship of the market" is not only insulting but abysmally ignorant.

It is true that a debtor is unfree. By contracting a budget deficit and debts, a country incurs the market's suspicion. Reforms have to be introduced to restore confidence in the national economy, otherwise the outside world will demand higher rates of interest on additional loans, or else, quite simply, stop lending. In this way a state, like Sweden at the beginning of the 90s, can find itself "in the hands of the market". But the government is to blame for this, not the market. If the government mismanages its finances and will not finance its expenditure out of its own funds, but with the market's, then it has decided to make itself dependent on the market.

The international financial markets were actually created by welfare states wishing to borrow for their expenditure during the crises of the 1970s. This was a way of increasing their scope for manoeuvre. Without financial markets the government would be forced to cut its cloth according to its yard – to live according to its means – while with financial markets the expenditure can be put off until later. In this way a policy which is credible and stable has a much wider range of options than before financial markets existed. But lenders have good historical reasons for distrusting states with a large national debt. Often those states have unilaterally reduced, by means of high inflation or devaluation – which reduces the value of a currency – the amounts which lenders can claim. So financial markets have cause to keep a watchful eye on the doings of governments and not to grant such favourable terms to those who do not seem to be making ends meet. But creditors lending money on their own terms cannot be likened to dictatorship. Governments are still at liberty to mismanage their economies, the only thing is that they cannot force others to finance the mismanagement.

Capitalism and democracy go hand in hand

Degree of economic freedom and democratic rights in 46 countries studied

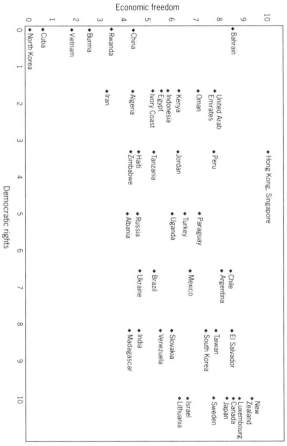

Source: Donway 2000.

255

"When national debts have once been accumulated to a certain degree, there is scarce, I believe, a single instance of their having been fairly and completely paid. The liberation of the public revenue, if it has ever been brought about by a bankruptcy; sometimes by an avowed one, but always by a real one, though frequently by a pretended payment."
Adam Smith 1776[126]

The market's assessment is often progressive. The Latin American dictatorships fell during the 1980s when the market abandoned their deeply indebted, crisis-ridden economies. Post-crisis, most of the Asian states are committed to openness and democratisation. Because they need information and the rule of law, investors hate secretiveness and corruption like poison. There is no better way of driving capital out of a country than suspicions of malpractice among the political élite. And there are few attractions so powerful as transparency, insight and illumination in the public sphere.

To some people, the very idea of the market passing judgement on politics is undemocratic. Lenders, as they see it, should keep quiet and willingly make their money available, even if governments look like blowing it all on inflation. By the same token, taxpayers placing their savings abroad is also undemocratic. But reacting to politics in order to protect one's interests is not anti-democratic, unless one equates democracy with total governmental control and implicit deference to the rulers of the nation. If so, then not only assessments by financial markets but also the compensatory pay claims put forward by trade unions and the close scrutiny undertaken by journalists are undemocratic. But this resembles a dictatorship insisting on total submission rather than a democracy based on civic liberty.[127]

---

126. Smith 1981, p. 929 f.

127. Svensson 2000.

What these critics really find threatened by the market is not democracy but the policy they want democracies to introduce, i.e. greater governmental power over people's economic decision-making. But, somehow, saying that the market threatens government control of our economic actions is less exciting than calling it a threat to democracy. And why should it be more democratic for a democratic government to have more powers of decision-making over us? Would Sweden be made more democratic by the government deciding whom we could marry, what work we could do or what we were entitled to write in a newspaper? Of course not. Democracy is a way to rule the state, not a way to rule society.

But if policy has to be changed owing to the demands of the market, this can sound like a threat to democracy. Suppose, for example, that the government has to abolish double taxation because otherwise companies will leave Sweden. This view again presupposes that people must always comply with political decisions and that the political process must have no other motive force than the conscious decision-making of government and parliament. But the normal state of affairs is that inspiration and challenges often come from outside, not from the politicians themselves. We acquired free radio and television broadcasting because technical progress threatened the old monopolies, and we acquired voting based on personal qualities because people are losing interest in politics, not as a result of politicians, of their own free will, making considered, long-term decisions on the subject. Democracy exists partly in order to adapt a country's policies to changing circumstances and new requirements, and this, when it happens, is not undemocratic. If it were, then all factors increasing the pressure of taxation and public spending more than political parties had promised would also be undemocratic. For example, the demands of pressure groups, the expansion by bureaucrats of their activities and efforts by politicians to keep their own party faithful happy. I have yet to hear anyone speak on this account of "the dictatorship of public spending".

257

The notion of the market forcing countries into a certain policy has, it seems to me, been created by craven politicians. Lacking the energy or the ability to justify economy measures or liberalisation measures they are taking, they declare them "necessary", forced upon them by globalisation. This is a handy cop-out, and a denigration of the market economy into the bargain.

There is reason to challenge the very premise of the argument that markets insist on a market-liberal policy. The players in the market do not demand a liberal ideology in order to "reward" a country with their localisation decisions, but they do require a well-ordered economy which is not on the verge of collapse. You yourself would hardly put your money into a pension fund which invested according to the degree of liberalisation rather than by economic criteria. And so the market's rating of the policy pursued is one reason for the good news of more and more countries having diminishing budgetary deficits, low inflation and low rates of interest. If the economy is equally well-ordered, investors will not treat a social democratic welfare state less well than a neo-liberal night watchman state. One of the world's most globalised countries is Sweden, which also happens to have the world's highest taxes. The past two decades of globalisation have witnessed an expansion of government machinery. Between 1980 and 1995, taxation in all the countries of the world rose from 22.6 to 25.9 per cent of their GDP, and public spending rose from 25.7 to 29.1 per cent of GDP.[128]

The fact of people and businesses being able to move freely does not necessarily mean that they will immediately relocate where taxes are lowest. They will move to wherever they feel that they get best value for their tax money. If citizens feel that they are getting security and service which are worth the money they pay in taxes, they will not leave the country. If businesses feel that they are getting research,

128. Larsson 2001a, p. 44.

258

education and infrastructure worth the money they pay in taxes, they will not leave the country either. It is only if taxes are used inefficiently or on things which people do not value (which does happen occasionally...) that they will cause problems in a world where we can move about more freely. It will be more difficult to maintain taxes which people feel give nothing in return. Which isn't exactly undemocratic, is it?

It may even be that globalisation augments the possibilities of maintaining the political system which the voters want, even if their choice falls on high taxes and a large public sector. This is because globalisation and free trade make it easier for us to obtain by exchange those things which our system disfavours, from countries with other systems. If the monopolisation of Swedish medical care disfavours the development of new technology and science in the medical sector, we can import these things from countries where the medical sector is more dynamic. If high taxes impede the emergence of broad financial markets, companies can procure capital in other countries. Globalisation enables countries to afford things they are not good at. There are of course problems with a certain policy, for example if a country's own citizens are denied opportunities and motive forces for education and production, so that they have nothing to trade with. But the main point is that the question whether or not we wish to have a certain political system, is something which we, the electorate, still decide on the basis of our values.

VII

Liberalise, don't standardise

The right to choose a culture

If children were forced to discover everything for themselves, they would develop very slowly. Happily they have parents who transmit their experience and things which they themselves have learned. In this way they can rapidly acquire knowledge which they could never have acquired on their own – what can be eaten, what is poisonous, how to find the centre of town and how to swim. One of the biggest advantages of globalisation is that young, new economies can learn from the older ones. Developing countries are not children and the industrialised countries are certainly not parents, but the economies of the industrialised nations have passed through the development which the developing countries have ahead of them. The developing countries which are growing today need not take as long to develop as the western world did. Instead they can take shortcuts and learn from our mistakes. Development which took Sweden 80 years to accomplish has been successfully reiterated by Taiwan in 25.

The developing countries can skip intermediate stages of development and benefit directly from the technology which is being produced, for example, in Europe and the USA. Mobile phones are a case in point. The developing countries need not incur the cost of constructing permanent telephone lines, they can utilise wireless technology. Mobile phones can, for example, be used by the poor to find out about prices of their goods. Many developing countries now have telephone rental companies, and villagers often club together for a mobile phone. This has meant steadier prices conforming to bigger markets and, due to more exact delivery times, less food wasted.

Halima Khatuun is an illiterate woman in a Bangladeshi village. She sells eggs to a dealer who comes by at regular intervals. She used to be compelled to sell at the price he proposed, because she did not have access to other buyers. But once, when he came and offered 12 taka for four eggs, she kept him waiting while she used the mobile phone to find out the market price in another village. Because the price there was 14 taka, she was able to go back and get 13 from the dealer. Market information saved her from being cheated.[129]

New information technology is now revolutionising old economic activities the world over. Hundreds of artisans, many of them women, in Morocco, Tunisia, Lebanon and Egypt who never had access to international markets before can now sell their products through an Internet network called Virtual Souk. Sales are climbing, and they are now able to retain a larger share of the earnings than was possible in the old markets.

Just as people in poor countries can perform service tasks for western companies by being on line to head office by satellite and the Internet, they can also obtain information. Thanks to the Internet, reliable medical advice and advanced education are no longer reserved for those living in the world's metropolitan cities. People may complain over the slowness of progress, with only about 5 per cent of the world's population, mostly in the affluent western countries, having access to the Internet, but this is to ignore the historical perspective. The Internet today is about 2,500 days old and has already reached one out of every twenty people on earth. This is the fastest spread of technology in world history. The telephone has existed for 125 years but even today, half the world's inhabitants have never made a phone call. This time things are moving with infinitely greater rapidity, and

---

129. World Bank 2000a, p. 73.

globalisation is the reason. One out of every ten families in Peking and Shanghai has a computer, and within a few years Chinese will be the web's biggest language.

The fact of the developing countries now being able to take "short-cuts" in development evokes the image of a common destination at the end of the road, one which all societies will be converging on. That picture troubles many people. They fear a "McDonaldisation" of the world, a standardisation in which everyone will end up wearing the same clothes, eating the same food and seeing the same films. But this is no accurate description of the globalisation process. Anyone going out in Stockholm today will of course have no trouble finding hamburgers and Coca-Cola, but just as easily we find kebab, sushi, Tex-Mex, Peking Duck, Thai, French cheeses or cappuccino. We know that Americans listen to Madonna and watch Bruce Willis films, but it occurs to us less often that this is also the country with 1,700 symphony orchestras, 7.5 million opera visits and 500 million museum visits a year.[130] Globalisation gives us not only docu-soaps and MTV but also classic films on Movie Channel, documentaries on Discovery and History Channel and news on CNN and CNBC. The masterpieces of music and literature are now just a few clicks away on the web, and the classics of cinema history are available in the video store round the corner.

With many reservations, one can say that developments are moving towards a common objective, but that objective is not the predominance of a particular culture. Instead it is pluralism, freedom to choose from a host of different paths and destinations. People's actual choices will then vary. Globalisation and greater exchange result, not in all the different countries choosing the same thing but in all options suddenly finding room in one country. When markets broaden and become international, this increases the prospects of even

---

130. Moore & Simon 2000, p. 218 f.

very narrow cultural manifestations surviving and flourishing. Perhaps not all that many Swedes are in the market for experimental electronic music or film versions of novels by Dostoevsky, and so the musicians and film makers concerned could never produce anything if they had only a Swedish audience to rely on. But even very narrow customer segments acquire purchasing power when combined with similar tastes in other countries. Globalisation can increase our chances of gaining access to exactly what we want, no matter how isolated we may feel in our liking for it. Moroccan folk art and French Roquefort cheese acquire better survival prospects when demand for them is aggregated worldwide. In this way the supply of goods and culture grows larger, coming from all four corners of the world. This is what makes people believe that differences are vanishing, because when you travel abroad things look almost the same as in their own countries: they too have goods and chains from different parts of the globe. But this is not due to uniformity and the elimination of differences but on the contrary, to a growth of pluralism everywhere. Americans are cultural leaders because they have been accustomed to producing commercially for a very large public (because of the language). Now other countries are being given the same chance.

This can be negative in certain situations, admittedly. When travelling to another country, we want to see something unique. Arriving in Rome and finding Hollywood films, Chinese food, Japanese Pokemon games and Swedish Volvo cars, we miss the local colour. And national specialities like pizza, pasta and espresso are already familiar to us, from our own locality. What we gain by being free to choose "everything" at home is that this makes it hard to find any place that feels really genuine, at least on the main tourist routes. This is a problem, but a luxury problem. A man from Prague was sometimes visited by Czech friends who had settled abroad. They deplored McDonald's having come to Prague, because it threatened the city's distinctive charm. This made the man indignant. How

265

could they regard his home city as a museum, a place for them to visit now and then in order to avoid fast food restaurants? He wanted a real city, including the convenient and inexpensive food which these exile Czechs themselves had access to. A real, living city cannot be a "Prague summer paradise" at the tourists' service. Other countries and populations do not exist in order to give us picturesque holiday experiences. They too are entitled like us to choose what they think suits them and that they feel in need of.[131]

Cultures change, and the greater the number of options, the faster change will be. If one can read about other lifestyles and values in the newspaper and see them on television, this may no longer be a very big step to take. But basically there is nothing new about cultures changing, colliding with each other and cross-pollinating. They always have done. Culture means cultivating, and change and renewal are inherent in the very definition. If we try to freeze certain cultural patterns in time and highlight them as distinctively Swedish, they cease to be culture. From being a part of ourselves they become museum relics and folklore. There is nothing wrong with that – museums can be pleasant places, but we can't live in one.

In a coming to terms with the idea of isolated and preserved culture, the Norwegian social anthropologist Thomas Hylland Eriksen has pointed out that culture is a process and therefore essentially unlimited:

When the government is to be the guarantor of the population's cultural identity, culture has to be defined and codified in the rigid administrative language of the bureaucracy. It ceases to be living, dynamic, changeable and manifold and becomes a package, a completed jigsaw puzzle from which none of the pieces can be removed without spoiling the picture.[132]

131. Goldberg 2000.

132. Hylland Eriksen 1999, p. 46.

Even what we experience as genuine traditions have generally resulted from cultural imports. Foreigners often find it hard to believe, but one of the most sacred Swedish traditions is that of watching Donald Duck on TV on Christmas Eve, and another, eleven days earlier, involved celebrating a Catholic Italian saint by adorning the hair of blonde girls with lighted candles. The Peruvian author Mario Vargas Llosa claims to have learned one thing from his lifelong studies of culture, French culture especially, which French politicians wish to protect with tariffs and subsidies:

> And the most important thing I have learned is that cultures do not need to be protected by bureaucrats and police forces or locked up behind bars or isolated by customs boundaries in order to survive and remain vigorous. They must live in the open, exposed to constant comparison with other cultures which enrich and renew them, enable them to develop and adapt to the constant flow of life. The threat to Flaubert and Debussy comes, not from the dinosaurs of Jurassic Park, but rather from the gang of small-time demagogues and chauvinists who speak of French culture as though it were a mummy which cannot be taken out of its chamber because fresh air would cause it to disintegrate.[133]

The cultural encounters of globalism reduce the risk of people being trapped in their culture. This may come as bad news to the guardians of tradition, but many people can imagine no greater triumph than escaping from the stereotypes and constraints of their own culture. This may be necessary in order to escape hidebound gender roles, to be allowed to live according to one's own values or to break the family tradition and enter an education of one's own choosing. Having other cultural expressions near one is a help. How can the élite maintain that their own way of life is the only possible one, with television

---

133. Vargas Llosa 1993.

and the computer carrying information about an infinite number of alternatives? How can the government insist on traditional family patterns when negotiating trade agreements with openly homosexual ministers in other countries? Regularly meeting people who do not think and live like oneself is an effective antidote to narrow-mindedness and smugness.

The British sociologist Anthony Giddens provides a striking illustration from his own recollections of how oppressive the one and only solutions of tradition can be:

> *If ever I am tempted to think that the traditional family might be best after all, I remember what my great aunt once said to me. She must have had one of the longest marriages of anyone, having been with her husband for over 60 years. She once confided that she had been deeply unhappy with him the whole of that time. In her day there was no escape.*[134]

There is no universal formula to show how much modernisation one must accept and how many traditions are to be preserved. This is why every balance has to be struck by people themselves. This can mean, but need not mean, earlier forms of culture dying out. Now that other people not born to the culture can gain access to it, its survival prospects are augmented in a different way – not by force of habit but by deliberate choice. The author Salman Rushdie has remarked that it is trees, not human beings, that have roots.

---

134. Giddens 1999, p. 66.

The onward march of freedom

Openness to influences makes it easy for the most tempting and convincing ideas to spread. This is why the idea of freedom and individualism has attained such tremendous force in the age of globalism. There are few ideas as inspiring as that of self-determination. When it is discovered that people in other countries have that right, it becomes almost irresistible. A dash of freedom to receive new impressions and to choose quickly leads people to make new demands for being allowed to choose and decide for themselves. This is why people who are allowed to enjoy economic freedom demand political democracy as well, and why those attaining democracy demand individual liberty. The idea of human rights is travelling the globe. If there is any elimination of differences in progress throughout the world, it is that societies are moving towards democratisation, more and more are being allowed to live as they please. The similarity consists in more and more people being allowed to be dissimilar.

"That contempt in which lower castes used to be held is almost disappearing completely. Now it is obvious for me to know that everyone, untouchables included, is a human being, with the same human dignity as myself. We all have the same colour blood."
The old Indian farmer Ram Vishal, himself of intermediate caste.[135]

---

135. Berg & Karlsson 2000, p. 51.

So much for ideas of cultural relativism, to the effect that certain peoples cannot cope with freedom, that they need a period of strong leaders, or that one cannot be entitled to interfere with other countries' policies. If other governments oppress, or even exterminate, their citizens, we are entitled, perhaps even duty bound, to combat this. The notion of human dignity meaning different things on different sides of frontiers has been badly dented. Even though it did not result in prosecution, a milepost was passed when a Spanish prosecutor prevailed on the British authorities to arrest former Chilean dictator Pinochet while he was visiting the UK. It was also logical that Cuban dictator Castro was furious over the decision, even though he has a different political complexion. He appreciated that the world now held fewer hiding places for dictators. Today dictators and mass murderers who, as little as a decade ago, could freely travel the world, now risk being hauled in front of war crimes tribunals and international courts. This in turn has spurred national judicial systems, which shows that the international measures supplement rather than supersede local law. In Rome in 1998 an agreement was signed for the setting up of an international criminal court to administer justice at global level concerning crimes against humanity, genocide and war crimes. More and more countries are acceding, and the court can start operating within a couple of years. In future perhaps crimes against humanity will not pay.

The future is not predetermined. There is no "single path" and there is nothing forcing us to accept globalisation. The anti-globalists are perfectly right about that. Capital can be locked up, trade flows blocked and frontiers barricaded. This has happened once before, following the globalisation of the late 19th century. The world had then experienced several decades of democratisation and greater openness. People could cross frontiers without passports and find jobs without work permits, and could easily become citizens of the country where they settled. But, following decades of anti-liberal propaganda and nationalistic sabre-rattling, this was replaced at the beginning of the 20th century by centralisation and closed frontiers. Countries which were really friends in trade and in the creation of new values began seeing one another as enemies to be fought for old values. Markets were to be conquered by force, not through free competition. The outbreak of the First World War in 1914 marks the end of that period's globalisation. Protectionism and passport requirements were introduced for the first time in a couple of generations.

Globalisation brings with it numbers of problems in which suspicion is easily cast: painful economic adjustments, interests undermined, cultures which are challenged and traditional power centres which are eroded. When boundaries become less important, not only can people, goods and capital move more freely but so too, for example, can crime and disease. The adherents of globalisation have to show that greater freedom and greater opportunities counterbalance such problems, and they must point to the possibilities of dealing with them, perhaps more effectively than before. Otherwise there is a serious risk of anti-globalist ideas taking root in the western world, in which case a downturn or a trivial tariff war, for example, could evoke a powerful protectionist reaction. After the Wall Street Crash of 1929, the USA switched to a drastic policy of protectionism, and after that all it exported was depression. Other governments responded in kind, and world trade collapsed, diminishing by two-thirds in just three years. In this way a national crisis led to worldwide depression. The return of protectionism today would mean stagnation in the affluent world and deeper poverty in the developing countries. At worst it would once again lead to conflicts, to countries starting to regard each other as enemies. Governments turn in upon themselves, regarding what is foreign as a threat rather than an opportunity. When that happens, the simplest and coarsest forms of enclosure and nationalism will gain ground.

There is less risk of globalism crash-landing in the same way today.

Imperialist ambitions have been dashed and globalisation is based on a host of democratic governments. Ideas of democracy and human rights are becoming more and more influential, and Asia and Latin America are more closely integrated with the world economy than ever, by their own choice. Most countries aim for regulated, mutual trade agreements within, say, the WTO, so that powerful governments will not be able to crush free trade just like that. But even if democracy and the market should continue to spread, there is no single path for everyone. Countries like Burma and North Korea show that it is possible to cut oneself off from the global environment, so long as one is prepared to pay heavily for doing so in terms of oppression and poverty. Nor is there anything forcing the EU to liberalise our markets, if we are prepared to take the losses of freedom and prosperity this implies – and if we are prepared to let the poor of the developing countries suffer through our decision to retain tariff walls. It is not "necessary" to follow the globalisation trend, it is merely desirable. Globalisation will not keep moving under its own steam if no one stands up for it and if no one challenges isolationism.

All change arouses suspicion and anxiety, sometimes justifiably so – even positive changes can have troublesome consequences in the short term. Decision-makers are unwilling to shoulder responsibility for failures and problems. It is preferable to be able to blame someone else. Globalisation makes an excellent scapegoat. It contains all the anonymous forces which have served this purpose throughout history – other countries, the market, evasive decision-making. Globalisation does not contradict when politicians blame it for overturning economies, increasing poverty and enriching a tiny minority, or when entrepreneurs say that it is globalisation, rather than their own decisions, which force them to pollute the environment, axe jobs or – raise their own salaries. And globalisation does not harvest any good will when good things happen, when the environment improves, the economy runs at high speed and poverty diminishes. Then there are plenty of people willing to accept full responsibility for the course of events. Globalisation does not defend itself. So if the trend towards greater globalisation is to continue, an ideological defence will be needed for freedom from frontiers and controls.

In 25 years' time there are likely to be two billion more of us on this planet. 97 per cent of that population increase will occur in the developing countries. There are no automatic, predetermined processes deciding what sort of a world they will experience and what their opportunities will be. Most will depend on what people like you and me believe, think and fight for.

***

In the Chinese village of Tau Hua Lin, Lasse Berg and Stig Karlsson meet people who describe the change that has occurred in ways of thinking since they were last there: "The last time you were here, people's thoughts and minds were closed, bound up," Yang Zhengming, one of the farmers, explains. But when they acquired power over their own land, they became entitled, for the first time, to decide something for themselves. Even a modest freedom like that was revolutionary. They were forced to think for themselves, to think along new lines, they were allowed to start thinking more about themselves and their loved ones instead of the leader's dictates. Individuals are not means to a higher end, they are the end in itself. Yang goes on to say that "a farmer could then own himself. He did not need to submit. He decided himself what he was going to do, how and when. The proceeds of his work were his own. It was freedom that came to us. We were allowed to think for ourselves." The author Lasse Berg sums up his impressions in a more universal observation:

It is not only inside the Chinese that a Chinese wall is now being torn down. Something similar is happening all over the world, in Bihar,

East Timor, Ovamboland. Human beings are discovering that the individual is entitled to be his own. This has by no means been self-evident before. The discovery engenders a longing, not only for freedom but also for the good things in life, for prosperity.[136]

It is this mentality which, all reservations notwithstanding, must inspire optimism. We have not travelled the full distance, coercion and poverty still cover large areas of our globe. Great set-backs can and will occur. But people who know that living in a state of oppression and ignorance is not a natural necessity will no longer accept this as the only conceivable state of affairs. People who realise that they are not merely the tools of society and the collective but are ends in themselves will not be submissive. People who have acquired a taste for freedom will not consent to be shut in with walls and fences. They will work to create a better existence for themselves and to improve the world we live in. They will demand freedom and democracy. The aim of politics should be to give them that freedom.

136. Berg & Karlsson 2000, pp. 162–171.

References

Ades, Alberto F & Glaeser, Edward L, "Evidence on Growth, Increasing Returns, and the Extent of the Market," in *Quarterly Journal of Economics*, vol 114, No 3, August 1999.

Altenberg, Per & Kleen, Peter, *Globalisering under attack*. Stockholm: SNS, 2001.

Anderson, Kym, Hoekman, Bernard & Strutt, Anna, *Agriculture and the WTO : Next Steps*. Washington, DC: World Bank/CEPR, August 1999, (http://wbweb4.worldbank.org/wbiep/trade/papers_2000/ag-rie-sept.pdf)

Aronsson, Gunnar & Gustafsson, Klas, "Kritik eller tystnad : en studie av arbetsmarknads- och anställningsförhållandens betydelse för arbetsmiljökritik," in *Arbetsmarknad & Arbetsliv*, No 3 1999.

Attac: "Platform of the association Attac," June 3rd, 1998, (http://www.attac.org/fra/asso/doc/plateformeen.htm)

Bajpai, Nirupam & Sachs, Jeffrey, *The Progress of Policy Reform and Variations in Performance at the Sub-National Level in India*. Cambridge, MA: Harvard Institute for International Development, 1999 (Development Discussion paper No 730).

Barnevik, Percy, *Global Forces of Change : Lecture at the 1997 International Industrial Conference*. San Francisco, September 29th, 1997.

Bartlett, Bruce, "The Truth About Trade in History," in *Freedom To Trade : Refuting the New Protectionism*. Washington, DC: Cato Institute, 1997.

Bastiat, Frédéric, *Det man ser och det man inte ser*. (A selection of essays by Frédéric Bastiat.) Stockholm: Timbro, 1999.

Bellamy, Carol, *The State of World's Children 1997*. New York: UNICEF, 1997, (http://www.unicef.org/sowc97/)

Ben-David, Dan & Winters, L Alan, *Trade, Income Disparity and Poverty*. Geneva: WTO, 2000 (WTO Special Study No 5, 2000), (http://www.wto.org/english/news_e/pres00_e/pr181_e.htm)

Berg, Lasse & Karlsson, Stig T, *I Asiens tid : Indien, Japan, Kina 1966–1999*. Stockholm: Ordfront, 2000.

Berggren, Niclas, "Economic Freedom and Equality : Friends or Foes?," in *Public Choice* (Vol 100) 1999.

Bhagwati, Jagdish, *Protectionism*. Cambridge, MA: MIT Press, 1988.

–, "Why Free Capital Mobility May be Hazardous to Your Health : Lessons From the Latest Financial Crisis," paper presented at the NBER Conference on capital controls in Cambridge, MA, November 7th, 1998, (http://www.columbia.edu/~jb38/papers/NBER_comments.pdf)

Bigsten, Arne & Levin, Jörgen, *Tillväxt, inkomstfördelning och fattigdom i u-länderna*. Stockholm: Globkom, September 2000, (http://www.globkom.net/rapporter.phtml)

Burnside, Craig & Dollar, David, "Aid, Policies, and Growth," in *American Economic Review*, Vol 90 (September 2000) No 4.

Burtless, Gary, Lawrence, Robert & Shapiro, Robert, *Globaphobia : Confronting Fears about Open Trade*. Washington, DC: Brookings Institution, 1998.

Cassen, Bernard, "Who are the Winners, and Who are the Losers of Globalisation?," speech in London June 17th, 2000 at The Amis UK Conference "Globalization in Whose Interest?," Conway Hall, London.

–, (2001a), interview by Lars Mogensen, "ATTAC lider af børne-sygdomme," in Danish *Information*, February 23rd, 2001.

–, (2001b), interview by John Einar Sandvand, "Globalisering kun til besvær," in Norwegian *Aftenposten*, March 2nd, 2001.

Clinell, Bim, *Attac : gräsrötternas revolt mot marknaden*. Stockholm: Agora, 2000.

Cox, W Michael & Alm, Richard, *Myths of Rich and Poor : Why We're Better Off than We Think*. New York: Basic Books, 1999.

Crook, Clive, "Third World Economic Development," in David Henderson (ed), *The Fortune Encyclopedia of Economics*. New York: Warner Books, 1993.

Dasgupta, Susmita, Mody, Ashoka, Roy, Subhendu & Wheeler, David, *Environmental Regulation and Development : A Cross-Country Empirical Analysis*. Washington, DC: World Bank, March 1995 (Working Paper).

Deininger, Klaus & Olinto, P, *Asset Distribution, Inequality and Growth*. Washington, DC: World Bank, 2000 (RP, 2375).

–, & Squire, Lyn, "New Ways of Looking at the Old Issues : Asset Inequality and Growth," in *Journal of Development Economics*, Vol 57 (1998), pp 259–87.

Demery, Lionel & Squire, Lyn, "Macroeconomic Adjustment and Poverty in Africa : An Emerging Picture," in *The World Bank Research Observer*, Vol 11, No 1, February 1996.

Dollar, David & Kraay, Aart (2000a), *Growth is Good for the Poor*. Washington, DC: World Bank, March 2000 (forthcoming Working Paper), http://www.worldbank.org/research/growth/pdfiles/growthgoodforpoor.pdf

–, (2000b), *Property Rights, Political Rights, and the Development of Poor Countries in the Post-Colonial Period*. Washington, DC: World Bank, 2000 (Preliminary draft, October 2000).

–, *Trade, Growth and Poverty*. Washington, DC: World Bank, 2001 (Preliminary Draft, January 2001).

Donway, Roger, "Lands of Liberty," in *Navigator*, No 4, 2000.

Easterly, William, *How Did Highly Indebted Countries Become Highly Indebted? Reviewing Two Decades of Debt Relief*. Washington, DC: World Bank, 1999 (World Bank Working Paper 2225) (http://wbln0018.worldbank.org/Research\workpapers.nsf/View+to+Link+WebPages/FEACC810073AEEAC8525682C005C94C4?OpenDocument)

Edwards, James Rolph, "The Myth of Capital Power," in *Liberty*, January 2001.

Edwards, Sebastian, *Openness, Productivity and Growth*. Cambridge, MA: NBER, National Bureau of Economic Research, 1997 (Working Paper 5978).

–, "A Capital Idea?," in *Foreign Affairs*, May/June 1999.

Ehnmark, Anders, *Minnets hemlighet : en bok om Erik Gustaf Geijer*. Stockholm: Norstedts, 1999.

Eichengreen, Barry & Mussa, Michael et al, *Capital Account Liberalization : Theoretical and Practical Aspects*. Washington, DC: IMF, 1998.

Eklund, Klas, "Globala kapitalrörelser," chapter from the anthology *Välfärd, politik och ekonomi i en ny värld*. Stockholm: Arbetar-rörelsens Ekonomiska Råd, 1999.

Elmbrant, Björn, *Hyperkapitalismen*. Stockholm: Atlas 2000.

Eriksen, Thomas Hylland, *Kulturterrorismen : en uppgörelse med tanken om kulturell renhet*. Nora: Nya Doxa, 1999.

Fakta och myter om globalisering : en artikelserie ur The Economist. Stockholm: Timbro, 1998. ("School Briefs on Globalization", from *The Economist*, Autumn 1997.)

Featherstone, Liza & Henwood, Doug, "Clothes Encounters : Activists and Economists Clash over Sweatshops," in *Lingua Franca*, Vol 11, No 2, March 2001.

Forrester, Viviane, *The Economic Horror*. Oxford: Polity Press, 1999.

François, Joseph, Glismann, Hans H & Spinanger, Dean, *The Cost of EU Trade Protection in Textiles and Clothing*. Stockholm: The Ministry for Foreign Affairs, March 2000.

Frankel, Jeffrey & Romer, David, "Does Trade Growth Cause Growth?," in *The American Economic Review*, Vol 89, No 3, June 1999.

Freedom House, *Freedom in the World 2000–2001*. New York: Freedom House, 2001, (http://www.freedomhouse.org/research/freeworld/2001/essay1.htm)

Freedom House, "Democracy's Century : A Survey of Global Politial Change in the 20th Century". New York: Freedom House, 2000, (http://www.freedomhouse.org/reports/century.pdf)

Friedman, Thomas L, *The Lexus and the Olive Tree : Understanding Globalization*. New York: HarperCollins, 1999.

Gallup, John Luke, Radelet, Steven & Warner, Andrew, *Economic Growth and the Income of the Poor*. Cambridge, MA: Harvard Institute for International Development, November 1998 (CAER II Discussion Paper no 36), (http://www.hiid.harvard.edu/caer2/htm/content/papers/confpubs/paper36/paper36.htm)

George, Susan, interview by Bim Clinell, "Dom kallar oss huliganer," in *Ordfront*, No 12, 2000.

Ghose, Ajit K, *Trade Liberalization and Manufacture Employment*. Geneva: International Labour Office, 2000 (Employment Paper

2000/3), (http://www.ilo.org/public/english/employment/strat/publ/ep00-3.htm)

Giddens, Anthony, *Runaway World : How Globalization is Reshaping our Lives*. London: Profile Books, 1999.

Goldberg, Jonah, "The Specter of McDonald's : An Object of Bottomless Hatred," in *National Review*, June 5th, 2000.

Goldsmith, Arthur, *Institutions and Economic Growth in Africa*. Cambridge, MA: Harvard Institute for International Development, 1998 (African Economic Policy Paper, Discussion paper No 7, July 1998), (http://www.eagerproject.com/discussion7.shtml)

Greenhouse, Steven & Khan, Joseph, "Workers' Rights : U S Effort to Add Labor Standards to Agenda Fails," in *New York Times*, December 3rd, 1999.

Grossman, Gene M & Krueger, Alan B, *Economic Growth and the Environment*. Cambridge, MA: National Bureau of Economic Research, 1994 (Working Paper 4634).

Gunnarsson, Christer & Rojas, Mauricio, *Tillväxt, stagnation, kaos : en institutionell studie av underutvecklingens orsaker och utvecklingens möjligheter*. Stockholm: SNS, 1997.

Gwartney, James, Lawson, Robert & Samida, Dexter (eds), *Economic Freedom of the World 2000*. Vancouver: Fraser Institute, 2000, (http://www.fraserinstitute.ca/publications/books/econ_free_2000/)

–, Lawson, Robert, Park, Walter & Skipton, Charles (eds), *Economic Freedom of the World 2000*. Vancouver: Fraser Institute, 2001,

(http://www.fraserinstitute.ca/publications/books/efw_2001/)

Hammar, K G, Motika, Dositej, Andersson, Krister, Thordson, Thord-Ove & Molin, Lennart, "Kd-ledaren ohederlig," in *Dagens Nyheter*, October 1st, 2000.

–, interview by Håkan A Bengtsson & Per Wirtén, "Att vända maktens pyramider," in *Arena*, No 6/2000.

Hansson, Åsa, *Limits of Tax Policy*. Lund: The University, 2000 (Lund Economic Studies. 90).

Hedström, Ingrid & Stenberg, Ewa, "Flyktingar får inte chansen att söka asyl," in *Dagens Nyheter*, March 11th, 2001.

Hertel, Thomas W & Martin, Will, *Would Developing Countries Gain from Inclusion of Manufactures in the WTO Negotiations?* Geneva: WTO, Centre William Rappard, 1999, (Paper presented at the WTO/World Bank Conference on Developing Countries in a Millennium Round, September 20–21st, 1999), (http://www.itd.org/wb/hertel.doc)

Hirst, Paul & Thompson, Grahame, *Globalization in Question*. Cambridge, UK: Polity Press, 1996.

Horesh, Ronnie, "Trade and Agriculture : The Unimportance of Being Rational," in *New Zealand Orchardist*, April 2000.

Illarionov, Andrei, "Russia's Potemkin Capitalism," in Ian Vásquez (ed), *Global Fortune*. Washington, DC: Cato, 2000.

Jaffe, Adam B, Peterson, Steven R, Portney, Paul R & Stavins,

Robert, "Environmental Regulation and the Competitiveness of U S Manufacturing : What Does the Evidence Tell Us?," in *Journal of Economic Literature*, Vol 33, No 1, March 1995.

Klein, Naomi, *No Logo : Taking Aim at the Brand Bullies*. London: Flamingo Books, 2000.

Kuznets, Simon, "Economic Growth and Income Inequality," in *American Economic Review*, Vol 45, March 1955, p 26.

Larsson, Tomas, "Asia's Crisis of Corporatism," in Vásquez, Ian (ed), *Global Fortune*. Washington, DC: Cato, 2000.

–, *Falska mantran : globaliseringsdebatten efter Seattle*. Stockholm: Timbro, 2001a, (http://www.timbro.se/bokhandel/pdf/75664801.pdf)

–, *The Race to the Top : The Real Story of Globalization*. Washington, DC: Cato, 2001b.

Leufstedt, Sofia & Voltaire, Fredrik, *Vad säger empirin om skatter och sysselsättning?* Stockholm: Svensk Handel, September 1998, (http://beta.svenskhandel.se/Filer/empiri.pdf)

Llosa, Mario Vargas, "Konstnärliga verk är också varor," in *Dagens Nyheter*, October 28th, 1993.

Lomborg, Bjørn, *The Sceptical Environmentalist : Measuring the Real State of the World*. Cambridge: Cambridge University Press, 2001.

Low, Patrick, Olarrega, Marcelo & Suarez, Javier, *Does Globalization Cause a Higher Concentration of International Trade and Investment Flows?* Geneva: World Trade Organization, 1998 (WTO Staff

Working Paper ERAD).

Lukas, Aaron, *Globalization and Developing Countries*. Washington, DC: CATO Institute, 2000 (WTO Report Card III, Trade Briefing Paper), (http://www.freetrade.org/pubs/briefs/tbp-010.pdf)

Maddison, Angus, *Monitoring the World Economy 1820–1992*. Paris: Development Centre of the Organisation for Economic Co-operation and Development, 1995.

Martin, Hans-Peter & Schumann, Harald, *The Global Trap : Globalization and the Assault on Prosperity and Democracy*. London: Zed Books, 1997.

Mausz, Steven J & Tarr, David, *Adjusting to Trade Policy Reform*. Washington, DC: World Bank, 1999 (Working Paper), (http://www.worldbank.org/html/dec/Publications/Workpapers/wps 2000series/wps2142/wps2142.pdf)

McNulty, Sheila, "Investors Lose Faith in Malaysia's Weak Reforms," in *Financial Times*, January 17th, 2001.

Melchior, Arne, Telle, Kjetil & Wiig, Henrik, *Globalisering och ulikhet: Verdens inntektsfordeling og levestandard 1960–1998.* Oslo: Royal Norwegian Ministry of Foreign Affairs, 2000. Also in an abridged English version: *Globalization and Inequality : World Income Distribution and Living Standards, 1960–1998.* (Studies on Foreign Policy Issues, Report 6:B, 2000) (http://xodin.dep.no/ud/ engelsk/publ/rapporter/032001-990349/index-dok000-b-n-a.html)

Messerlin, Patrick, *Measuring the Costs of Protection in Europe*. Washington, DC: Institute for International Economics, 2001.

Micklethwait, John & Wooldridge, Adrian, *A Future Perfect*. New York: Random House, 2000.

Moore, Stephen & Simon, Julian L, *It's Getting Better All the Time : Greatest Trends of the Last 100 Years*. Washington DC: Cato, 2000.

Norberg, Johan & Röttorp, Paula Werenfels, *Från Lutherhjälpen till skyltfönsterkrossare – en kartläggning av frihandelsmotståndet*. New rev ed. Stockholm: Svensk Handel, 2001, (http://beta.svenskhandel.se/Filer/frihandel2.pdf)

Nordin, Ingemar, *Etik, teknik och samhälle*. Stockholm: Timbro, 1992.

Nordström, Håkan, *The Trade and Development Debate : An Introductory Note with Emphasis on WTO Issues*. Stockholm: Kommittén om Sveriges politik för global utveckling, Globkom, March 2000, (http://www.globkom.net/rapporter.phtml)

–, & Vaughan, Scott, *Trade and Environment*. Geneva: WTO publications, 1999 (WTO Special Study).

Obstfeld, Maurice & Rogoff, Kenneth, "The Mirage of Fixed Exchange Rates," in *Journal of Economic Perpectives*, Fall 1995.

O'Driscoll, Gerald P Jr, Holmes, Kim R & Kirkpatrick, Melanie, *The 2001 Index of Economic Freedom*. Washington, DC: Heritage Foundation & Wall Street Journal, 2001, (http://www.heritage.org/index/2001/)

OECD, *Survey of OECD Work on International Investment*. Paris: OECD, 1998 (Working Paper on International Investment).

OECD, *International Trade and Core Labour Standards*. Paris: OECD, 2000.

Overseas Development Institute, *Developing Countries in the WTO*. London: Overseas Development Institute, 1995 (Briefing Paper 3).

Oxfam, "The Clothes Trade in Bangladesh" (Internet article). Oxford: Oxfam, (http://www.oxfam.org.uk/campaign/clothes/clobanfo.htm)

Pagrotsky, Leif, "Varför en ny WTO-runda?," speech at the EU committee's WTO-hearing, November 25th, 1999.

Pomfret, John, "Chinese Are Split Over WTO Entry," in *Washington Post*, March 13th, 2000.

–, & Laris, Michael, "Chinese Liberals Welcome WTO Bid," in *Washington Post*, November 18th, 1999.

Radelet, Steven & Sachs, Jeffrey, *What Have We Learned, So Far, From the Asian Financial Crisis?* Cambridge, MA: Harvard Institute for International Development, 1999 (CAER II discussion paper No 37, March), (http://www.hiid.harvard.edu/caer2/htm/content/papers/paper37/paper37.htm)

Radetzki, Marian, *Den gröna myten : ekonomisk tillväxt och miljöns kvalitet*. Stockholm: SNS, 2001.

Rand, Ayn, *Capitalism : The Unknown Ideal*. New York: New American Library, 1966.

Rankka, Maria, *Frihet med förhinder : in- och utvandring i vår tid*.

Stockholm: Timbro, 2000, (http://www.timbro.se/bokhandel/pdf/917566481x.pdf)

Rodriguez, Francisco & Rodrik, Dani, *Trade Policy and Economic Growth : A Skeptic's Guide to The Cross-National Evidence*. Cambridge, MA: National Bureau of Economic Research, 1999 (Working paper series 7081).

Rojas, Mauricio, *Millennium Doom : Fallacies About the End of Work*. London: Social Market Foundation, 1999.

Roodman, David, "Worldwatch Proposes $ 2 000 Tax Cut per Family to Save the Planet". Washington, DC: Worldwatch Institute, 1998 (Worldwatch Briefing, 12 september 1998), (http://www.worldwatch.org/alerts/pr980912.html)

Rosenberg, Nathan & Birdzell, L E Jr, *How the West Grew Rich : the Economic Transformation of the Industrial World*. New York: Basic Books, 1986.

Rudbeck, Carl, *Creole love call : kultur i den globala eran*. Stockholm: Timbro, 1998, (http://www.timbro.se/bokhandel/pejling/pdf/75663805.pdf)

Rädda Barnen, "Faktablad om barnarbete". http://www.raddabarnen.se/fakta/arbBarn2000/

Sachs, Jeffrey, "External Debt, Structural Adjustment, and Economic Growth," Paper addressed to the G-24 Research Group in Washington DC September 18th, 1996. Geneva: Intergovernmental Group of 24 on International Monetary Affairs.

–, & Warner, Andrew, "Economic Reform and the Process of Global Integration," i *Brookings Papers on Economic Activity*, 1995 No 1.

–, & Warner, Andrew, "Sources of Slow Growth in African Economies," in *Journal of African Economies*, Vol 6 (1997) No 3, pp 335–76.

Sally, Razeen, "Free Trade in Practice : Estonia in the 1990s," in *Central Europe Review*, No 27, 2000.

Scully, GW, *Constitutional Environments and Economic Growth*. Princeton, NJ: Princeton University Press, 1992.

Sen, Amartya, *Development as Freedom*. New York: Anchor Books, 1999.

Short, Clare, *Eliminating World Poverty : Making Globalisation Work for the Poor*. London: HMSO, 2000 (White Paper on International Development, December 2000), (http://www.globalisation.gov.uk/intro.htm)

Sifo, "Stress i arbetslivet, pensioner : en undersökning för Pensions-forum i januari 2001". Stockholm: Sifo, February 13th, 2001.

Simon, Julian, *The State of Humanity*. Oxford: Blackwell Publishers, 1995.

Smith, Adam, *An Inquiry Into the Nature and Causes of The Wealth of Nations*. Indianapolis: Liberty Classics, 1981.

de Soto, Hernando, *The Mystery of Capital : Why Capitalism Triumphs in the West and Fails Everywhere Else*. London: Bantam

Press, 2000.

Srinivasan, T N & Bhagwati, Jagdish, "Outward-Orientation and Development : are Revisionists Right?," in *Professor Anne Krueger Festschrift*. September 1999
(http://www.columbia.edu/~jb38/Krueger.pdf)

Svensson, Mattias, *Mer demokrati – mindre politik*. Stockholm: Timbro, 2000.
(http://www.timbro.se/bokhandel/pejling/pdf/75664666.pdf)

Tobin, James, "Financial Globalization : Can national Currencies Survive?," paper presented at *The Annual World Bank Conference on Development Economics April 20–21st, 1998*. Washington, DC: World Bank.

–, interview by Radio Australia November 17th, 1998.
(http://www.abc.gov.au/money/vault/extras/extra14.htm)

Todaro, Michael P, *Economic Development*. 6 ed. Reading, MA: Addison Wesley Longman, 1997.

UNDP, *Human Development Report 1997*. New York: Oxford University Press for the United Nations Development Programme (UNDP), 1997.

Vásquez, Ian (ed), *Global Fortune : The Stumble and Rise of World Capitalism*. Washington, DC: Cato Institute, 2000.

Vlachos, Jonas, *Är ekonomisk tillväxt bra för de fattiga? : en översikt över debatten*. Stockholm: Globkom, 2000,
(http://www.globkom.net/rapporter/vlachos.pdf)

Wheeler, David, *Racing to the Bottom? : Foreign Investment and Air Pollution in Developing Countries*. Washington, DC: World Bank, 2000 (Working paper 2524) (http://econ.worldbank.org/view.php?type=5&id=1340)

–, Huq, M & Martin, P, *Process Change, Economic Policy and Industrial Pollution : Cross Country Evidence from the Wood Pulp and Steel Industries*. Paper presented at The Annual Meeting of the American Economic Association, 1993.

World Bank, *World Development Report 1992 : Development and the Environment*. Washington, DC: World Bank, 1992.

–, *The East Asian Miracle : Economic Growth and Public Policy*. New York: Oxford University Press/World Bank, 1993.

–, *Assessing Aid : What Works, What Doesn't, and Why*. New York: Oxford University Press/World Bank, 1998.

–, *World Development Report 2000/2001 : Attacking Poverty*, (2000a). New York: Oxford University Press/World Bank, 2000, (http://www.worldbank.org/poverty/wdrpoverty/report/index.htm)

–, *Does More International Trade Openness Increase World Poverty?* Vol 2 of *Assessing Globalization*, (2000b). Washington, DC: World Bank/PREM Economic Policy Group and Development Economics Group, 2000 (World Bank briefing papers), (http://www.worldbank.org/html/extdr/pb/globalization/)

–, *Income Poverty : Trends in Inequality*, (2000c). Washington, DC: World Bank, 2000, (http://www.worldbank.org/poverty/data/trends/inequal.htm)

–, *Making Transition Work for Everyone : Poverty and Inequality in Europe and Central Asia*, (2000d). Washington, DC: World Bank, 2000.

–, *World Development Indicators 2000*, (2000e). Washington, DC: World Bank, 2000.

Yago, Glenn & Goldman, David, *Capital Access Index Fall 1998 : Emerging and Submerging Markets.* Santa Monica: Milken Institute, 1998, (http://www.milkeninstitute.org/poe.cfm?point=pub03)

Yao, Shuije, "Economic Development and Poverty Reduction in China over 20 Years of Reform," in *Economic Development and Cultural Change*, Vol 48 (2000), No 3, pp 447–74.

Yergin, Daniel & Stanislaw, Joseph, *The Commanding Heights : The Battle Between Government and the Marketplace that is Remaking the Modern World.* New York: Free Press, 1998.

Åslund, Anders, "Därför har Estland lyckats," in *Svenska Dagbladet*, August 2nd, 2000.

Örn, Gunnar, *Nationalekonomi för noviser.* Stockholm: Timbro, 1996.

Österberg, Torun, *Economic Perspectives on Immigrants and Inter-Generational Transmissions.* [Diss.] Gothenburg: The University, 2000.